**1,00**
are a

# Forgotten Books

www.ForgottenBooks.com

Read online
Download PDF
Purchase in print

ISBN 978-0-282-38572-9
PIBN 10849843

This book is a reproduction of an important historical work. Forgotten Books uses state-of-the-art technology to digitally reconstruct the work, preserving the original format whilst repairing imperfections present in the aged copy. In rare cases, an imperfection in the original, such as a blemish or missing page, may be replicated in our edition. We do, however, repair the vast majority of imperfections successfully; any imperfections that remain are intentionally left to preserve the state of such historical works.

Forgotten Books is a registered trademark of FB &c Ltd.
Copyright © 2018 FB &c Ltd.
FB &c Ltd, Dalton House, 60 Windsor Avenue, London, SW19 2RR.
Company number 08720141. Registered in England and Wales.

For support please visit www.forgottenbooks.com

# 1 MONTH OF FREE READING

at

www.ForgottenBooks.com

By purchasing this book you are eligible for one month membership to ForgottenBooks.com, giving you unlimited access to our entire collection of over 1,000,000 titles via our web site and mobile apps.

To claim your free month visit: www.forgottenbooks.com/free849843

\* Offer is valid for 45 days from date of purchase. Terms and conditions apply.

English
Français
Deutsche
Italiano
Español
Português

# www.forgottenbooks.com

**Mythology** Photography **Fiction** Fishing Christianity **Art** Cooking Essays Buddhism Freemasonry Medicine **Biology** Music **Ancient Egypt** Evolution Carpentry Physics Dance Geology **Mathematics** Fitness Shakespeare **Folklore** Yoga Marketing **Confidence** Immortality Biographies Poetry **Psychology** Witchcraft Electronics Chemistry History **Law** Accounting **Philosophy** Anthropology Alchemy Drama Quantum Mechanics Atheism Sexual Health **Ancient History** **Entrepreneurship** Languages Sport Paleontology Needlework Islam **Metaphysics** Investment Archaeology Parenting Statistics Criminology **Motivational**

# AN ACCOUNT

## OF

# CORSICA.

𝕰𝖓𝖙𝖊𝖗𝖊𝖉 𝖎𝖓 𝕾𝖙𝖆𝖙𝖎𝖔𝖓𝖊𝖗𝖘 𝕳𝖆𝖑𝖑 𝖆𝖈𝖈𝖔𝖗𝖉𝖎𝖓𝖌 𝖙𝖔 𝕬𝖈𝖙 𝖔𝖋 𝕻𝖆𝖗𝖑𝖎𝖆𝖒𝖊𝖓𝖙.

# AN ACCOUNT OF CORSICA,

## THE JOURNAL OF A TOUR TO THAT ISLAND;

## AND MEMOIRS OF PASCAL PAOLI.

### BY JAMES BOSWELL, Esq;

ILLUSTRATED with a New and Accurate MAP of CORSICA.

Non enim propter gloriam, divitias aut honores pugnamus, sed propter libertatem solummodo, quam nemo bonus nisi simul cum vita amittit.
Lit. Comit. et Baron. Scotiæ ad Pap. A. D. 1320.

GLASGOW,
PRINTED BY ROBERT AND ANDREW FOULIS FOR
EDWARD AND CHARLES DILLY IN THE POULTRY, LONDON;
M DCC LXVIII.

# DEDICATION

## TO

# PASCAL PAOLI

## GENERAL OF

## THE CORSICANS.

SIR,

Dedications are for most part the offerings of interested servility, or the effusions of partial zeal; enumerating the virtues of men in whom no virtues can be found, or predicting greatness to those who afterwards pass their days in unambitious indolence, and die leaving no memorial of their exis-

a

tence, but a dedication, in which all their merit is confessedly future, and which time has turned into a silent reproach.

He who has any experience of mankind, will be cautious to whom he dedicates. Publickly to bestow praise on merit of which the publick is not sensible, or to raise flattering expectations which are never fulfilled, must sink the character of an authour, and make him appear a cringing parasite, or a fond enthusiast.

I am under no apprehensions of that nature, when I inscribe this book to Pascal Paoli. Your virtues, Sir, are universally acknowledged; they dignify the

## DEDICATION.

pages which I venture to present to you; and it is my singular felicity that my book is the voucher of its dedication.

' In thus addressing you, my intention is not to attempt your panegyrick. That may in some measure be collected from my imperfect labours. But I wish to express to the world, the admiration and gratitude with which you have inspired me.

This, Sir, is all the return that I can make for the many favours which you have deigned to confer upon me. I intreat you to receive it as a testimony of my disposition. I regret that I have neither power nor interest to enable me to render any

## DEDICATION.

essential service to you and to the brave Corsicans. I can only assure you of the most fervent wishes of a private gentleman. I have the honour to be, with all respect and affection,

Sir,

Auchinleck, Ayrshire,
29 October 1767.

Your ever devoted

obliged humble servant

JAMES BOSWELL.

# PREFACE.

No apology shall be made for presenting the world with An Account of Corsica. It has been for some time expected from me; and I own that the ardour of publick curiosity has both encouraged and intimidated me. On my return from visiting Corsica, I found people wherever I went, desirous to hear what I could tell them concerning that island and its inhabitants. Unwilling to repeat my tale to every company, I thought it best to promise a book which should speak for me.

But I would not take upon me to do this, till I consulted with the General of the nation. I therefore informed him of my design. His answer is perhaps too flattering for me to publish: but I must beg leave to give it as the licence and sanction of this work.

Paoli was pleased to write to me thus;
‘ Non può esser piu generoso il di lei di-

# AN ACCOUNT OF CORSICA,

## THE JOURNAL OF A TOUR TO THAT ISLAND;

## AND MEMOIRS OF PASCAL PAOLI.

### BY JAMES BOSWELL, Esq;

ILLUSTRATED with a New and Accurate MAP of CORSICA.

Non enim propter gloriam, divitias aut honores pugnamus, sed propter libertatem solummodo, quam nemo bonus nisi simul cum vita amittit.
Lit. Comit. et Baron. Scotiæ ad Pap. A. D. 1320.

GLASGOW,
PRINTED BY ROBERT AND ANDREW FOULIS FOR
EDWARD AND CHARLES DILLY IN THE POULTRY, LONDON;
M DCC LXVIII.

lative to the subject. I am thus enabled to lay before the world such An Account of Corsica, as I flatter myself will give some satisfaction; for, in comparison of the very little that has been hitherto known concerning that island, this book may be said to contain a great deal.

It is indeed amazing that an island so considerable, and in which such noble things have been doing, should be so imperfectly known. Even the succession of Chiefs has been unperceived; and because we have read of Paoli being at the head of the Corsicans many years back, and Paoli still appears at their head, the command has been supposed all this time in the person of the same man. Hence all our newspapers have confounded the gallant Pascal Paoli in the vigour of manhood, with the venerable chief his deceased Father Giacinto Paoli. Nay the same errour has found its way into the page of the historian; for Dr. Smollet when mentioning Paoli at the siege of Furiani a few years ago, says he was then past fourscore.

I would in the first place return my

## PREFACE. xiii

moſt humble thanks to Paſcal Paoli, for the various communications with which he has been pleaſed to favour me; and as I have related his remarkable ſayings, I declare upon honour, that I have neither added nor diminiſhed; nay ſo ſcrupulous have I been, that I would not make the ſmalleſt variation even when my friends thought it would be an improvement. I know with how much pleaſure we read what is perfectly authentick.

Count Rivarola was ſo good as to return me full and diſtinct anſwers to a variety of queries which I ſent him with regard to many particulars concerning Corſica. I am much indebted to him for this, and particularly ſo, from the obliging manner in which he did it.

The reverend Mr. Burnaby, chaplain to the Britiſh factory at Leghorn, made a tour to Corſica in 1766, at the ſame time with the honourable and reverend Mr. Hervey now biſhop of Cloyne. Mr. Burnaby was abſent from Leghorn when I was there, ſo I had not the pleaſure of being personally known to him. But he with great politeness of his own accord, sent me a copy of the Journal which he made of what he observed in Corsica. I had the satisfaction to find that we agreed in every thing which both of us had considered. But I found in his Journal, observations on several things which I had omitted; and several things which I had remarked, I found set in a clearer light. As Mr. Burnaby was so obliging as to allow me to make what use I pleased of his Journal, I have freely interwoven it into my work.

I acknowledge my obligations to my esteemed friend John Dick Esquire, his Britannick Majesty's Consul at Leghorn, to Signor Gian Quilico Casa Bianca, to the learned Greek physician Signor Stefanopoli, to Colonel Buttafoco, and to the Abbé Rostini. These gentlemen have all contributed their aid in erecting my little monument to liberty.

I am also to thank an ingenious gentleman who has favoured me with the translations of Seneca's Epigrams. I made application for this favour, in the London Chronicle; and to the honour of literature, I found her votaries very liberal. Several tranflations were fent, of which I took the liberty to prefer thofe which had the fignature of Patricius, and which were improved by another ingenious correfpondent under the fignature of Plebeius. By a fubfequent application I begged that Patricius would let me know to whom I was obliged for what I confidered as a great ornament to my book. He has complied with my requeft; and beg leave in this publick manner, to acknowledge that I am indebted for thofe tranflations to Thomas Day Efquire, of Berkfhire, a gentleman whofe fituation in life is genteel, and his fortune affluent. I muft add that although his verfes have not only the fire of youth, but the maturity and correctnefs of age, Mr. Day is no more than nineteen.

Nor can I omit to exprefs my fenfe of the candour and politenefs with which

## PREFACE.

Sir James Steuart received the remark which I have ventured to make in oppofition to a paffage concerning the Corficans, in his Inquiry into the Principles of Political Oeconomy.

I have fubmitted my book to the revifal of feveral gentlemen who honour me with their regard, and I am fenfible how much it is improved by their corrections. It is therefore my duty to return thanks to the reverend Mr. Wyvill rectour of Black Notely in Effex, and to my old and moft intimate friend the reverend Mr. Temple rectour of Mamhead in Devonfhire. I am alfo obliged to My Lord Monboddo for many judicious remarks, which his thorough acquaintance with ancient learning enabled him to make. But I am principally indebted to the indulgence and friendly attention of My Lord Hailes, who under the name of Sir David Dalrymple\*, has been long

---

\* It is the cuftom in Scotland to give the Judges of the court of feffion the title of Lords by the names of their eftates. Thus Mr. Burnett is Lord Monboddo, and Sir David Dalrymple is Lord Hailes.

known to the world as an able Antiquarian, and an elegant and humourous Essayist; to whom the world has no fault but that he does not give them more of his own writings, when they value them so highly.

I would however have it understood, that although I received the corrections of my friends with deference, I have not always agreed with them. An authour should be glad to hear every candid remark. But I look upon a man as unworthy to write, who has not force of mind to determine for himself. I mention this, that the judgement of the friends I have named may not be considered as connected with every passage in this book.

Writing a book I have found to be like building a house. A man forms a plan, and collects materials. He thinks he has enough to raise a large and stately edifice; but after he has arranged, compacted and polished, his work turns out to be a very small performance. The authour however like the builder, knows how much labour his work has cost him; and therefore estimates it at a much higher rate than other people think it deserves.

I have endeavoured to avoid an ostentatious display of learning. By the idle and the frivolous indeed, any appearance of learning is called pedantry. But as I do not write for such readers, I pay no regard to their censures. Those by whom I wish to be judged, will I hope, approve of my adding dignity to Corsica, by shewing its consideration among the ancients, and will not be displeased to find my page sometimes embellished with a seasonable quotation from the Classicks. The translations are ascribed to their proper authours. What are not so ascribed are my own.

It may be necessary to say something in defence of my orthography. Of late it has become the fashion to render our language more neat and trim by leaving out k after c, and u in the last syllable of words which used to end in our. The illustrious Mr. Samuel Johnson, who has alone executed in England what was the talk of whole academies in other countries, has been careful in his Dictionary to preserve the k as a mark of Saxon original. He has for moſt part too, been careful to preſerve the u, but he has alſo omitted it in ſeveral words. I have retained the k, and have taken upon me to follow a general rule with regard to words ending in our. Wherever a word originally Latin has been tranſmitted to us through the medium of the French, I have written it with the characteriſtical u. An attention to this may appear trivial. But I own I am one of thoſe who are curious in the formation of language in its various modes; and therefore wiſh that the affinity of Engliſh with other tongues may not be forgotten. If this work ſhould at any future period be reprinted, I hope that care will be taken of my orthography.

He who publiſhes a book, affecting not to be an authour, and profeſſing an indifference for literary fame, may poſsibly impose upon many people such an idea of his consequence as he wishes may be received. For my part, I should be proud to be known as an authour; and I have an ardent ambition for literary fame; for of all possessions I should imagine literary fame to be the most valuable. A man who has been able to furnish a book which has been approved by the world, has established himself as a respectable character in distant society, without any danger of having that character lessened by the observation of his weaknesses. To preserve an uniform dignity among those who see us every day, is hardly possible; and to aim at it, must put us under the fetters of a perpetual restraint. The authour of an approved book may allow his natural disposition an easy play, and yet indulge the pride of superiour genius when he considers that by those who know him only as an authour, he never ceases to be respected. Such an authour when in his hours of gloom and discontent, may have the confolation to think that his writings are at that very time giving pleafure to numbers; and fuch an authour may cherifh the hope of being remembered after death, which has been a great object to the nobleft minds in all ages.

Whether I may merit any portion of literary fame, the publick will judge. Whatever my ambition may be, I truft that my confidence is not too great, nor my hopes too fanguine.

# CONTENTS.

INTRODUCTION. page 1

### CHAP. I.

Of the Situation, Extent, Air, Soil, and Productions, of Corsica. 11

### CHAP. II.

A concise view of the Revolutions which Corsica has undergone from the earliest times. 55

### CHAP. III.

The Present State of Corsica, with respect to Government, Religion, Arms, Commerce, Learning, the Genius and Character of its Inhabitants. 144

Appendix, containing Corsican State Papers. 141

The Journal of a Tour to Corsica; and Memoirs of Pascal Paoli. 259

# AN ACCOUNT OF CORSICA.

## INTRODUCTION.

LIBERTY is so natural, and so dear to mankind, whether as individuals, or as members of society, that it is indispensibly necessary to our happiness. Every thing worthy ariseth from it. Liberty gives health to the mind, and enables us to enjoy the full exercise of our faculties. He who is in chains cannot move either easily or gracefully; nothing elegant or noble can be expected from those, whose spirits are subdued by tyranny, and whose powers are cramped by restraint.

There are, indeed, who from the darkest prejudice, or most corrupt venality, would endeavour to reason mankind out of their original and genu-

## INTRODUCTION.

ine feelings, and perfuade them to fubstitute artificial fentiment in place of that which is implanted by God and Nature. They would maintain, that flavery will from habit become eafy, and, that mankind are truly better, when under confinement and fubjection to the arbitrary will of a few.

Such doctrine as this, could never have gained any ground, had it been addreffed to calm reafon alone. Its partifans therefore have found it neceffary to addrefs themfelves to the imagination and paffions; to call in the aid of enthufiafm and fuperftition; in fome countries to inftill a ftrange love and attachment to their fovereigns; and in others to propagate certain mystical notions, which the mind of man is wonderfully ready to receive, of a divine right to rule; as if their fovereigns had defcended from heaven. This laft idea has been cherifhed for ages, from the ' Cara Deûm foboles, The beloved offspring of the Gods,' among the Romans, to thofe various elevated and endearing epithets, which modern nations have thought proper to beftow upon their fovereigns.

But whatever fophifms may be devifed in favour of slavery, patience under it, can never be any thing but ' the effect of a sickly constitution, ' which creates a laziness and despondency, that ' puts men beyond hopes and fears: mortifying ' ambition, and other active qualities, which free-' dom begets; and instead of them, affording on-' ly a dull kind of pleasure, of being careless and ' insensible (*a*).'

There is no doubt, but by entering into society, mankind voluntarily give up a part of their natural rights, and bind themselves to the obedience of laws, calculated for the general good. But, we must distinguish between authority, and oppression; between laws, and capricious dictates; and keeping the original intention of government ever in view, we should take care that no more restraint be laid upon natural liberty, than what the necessities of society require.

Perhaps the limits between the power of government, and the liberty of the people, should not be too strictly marked out. Men of taste reckon that picture hard, where the outlines are so strong, as to be clearly seen. They admire a piece of painting, where the colours are delicately blend-

(*a*) My lord Molesworth's Account of Denmark, p. 69.

## INTRODUCTION.

ed, and the tints, which point out every particular object, are softened into each other, by an insensible gradation. So in a virtuous state, there should be such a mutual confidence between the government and the people, that the rights of each should not be expressly defined.

But flagrant injustice, on one side or other, is not to be concealed; and, without question, it is the priviledge of the side that is injured, to vindicate itself.

I have been led into these reflections from a consideration of the arguments by which ingenious men in the refinement of politics have endeavoured to amuse mankind, and turn away their attention from the plain and simple notions of liberty.

Liberty is indeed the parent of felicity, of every noble virtue, and even of every art and science. Whatever vain attempts have been made to raise the generous plants under an oppressive climate, have only shewn more evidently the value of freedom.

It is therefore no wonder that the world has at all times been roused at the mention of liberty; and that we read with admiration and a vir-

## INTRODUCTION. 5

tuous enthusiasm, the gallant achievements of those who have distinguished themselves in the glorious cause; and the history of states who were animated with the principle of freedom, and made it the basis of their constitution.

Should any one transmit to posterity the annals of an enslaved nation, we should sleep over whole ages of the humbling detail. Every thing would be so poor, so tame, and so abject, that one might as well peruse the records of a prison-house.

But we have a manly satisfaction in reading the history of the ancient Romans; even abstracting from their connections and their broils with other states. Their internal progress alone affords ample matter of speculation to a judicious and spirited observer of human nature. We love to trace the various springs of their conduct, and of their advancement in greatness. We contemplate with pleasure the ferments between the patricians and plebeians, the strong exertions of rude genius, the vigorous exercises and hardy virtues of men uncontrouled by timid subjection.

They who entertain an extravagant veneration for antiquity, would make us believe, that the divine fire of liberty has been long ago exhausted, and that any appearances of it which are to be found in modern times are but feeble and dim. They would make us believe that the world is grown old, that the strength of human nature is decayed, and that we are no more to expect those noble powers which dignified men in former ages.

But the truth is, that human nature is the same at all times, and appears in different lights merely from a difference of circumstances. In the language of the schoolmen, the substance is fixed, the accidents only vary. Rome has yet the seven hills on which the conquerors of the world dwelt, and these are inhabited by Romans. Athens still occupies the space from whence philosophy and genius diffused a radiance to all the nations around, and is possessed by Athenians. But neither of these people now retain any resemblance of their illustrious ancestors; this is entirely owing to the course of political events, which has produced a total change in their manners.

That the spirit of liberty has flourished in modern times, we may appeal to the histories of the Swiss, and of the Dutch; and the boldest proofs

# INTRODUCTION.

of it are to be found in the annals of our own country.

But a most distinguished example of it actually exists in the island of Corsica. There, a brave and resolute nation, has now for upwards of six and thirty years, maintained a constant struggle against the oppression of the republic of Genoa. These valiant islanders were for a long time looked upon as an inconsiderable band of malecontents, as a disorderly troop of rebels, who would speedily be compelled to resume those chains which they had frowardly shaken off. They have however continued steady to their purpose. Providence has favoured them; and Europe now turns her eyes upon them, and with astonishment sees them on the eve of emancipating themselves for ever from a foreign yoke, and becoming a free and independent people.

> Libertas quae sera tamen respexit———
> Respexit tamen et longo post tempore venit.
> 
> VIRG. Eclog. I.
> 
> When a long age of vent'rous toil was past,
> Celestial freedom blest their isle at last.

The smallness of the Corsican state does not render it less an object of admiration. On the contrary, we ought to admire it the more. The ingenious Mr. Hume (*a*) hath shewn us, that Rhodes, Thebes, and many of the famous ancient states were not so numerous as the people of Corsica now are. If the ten thousand Greeks have gained immortal honour because they were opposed to the armies of the Persian monarch, Shall not the Corsicans be found deserving of glory, who have set themselves against a republic, which has been aided at different times by the power of France, and by that of the empire of Germany?

The Corsicans have been obliged to shew particular force of spirit. The Swiss and the Dutch were both assisted by powerful nations in the recovery of their liberties: but during the long and bloody war which Corsica has carried on, the Powers of Europe, who might be supposed friendly to her, have stood aloof, and she has single and unsupported, weathered the storm, and arrived at the degree of consequence which she now holds.

To give an account of this island, is what I am now to attempt. The attempt is surely laudable; and I am persuaded that my readers will

(*a*) Essay on the populousness of ancient nations.

grant me every indulgence, when they confider how favourable is the fubject. They will confider that I am the firft Briton who has had the curiofity to vifit Corfica, and to receive fuch information as to enable him to form a juft idea of it; and they will readily make allowance for the enthufiafm of one who has been among the brave iflanders, when their patriotic virtue is at its height, and who has felt as it were a communication of their fpirit.

The plan which I have prefcribed to myfelf is, to give a Geographical and Phyfical defcription of the ifland, that my readers may be made acquainted with the country which in thefe latter days has produced fo heroic a race of patriots. To exhibit a concife view of the Revolutions it has undergone from the earlieft times, which will prepare the mind, and throw light on the fequel. To fhew the Prefent State of Corfica; and to fubjoin my Journal of a Tour to that ifland, in which I relate a variety of anecdotes, and treafure up many memoirs of the illuftrious General of the Corficans——MEMORABILIA PAOLI.

I do moft fincerely declare, that I feel myfelf inferiour to the tafk. But I hope the fketch which I give will be of some immediate service, and will induce others to execute a more perfect plan. I shall be happy if I contribute in a certain degree to give the world a just idea of Corsica, and to interest the generous in its favour; and I would adopt for this work a simple and beautiful inscription on the front of the Palazzo Tolomei at Siena,

>Quod potui feci; faciant meliora potentes.
>I've done my best; let abler men do more.

# CHAPTER I.

*Of the Situation, Extent, Air, Soil, and Productions, of* CORSICA.

CORSICA is an island of the Mediterranean sea, situated between the 41 and 43 degree of north latitude, and between the 8 and 10 degree of east longitude, reckoning from London. It hath on the north the Ligurian sea, and gulph of Genoa. On the east, the Tuscan sea; on the south, a strait of ten miles which separates it from Sardinia; and on the west the Mediterranean. It is about 100 miles south of Genoa, and 80 south-west of Leghorn, from whence it can plainly be seen when the weather is clear. It is 150 miles in length, and from 40 to 50 in breadth, being broadest about the middle. It is reckoned 322 miles in circumference; but an exact measurement round it would extend to 500 miles, as it is edged with many promontories, and with a variety of bays.

Pliny the elder hath given us a short, but very accurate account of the geography of Corsica;

' In Ligustico mari est Corsica quam Graeci Cyr-
' non appellavere, sed Thusco proprior, a septen-
' trione in meridiem projecta, longa passuum CL
' millia, lata majore ex parte L, circuitu CCCXXII,
' civitates habet XXXIII et colonias Marianam a
' Mario deductam, Aleriam a dictatore Sylla (*a*). 
' In the Ligurian sea, but nearer to Tuscany than
' to Liguria, is Corsica, which the Greeks called
' Cyrnus. It extendeth from north to south, and
' is about 150 miles in length, for the most part
' 50 in breadth, and 321 in circumference. It
' hath 33 states and two colonies, Mariana found-
' ed by Marius, and Aleria founded by the dicta-
' tor Sylla.' Of these 33 states, not above five
or six can now be traced; and the colonies are
only to be marked by their ruins. But the usual
fidelity of Pliny is to be credited in this account.
Pomponius Mela (*b*) describes the situation of
Corsica, as does Ptolemy (*c*).

Seneca the philosopher hath left us two most
horrid pictures of Corsica, very false indeed, but
executed with uncommon strength of fancy and
expression. Stoic as he was, of a grave and se-

---

(*a*) Plin. Nat. Hist. lib. ii. cap. 6.   (*b*) Pomp. Mel. lib. ii.
cap. 7.   (*c*) Ptol. Geog. lib. iii. cap. 2.

vere demeanour, he did not escape the Emperour's jealousy, but being accused as one of the many gallants with whom the profligate Julia had been guilty of adultery, he was banished to Corsica, where he remained for seven years; and where in the province of Capo Corso they still shew an old ruin called 'Il torre di Seneca, Seneca's Tower.' Here he composed his books de Consolatione to Polybius, and to his mother Helvia, with several other works; and here he indulged his fretted imagination in the following epigrams.

I.

Corsica Phocaeo tellus habitata colono,
    Corsica quae Graio nomine Cyrnus eras:
Corsica Sardinia brevior, porrectior Ilva;
    Corsica piscosis pervia fluminibus:
Corsica terribilis quum primum incanduit aestas;
    Saevior, ostendit quum ferus ora canis:
Parce relegatis, hoc est, jam parce sepultis,
    Vivorum cineri sit tua terra levis.

O sea-girt Corsica! whose rude domains,
First own'd the culture of Phocaean swains;
Cyrnus, since thus the Greeks thy isle express,
Greater than Ilva, than Sardinia less;
O Corsica! whose winding rivers feed,
Unnumber'd as their sands, the finny breed:
O Corsica! whose raging heats dismay,
When first returning summer pours her ray;

Yet fiercer plagues thy scorching shores dispense,
When Sirius sheds his baneful influence:
Spare, spare the banish'd! spare, since such his doom,
A wretch, who living, seeks in thee a tomb!
Light lay thy earth, in pity to his pains,
Light lay thy earth upon his sad remains.

## II.

Barbara praeruptis inclusa est Corsica saxis;
   Horrida, desertis undique vasta locis.
Non poma autumnus, segetes non educat aestas;
   Canaque Palladio munere bruma caret;

Umbrarum nullo ver est laetabile foetu,
   Nullaque in infausto nascitur herba solo:
Non panis, non haustus aquae, non ultimus ignis,
   Hìc sola haec duo sunt, exsul, et exsilium.

O! Corsica, whom rocks terrific bound,
Where nature spreads her wildest desarts round,
In vain revolving seasons cheer thy soil,
Nor rip'ning fruits, nor waving harvests smile:
Nor blooms the olive mid the winter drear;
The votive olive to Minerva dear.
See, spring returning, spreads her milder reign!
Yet shoots no herb, no verdure clothes the plain.
No cooling springs to quench the traveller's thirst
From thy parch'd hills in grateful murmurs burst;
Nor, hapless isle! thy barren shores around,
Is wholesome food, fair Ceres' bounty, found.
Nor ev'n the last sad gift, the wretched claim,
The pile funereal, and the sacred flame.
Nought here, alas! surrounding seas enclose,
Nought but an exile, and an exile's woes.

He hath alfo vented his fpleen againft the place of his exile, in the fame extravagant manner, in his books De Confolatione. But we muft confider, that notwithftanding all the boafted firmnefs of Seneca, his mind was then clouded with melancholy, and every object around him, appeared in rueful colours.

Corfica is in reality, a moft agreeable ifland. It had from the ancient Greeks the name of Callifta, Κάλλιϛη on account of its beauty; and we may believe it was held in confiderable eftimation, fince Callimachus places it next to his favourite Delus,

Η δ'όπιθεν Φοινίσσα μετ' ίχνια Κύρνος όπηδεῖ
Οὐκ ὀνοτή——    CALLIM. Hymn. in Del. l. 19.

Next in the rank, Phoenician Cyrnus came,
A fruitful ifle, of no ignoble name.

It is charmingly fituated in the Mediterranean, from whence continual breezes fan and cool it in fummer, and the furrounding body of water keeps it warm in winter, fo that it is one of the moft temperate countries in that quarter of Europe. Its air is frefh and healthful, except in one or two places, which are moift, and where the air, efpecially in fummer, is fuffocating and fickly; but in general, the Corsicans breathe a pure atmosphere, which is also keen enough to brace their fibres more than one would expect under so warm a sun.

Corsica has indeed been pretty generally represented as unwholesome, which, I suppose, has been owing to the bad report given of it by the Romans, who established their colonies at Aleria and Mariana, which from their damp situation, occasioned a great death among the inhabitants, and accordingly these colonies soon went to ruin. But all the interiour parts of the Island are extremely well aired.

Corsica is remarkably well furnished with good harbours, so that we may apply to it what Florus says of the Campania, 'Nihil hospitalius mari (*a*). Nothing more hospitable to the sea.' It has on the north Centuri. On the west San Fiorenzo, Isola Rossa, Calvi, Ajaccio. On the South it has Bonifaccio. And on the east Porto-Vecchio, Bastia and Macinajo. Of each of these I shall give some account.

Centuri, though at present but a small harbour, may be greatly enlarged, as its situation is very convenient.

(*a*) Flor. Lib. i. Cap. 16.

San Fiorenzo is an extensive gulph. It runs about fifteen miles up into the country, and is about five miles across, and many fathom deep. The gulf itself hath often a violent surge, being exposed to the westerly winds; but there are several creeks and bays, particularly on the south side of it, which are quite secure. There is in particular, a bay under the tower of Fornali, about two miles from San Fiorenzo, which is highly esteemed, and where vessels of considerable burden may be safely stationed.

Isola Rossa is but a little harbour; but has a considerable depth of water, and is defended by a small Island against the westerly winds. They talk of erecting a mole to lock it in on every quarter. It is at present one of the principal ports for Commerce in the possession of the Corsicans.

Calvi (*a*) is a large and excellent harbour. Cluverius calls it 'Celeberrimus insulae portus (*b*),

---

(*a*) Postlethwayt in his translation of Savary's Dictionary of Trade and Commerce, has a most absurd observation concerning Calvi; 'Its inhabitants,' says he, 'are called Calves.' Who told him this? What connection is there between the English word calves and the Italian word Calvi? Perhaps he intended it as wit. If so, how clumsy are the jests of this Lexicographer!

(*b*) Cluver. Corsic. Antiq.

B

The moſt famous port of this Iſland.' The only objection I ever heard made to it, was by a French Gentleman, who told me, that the bottom of it was full of ſharp rocks, which were apt to cut the cables of ſhips which entered it. And he inſtanced one of the tranſports, which had landed ſome of the French troops in the year 1764. He however, was under a miſtake; for I have been at pains to enquire very particularly concerning this, and am informed from the beſt authority, that there is nothing to fear from rocks at Calvi, and that the French tranſport which ſuffered a little there, happened to be run foul of by ſome of the reſt, which was the occaſion of any damage it ſuſtained.

Ajaccio is a wide and commodious harbour, with a good mole, and perfectly ſafe. It wants only to have a ſmall rock in front of the mole removed, which might be done at no great charge.

Corſica hath alſo in this quarter ſeveral ſmaller havens, which are uſeful for the reception of little veſſels.

Bonifaccio is an uſeful harbour, much frequented ſince the oldeſt times, and very fit for Trade.

Baſtia is not a port of the firſt conſideration, as

ships of war cannot enter it. But it hath a mole for the convenience of small vessels, for which it is very well fitted. The islands of Gorgona, Capraja and Ilva, or the Elbe, are placed at no great distance in the sea which rolls between the east coast of Corsica and Tuscany, with the Pope's dominions; so that small vessels can never be at a loss for protection, should any sudden storm come upon them, as they can run into any of these Islands.

Macinajo is none of the principal harbours in Corsica, though it is very safe and commodious for vessels of a light construction. I mention Macinajo, because it was from thence that the expedition set sail against Capraja, as will be afterwards seen.

Diodorus Siculus celebrates Corsica for the excellency of its harbours, Αὕτη δὲ ἡ νῆσος εὐπρόσορμιςος οὖσα, κάλλιςον ἔχει λιμένα τὸν ὀνομάζομενον Συρακύσιον (a). 'The island being of very easy access, has a most beautiful port, called the Syracusian.' This, which was anciently called the Syracusian, has now the name of Porto Vecchio;

---

(a) Diodor. Sicul. lib. v.

of which it is proper to take particular notice.

Porto Vecchio is a spacious haven, capable of containing a very large fleet. It is 5 miles long, above a mile and a half broad, has a great depth of water, and a good bottom, and being land-locked on every side, is well sheltered from storms. I may add, that a high and rocky mountain nature has placed like a stately column to point it out at a great distance. In short, Porto Vecchio may vie with the most distinguished harbours in Europe.

The only objection to it, is the badness of its air, occasioned by the marshy grounds which lie in its neighbourhood. But this disadvantage may be remedied, as has been done at Leghorn. ' The
' country about Leghorn was formely a vile mo-
' rass or rather quagmire, the noxious steams of
' which, rendered the air unwholesome; but by the
' skill and pains of an Englishman, sir Robert
' Dudley son to Queen Elizabeth's potent favou-
' rite, the Earl of Leicester, the soil was render-
' ed habitable, the air much less unwholesome, and
' the port improved, so as to become the best in
' Italy (a).'

---

(a) Present State of Europe, p. 411.

From this account of the harbours of Corsica, it will appear of how great consequence an alliance with this island might be to any of the maritime powers of Europe. For a fleet stationed there, might command the navigation of Genoa, Tuscany, and the ecclesiastical state, that between Spain and Naples, and a good share of that to the Levant; not to mention its influence over that of Sardinia. And it may be material to observe, that vessels stationed in the ports of Corsica might be formidable to France, as the western side of the island is directly opposite to the extensive coast of Provence, on which a descent might be made with cruisers in a very short time.

The northern point of Corsica, called Capo Corso (*b*), is about 30 miles long, very mountainous and rocky, but covered with vines and olives.

There are, in several parts of the island, but particularly in Capo Corso, a great many ancient towers, built about three or four hundred years ago, to defend the inhabitants against the incursions of the Turks and other pirates. There is there a little village called Tomino, strong by situation.

(*b*) There is a place in Guinea, which has also the name of Capo Corso. I know not from what.    Cluver. Geog. p. 537.

The Genoese have made several attacks upon it during the late troubles, but were never able to carry it. The inhabitants are very deservedly proud of this. They shew with particular triumph, a shell which the enemy threw into their village, to oblige them to surrender. They have placed it in a niche on the outside of their church, to serve as a memorial of their deliverance, and to inspire them with greater zeal and devotion when they go to divine worship.

From Tomino east to Bastia, is about 26 miles of a country much diversified with hills, and abounding in springs. On the coast are a number of poor fishing towns, and a little up the country, there are several villages or hamlets prettily enough situated.

Bastia has of a long time been reckoned the capital of Corsica. It was here that the Genoese held the seat of their sovereign power: and indeed Bastia is still the largest town in the island. It has a stately appearance from the sea, being built on the declivity of a hill; though upon entering the town, one is a good deal disappointed; for the houses are in general ill built, and the streets narrow, and from the situation of the

## OF CORSICA. 23

town, are necessarily very steep. There are however several pretty good buildings here. It hath a castle, which commands the town and harbour, which, though but a sorry fortification at present, is capable of being made a place of considerable strength, as it hath a range of hills behind it, on which little redoubts might be erected; and with these, and a few substantial outworks towards the sea, it might stand a pretty long siege. The castle is properly on a separate territory, called TERRA NUOVA, the New Land, as is also the cathedral of Bastia, which has nothing very remarkable. It belongs to the bishopric of Mariana.

The church of St. John in this city, by no means an inelegant building, belongs to the Jesuits, who have here a college. Their garden is finely situated, large, and well laid out. This they owe in a great measure to the French, who have been stationed in Corsica at different times. From them the inhabitants have learned much of what they know of the arts and conveniences of life. There is here a convent of Lazarists or missionaries, a vast and magnificent house, almost overhanging the sea. The convent of the Franciscans, and that of the Capuchins, are situated on the rising grounds behind Bastia. The last stands in a beautiful exposure, and has really a very pretty front.

From Bastia south to beyond Aleria, is one continued plain, between 50 and 60 miles in length, proper for raising all sorts of grain, as well as for pasturage.

I say nothing of the ruins of Mariana and Aleria, the two Roman colonies which stood on this plain; for as Corsica was much disregarded by the Romans, they did not think it worthy of having any of their taste and magnificence employed in it. So there are no vestiges of ancient grandeur. As however even the dregs of the Romans could not be without some skill in the arts, several antiques, such as rings, and seals with engravings on precious stones have been found here, and sometimes pretty good ones. The ruins of an old town called Nicæa, said to be built by the Etruscans, are still to be seen on this plain, but without any thing remarkable.

Beyond Aleria the country rises into small hills, proper for vines, olives, mulberry-trees, and many of them for corn. It is traversed by some ridges of mountains, upon which, not far from Porto

Vecchio, are great numbers of very fine oaks, the best being to be found here, and at Campoloro. A rich waved country with some few interruptions, reaches along the east and south coasts to Bonifaccio, which is a pretty confiderable town, well inhabited, and strongly fortified; and from thence is continued to the plain of Ajaccio.

Ajaccio is the prettiest town in Corsica. It hath many very handsome streets and beautiful walks; a citadel, and a palace for the Genoese governour. The inhabitants of this town are the genteelest people in the island, having had a good deal of intercourse with the French. In Ajaccio are the remains of a colony of Greeks settled in Corsica, of which colony a particular account I shall be given in the next chapter.

From the plain of Ajaccio, after passing some more ridges, you advance along the west shore to the provinces of Balagna and Nebbio, which are very rich, and afford an agreeable prospect, particularly Balagna, which may be called the garden of Corsica, being highly favoured by nature, and having also had in a superiour degree the advantages of cultivation.

You next arrive at San Fiorenzo, which is but

an inconsiderable place, and of no great strength. About a quarter of a mile to the southward of the town, are some low marshy grounds, which make San Fiorenzo so sickly, that few people choose to inhabit it, and the garrison there must be changed every month.

On the northern shore of the gulph, are two or three villages, of which the principal is Nonza. This is properly the key of Capo Corso; because from the cape into the interiour parts of the island on the western side, there is only one pass, and that leads through this place. Nonza is a little village, on a high rock, on the extreme pinnacle of which, some hundred fathoms above the gulph, and directly perpendicular, stands a tower or small fortress, which commands the avenue to it. Nonza is literally what Cicero calls Ithaca, ' In asperrimis saxulis tanquam nidulum affixam (*a*). Stuck on the rudest cliffs like a little nest.' After this, the cape begins, which finishes at Ersa.

I have thus reviewed the Corsican harbours, and travelled round the skirts of the country, along its shores.

Diodorus Siculus describes Corsica as an exten-

(*a*) Cic. De Orat. lib. i. cap. 44.

sive island, very mountainous, abounding in large forrests, and watered with many rivulets, Η δὲ ὅλη νῆσος εὐμεγέθης ὖσα, πολλὴν τῆς χώρας ὀρεινὴν ἔχει πεπυκασμένην δρυμοῖς συνεχέσι κὴ ποταμοῖς διαρ̱ρεομένην μικροῖς (a).

Indeed the interiour parts of the island are in general mountainous, though interspersed with fruitful valleys; but have a peculiar grand appearance, and inspire one with the genius of the place; with that undaunted and inflexible spirit, which will not bow to oppression. As Homer says of Ithaca,

Τρηχεῖ, ἀλλ' ἀγαθή κουροτρόφος.

Odyss. lib. ix. l. 27.

Strong are her sons, tho' rocky are her shores.

POPE.

The great division of Corsica, is into the DI QUA and the DI LA DEI MONTI. The country on this side, and the country on the other side of the mountains, reckoning from Bastia. By the mountains is understood, that great range of them which rises beyond Aleria, and stretches across the island, intersecting it however by no means equally; for, the country DI QUA, is a third more, than that DI LA. Another old di-

(a) Diodor. Sicul. lib. v.

vision of this island was, to suppose a line drawn from Porto Vecchio, to the gulph of San Fiorenzo; and the division upon the east, was called BANDA DI DENTRO, the side within; and that on the west, was called BANDA DI FUORI, the side without. I never could learn the meaning of this division farther, than that, I suppose, those who inhabited Bastia and the plain of Aleria, looked upon themselves as the most civilized; and so were for calling those on the opposite side of the island to them 'forrestieri, foreigners.'

The next division is into provinces, of which there are nine; for although a great part of this country long went under the denomination of 'FEUDOS, feus,' and is still called so in the maps; the jurisdiction of the signors is now gradually wearing out, and will soon be sunk into the general power of the state.

Another division of Corsica is into PIEVES. A Pieve is properly an ecclesiastical appointment, containing a certain number of parishes, over which is placed a PIEVANO, who superintends the priests, and draws a certain part of the tithes. But this division is as much used for civil affairs, as for those of the church.

There are large tracts of uninhabited land in Corsica, mostly covered with woods; to some parts of which the peasants resort in summer to feed their cattle, and to gather chesnuts, making little sheds for themselves to lie under. There is hardly such a thing as a detached farm-house to be seen in the island, like what are scattered every where over Great Britain; for, the Corsicans gather together in little villages, which they call by corruption 'PAESES, countries.' I remember when I was once told in Corsica, that I should travel a great many miles 'Senza veder un paese, without seeing a country.' I could not conceive what they meant. The Corsicans are in greater safety, and have more society with each other by thus living in villages; which is much the custom in the cantons of Switzerland, and some parts of Germany; as it was anciently among all nations.

The Corsican villages are frequently built upon the very summits of their mountains, on craggy cliffs of so stupenduous a height, that the houses can hardly be distinguished during the day; but at night, when the shepherds kindle their fires, the reflection of such a variety of lights, makes these aerial villages have a most picturesque and pleasing appearance.

In the center of the Island stands Corte, which is properly its capital, and will undoubtedly be one day a city of eminence. Here is the general's palace; and here is the supreme seat of justice, where the executive power constantly resides, and where the legislature is annually assembled; and here also is the university, which in time may become a distinguished seat of learning, though I must not allow my enthusiasm to indulge itself in too eager hopes of seeing Corsica an Athens, as well as a Thebes.

Corte is situated part at the foot, and part on the declivity of a rock, in a plain surrounded with prodigious high mountains, and at the conflux of two rivers, the Tavignano and Restonica. It hath a great deal of rich country about it, and a wonderful natural strength, being hemmed in by almost impassable mountains and narrow defiles, which may be defended with a handful of men, against very large armies.

Upon a point of the rock, prominent above the rest, and on every side perpendicular, stands the caftle or citadel. It is at the back of the town, and is almoft impregnable; there being only one winding paffage to climb up to it, and that not capable of admitting more than two perfons abreaft. Thuanus thus defcribes it, 'Curiae arx faxo fere undique praerupto impofita (*a*), The caftle of Corte placed upon a rock, broken and ragged almoft on every fide.' In the year 1554, it was in poffeffion of the French. (*b*) A Capitaine la Chambre betrayed it, for which he was afterwards hanged at Marfeilles. The fame hiftorian informs us, that after the Corficans had thus got back the citadel of Corte, it ftood a fiege by the French general de Thermes, from Auguft to October, and that it was a fcarcity of water, which at laft occafioned its furrender.

In the plain, on the north of Corte, there is a convent of Capuchins, and on the fide of the hill, to the fouth of the City, there is a convent of Francifcans. Here the general lived while his palace was repairing; and here all ftrangers of refpect are lodged. From this convent, one has the beft view of the city of Corte.

(*a*) Thuan. Hift. tom. 1. p. 507.
(*b*) Ibid.

The learned and ingenious Meſſieurs Hervey and Burnaby, when they were at this convent, were greatly ſtruck with the romantick appearance of Corte.

'We could ſcarce help fancying ourſelves at
' Lacedemon, or ſome other ancient Grecian City.
' Livy ſpeaking of Heraclea, has given a deſcrip-
' tion of it very like Corte. Sita eſt Heraclea in
' radicibus Aetae montis, ipſa in Campo, arcem
' imminentem loco alto et undique praecipiti ha-
' bet. Lib. 86. cap. 22. Heraclea is ſituated
' at the foot of mount Aeta; itſelf on a plain, but
' hanging over it, is a citadel, on a cliff very high
' and ſteep on every ſide. One would think he
' was ſpeaking of the very place. At Lacedemon in-
' deed, as appears from Pauſanias, there was no
' Acropolis or citadel, and they only called the
' higheſt point or eminence in the city by that
' name; from its anſwering probably the ſame
' purpoſe to them, as the Acropolis did to the
' other cities of Greece, it being more difficult of
' acceſs to an enemy, and admitting of an eaſier
' defence. Λακεδαιμονίοις δὲ ἡ ἀκρόπολις μέν ἐς
' ὕψος περιφανὲς ἐξίχουσα οὐκ ἔστι, καθὰ δὴ Θηβαί-
' οις τε ἡ Καδμεία, κ̄ ἡ Λάρισσα Ἀργείοις, ὄντων δὲ ἐν

' τῇ πόλει λόφων κỳ ἄλλων τὸ μάλιϛα ἐς μετέω-
' ρον ἀνήκον ὀνομάζῃσιν ἀκρόπολιν, ἐνταῦθα Ἀθῆνας
' ἱερὸν πεποίηται. Pausan. lib. iii. cap. 17. The
' Lacedemonians have no citadel built upon a
' high place, like Cadmaea of the Thebans, or
' Larissa of the Argives. But as there are in the
' city many hills, they give the most elevated of
' them the name of the citadel. Upon this hill is
' a temple to Minerva.' And Livy, speaking of
' its being besieged by Flaminius, observes nearly
' the same thing. ' Altiora loca et difficiliora aditu
' stationibus armatorum, pro munimento objectis
' tutabantur. lib. xxxiv. cap. 38. The higher
' places, and those more difficult of access, were
' defended by natural strength of situation; being
' to the soldiers equal to a fortification.'

' According to the institution of Lycurgus,
' the Spartans were not allowed to have any for-
' tifications; but were to rely for their defence
' upon their own valour. Towards the decline of
' the Grecian liberty however, they erected walls
' in the plainer and more open avenues; Locis
' patentibus plerisque objecerunt murum, says
' Livy. The remainder was still confided to the
' valour of its citizens. However, notwithstand-

C

'ing this, there was sufficient likeness to form a
'comparison between Corte and Lacedemon;
'especially as the Acropolis was built upon; the
'temple of Minerva being placed there. We
'could not help imagining, that yonder was the
'Taygetus, here the Eurotas; and what made
'the comparison more striking, was the resem-
'blance, we fancied, between Lycurgus and
'Paoli (*a*).'

Corsica is extremely well watered. Its principal lakes, are those of Ino and Crena, about two
miles from each other; both situated on the highest mountain in the island, called by the ancients
Mons Aureus, and now Gradaccio or Monte Ro-
tondo. It is of an amazing height, and may
equal any of the Alps. From the top of it there
is a most extensive view of all Corsica, of the
seas and of Sardinia, with distant prospects of Italy
and France; while the Mediterranean and many
of its little isles are also under the eye. But people
seldom go to take this view; for the upper part
of the mountain is almost a perpendicular rock,
so that a man must climb two miles with the
help of his hands and knees; and for the greatest

(*a*) Mr. Burnaby's Journal.

part of the year, this immense mountain is covered with snow. These two lakes of Ino and Crena, are both of considerable extent.

In the plain of Aleria, near to Mariana, is a lake called Chiurlina or Biguglia, which is pretty large, and communicates with the sea; and near to Aleria, is a lake called Il Stagno di Diana, which also communicates with the sea; and it is remarkable, that in summer, when the heat of the sun has exhaled part of the water, and the rest of it is absorbed by the sandy bottom, there remains a kind of natural salt, which the Corsicans find very good, and constantly make use of.

The rivers of Corsica are, the Golo, a large and beautiful river, which takes its rise from the lake of Ino, traverses several provinces, and after a course of above seventy miles, empties itself into the sea, just by the ancient city of Mariana. The Tavignano, also a considerable river, which takes its rise from the lake of Crena, and after traversing a long tract of rude country, empties itself into the sea, just by the ancient city of Aleria. The Restonica, which, though but a small river, is famous in Corsica, on account of its particular qualities. Its water is clear as chrystal, and moſt agreeable to drink; ſo that Seneca certainly never ſaw the Reſtonica, otherwiſe he would never have ſaid, 'that Corſica had not ʽhauſtus aquae, a draught of water.' The Reſtonica is ſaid to be of a mineral nature, and very wholeſome. It hath a virtue of whitening every thing. The ſtones in its channel are like as many pieces of chalk. I remember on the road between Rome and Naples, a run from a ſulphureous ſpring, which had ſomething of the ſame quality, only it did not give ſo very white a tincture as that of the Reſtonica, which will make iron look almoſt like ſilver, and never ruſt. The Corſicans frequently dip the barrels and locks of their guns in it.

There are ſeveral other rivers, of which I ſhall not give a particular deſcription; the Prunella, Fiumorbo, Gravonne, Valinco, Talavo, Liamone, fine poetical names. There are alſo a great many rivulets, which ſerve to enrich the country, and keep it conſtantly freſh.

It hath been ſaid, that with proper care and expence, ſome of the Corſican rivers might be rendered navigable; but this, I think, would be a very idle project; for their courſes are exceedingly, rapid, and when there has been a great deal of rain, the torrents which tumble from the mountains often bring down large fragments of rock, which would dash in pieces any vessels that they should encounter.

There are many mineral springs, both of the hot and cold kind, in different parts of the island, which the inhabitants of the country find to be very efficacious for the cure of most distempers; and people of skill, particularly some French physicians, have examined them by a chymical analysis, and approved of them.

Corsica is extremely well supplied with fish. I never indeed could hear of any other fish in their rivers or fresh water lakes, except trout and eel. These however are found in great plenty, very fat, and of an uncommon size.

But the rich treasure of fish for Corsica, is in its sea; for on all its coasts, there is the greatest variety of all the best kinds, and in particular a sort of ton or sturgeon, and the small fish called Sardinas, which is of an exquisite taste. And in several places, the Corsicans have beds of oysters, remarkably large; of which they have not only a sufficiency for their own consumption, but export a great many to Italy.

From the earliest times, Corsica has been famous for its excellent fish. Juvenal, when satyrising the excessive luxury of the Romans in his time, who brought every delicacy from the greatest distance, says,

> Mullus erit domini quem misit Corsica.
> Juv. Sat. v. l. 92.
> A precious mullet from the Corsic seas,
> Nor less the master's pamper'd taste can please.

And since I am talking of the productions of the Corsican sea, I may observe, that they here fish great quantities of coral, of all the three kinds, white, red and black. But I shall say more of this, when I come to the commerce of Corsica.

Corsica hath as great a variety of animals as most countries. The horses here, are in general of a very small breed. Procopius in his wars of the Goths, says, they run about in herds, and were little bigger than sheep (*a*). They are, however, remarkably lively, and very hardy; somewhat of the nature of Welch ponies, or of the little horses called shelties, which are found in the highlands and

---

(*a*) Procop. de Bell. Goth. lib. iii. cap. 24.

islands of Scotland; though I have seen Corsican horses of a very good size. The asses and mules here, are also small, but very strong and wonderfully agile in scrambling along the steep rocky mountains; for there are hardly any made roads in the Island. Sir Alexander Dick, whose publick spirit in promoting good roads in an improved age, is well known to all his countrymen, observed that this has been no loss to the Corsicans during the time that they have been employed only in defending themselves in a state of natural freedom. Had their country been open and accessible, they had been easily subdued by regular troops. It was in a good measure owing to her rugged hills, that ancient Scotland preserved her independency.

The black cattle are larger in proportion than the horses, but the greatest part of the Island is not very proper pasture for them; so in general, they do not give much milk, and their beef is lean and tough. There is not so great occasion for milk in Corsica, as they make no butter, oil supplying its place, as in Italy, and most warm countries. They however make a good deal of cheese in some pieves.

There are here a vast number of goats, which browse upon the wild hills, and put one in mind of Virgil's Bucolicks, where mention is so often made of this animal. Sheep are also very plentiful, and have fine feeding; so that their mutton is as sweet and juicy as one could desire, and atones for the badness of the beef.

The Corsican sheep are generally black, or of a dusky colour; a white sheep being here and there to be met with in a flock, as black ones are amongst our sheep. The wool is coarse and hairy; which the people of the country impute to their sheep being of a mongrel race. They have had thoughts of helping this, by importing a good breed from England or Spain. But I have been told by the breeders of sheep, that the quality of wool is not so much owing to the kind of sheep, as to the nature of their pasture; for those sheep who bear very rough fleeces when upon one farm, will, when put upon another of a different soil, bear fleeces exceedingly fine. It is very common here, for sheep to have more horns than two: many of them have six.

The forrests of this island abound in deer. And there is here a curious animal, called a Musfoli. It resembles a stag, but has horns like a ram, and a skin uncommonly hard. It is very wild, and lives on the highest mountains, where it can hardly be approached, it is so nimble. It will jump from rock to rock, at the distance of many feet, and if hard chaced to the extremity of a cliff, from whence it can reach no other, it will throw itself over, and with surprizing agility pitch upon its horns, without receiving any hurt. Yet when these creatures are taken young, they are very easily tamed. M. de Marboeuf, the French commander at the time I was in Corsica, had then one of them; and there are now two of them at Shugborough in Staffordshire, the seat of Mr. Anson, who has a rich assemblage of what is curious in nature, as well as of what is elegant in art.

The Corsican animals in general, appear'd wild to strangers. Polybius gives us a reason for it. Δοκεῖ γε μὴν πάντ᾽ εἶναι τὰ ζῶα κατὰ τὴν νῆσον ἄγρια διὰ ταιαύτην αἰτίαν. Οὐ δύνανται κατὰ τὰς νομὰς συνακολυθεῖν οἱ ποιμένες τοῖς θρέμμασι, διὰ τὸ σύνδενδρον κ᾽ κρημνῶδη κ᾽ τραχεῖαν εἶναι τὴν νῆσον (a). 'All the animals in the island appear to

(a) Polyb. hist. lib. xii.

' be wild, on this account, that it is so rude
' and steep, and so thick set with trees, that the
' shepherds are not able to follow their flocks.'
The wild boar is found here in great plenty. Indeed their swine which are very numerous, have all a mixture of the wild breed, and being fed on chestnuts, they are agreeable food.

The Corsicans are very fond of the diversion of hunting the wild boar, for which there is here a race of dogs, particularly excellent. They have smooth hair, and are something between a mastiff, and a strong shepherd's dog. They are large, and exceedingly fierce; but when once they have taken an attachment, they are very faithful to their master, watch him night and day, and are most undaunted in his defence.

Procopius (*b*) tells us, that there were in Corsica, apes wonderfully resembling men; and indeed, this island, and all that quarter of Europe before it was well inhabited, must on account of its vicinity to Africa, have swarmed with apes. Of these, however, there are at present no remains, which is a proof, that different species of animals migrate from one country to another, and when

(*b*) Procop. de Bell. Goth. lib. iii. cap. 24.

their race wears out in a particular part of the globe, it may be very numerous somewhere else. Certain it is, that in many countries, the race of several animals, well known there in ancient times, is totally extinguished. But I am not inclined to believe that our Creatour allows any of the various creatures which his almighty hand hath formed, to be absolutely annihilated.

There are hares enough in Corsica, but no rabbits; though Polybius, when talking of the animals of this island, says there are rabbits, and is very minute as to their form and qualities; saying, that at a distance, one would take them to be little hares, but when they are caught, a great difference is perceived, both in their appearance and taste. There are here no Wolves, nor any of the larger wild beasts, unless foxes can be reckoned so, which are here indeed extremely large and ravenous. It is said, they not only destroy sheep, but have been known to devour even foals.

There is also a variety of birds in Corsica; the eagle, the vulture, wood pidgeon, turtle, thrush, blackbird, and many of the smaller species; and plenty of game, as partridges, woodcocks, snipes, and water-fowl in the lakes. The poor thrushes and blackbirds too, must be reckoned as part of the game, for they are very numerous; and from there being a great quantity of the arbutus fruit in the island, they are exceedingly fat, and are esteemed a particular delicacy. It is barbarous to destroy, for the mere luxury of the table, birds which make such fine musick; surely their melody affords more enjoyment, than what can be had from eating them. They are however, a very common dish in the southern countries, particularly in France.

In general, it may be observed that this island is so privileged by nature, that there is no poisonous animal in it. For although there are some scorpions, their bite carries no venom. The creature in Corsica, which approaches nearest to a poisonous animal is a spider, of an extraordinary size. Its bite will irritate, and inflame to a great degree, and the swelling which it occasions, is very alarming to one unacquainted with it; but it soon goes away, and no bad consequences follow, more than from the stinging of our bees. This spider, has by some been mistaken for the famous tarantula of the kingdom of Naples.

Trees grow remarkably well in Corsica. There

is here almoſt every ſort of forreſt trees, but it is principally adorned with pines of different kinds, oaks, and cheſtnut trees. All of theſe are to be found of a great ſize; ſome of the pines in particular, are exceedingly lofty, and the cheſtnut tree grows to a prodigious bigneſs.

There are extenſive forreſts in different places. That of Vico is moſt remarkable. There is in Corſica, timber ſufficient to maintain a very large fleet, and the timber here, is much harder than one would expect in ſo ſouthern a latitude, owing to the rocky ſoil of the country, to the perpetual currents of freſh air through its valleys, and to the temperature that proceeds from ſome of its mountains being half of the year in ſnow, and this is alſo one great cauſe of the ſalubrity of the climate, in which Corſica has much the advantage of Sardinia.

The Ilex, or ever-green oak, is very common here, and gives the country a chearful look even in the depth of winter. The lemon, the orange, the fig and the almon trees are alſo frequent. There are however, few walnut trees, and the apple, pear, plumb and cherry are not remarkably good, which is probably, owing to no care being taken of them. Corſica has the pomegranate in great perfection, also the Indian fig and the aloe; which last is said to flower here, as well as in the East.

The Corsican mountains are covered with the arbutus or strawberry tree, which gives a rich glowing appearance as far as the eye can reach. Indeed the island is very like the country which Virgil describes as the seat of rural felicity.

> Glande sues laeti redeunt, dant arbuta sylvae:
> Et varios ponit foetus autumnus et alte
> Mitis in apricis coquitur vindemia saxis.
> VIRG. Georg. lib. ii. l. 520.
> On fatning mast, the swine well pleas'd, are fed;
> And every wood with arbutus is red.
> Benignant autumn smiling on the fields,
> All various fruits in rich abundance yields;
> While ev'ry rocky mountain vines displays,
> Whose grapes are mellow'd by the sun's warm rays.

The mulberry grows well here, and is not so much in danger from blights and thunderstorms as in Italy, and the south of France; so that whenever Corsica enjoys tranquillity, it may have abundance of silk. We must not omit the laurel, to which Corsica has surely a very good claim. The box tree is a very common plant here. In most countries it is dwarfish, and generally used only for hedges; but it grows to a good size in Corsica, and may be reckoned a timber tree. Bochart (*a*) has very ingeniously shewn, that the benches of the Tyrian ships, which according to the common translation of Ezechiel, chap. xxvii. ver. 6. are said to have been made of ivory brought out of the isles of Chittim, were most probably made of Corsican boxwood.

Theophrastus in his history of plants expatiates on the wonderful size of the Corsican trees; to which, he says, the pines of Latium were nothing at all. He also says, the trees were immensely thick here; his expression is very strong, Καὶ ὅλως πᾶσαν τὴν νῆσον δασεῖαν κὶ ὥσπερ ἠγριωμένην τῇ ὕλη *b*). 'The whole island seemed crouded and savage with woods.' He relates a strange tradition, that the Romans, who were struck with the vastness of these woods, built here a prodigious large ship, which carried no less than fifty sails, but was lost in the ocean (*c*). This authour gives another ancient testimony to the goodness of the climate, soil, and air of the island, Κύρνος μὲν ὂν εἴτε διὰ τὴν ἄνεσιν, εἴτε κὶ τὸ ἔδαφος,

---

(*a*) Bochart Geog. Sac. pars i. lib. i. cap. 5.   (*b*) Theophrast. Hist. lib. v. cap. 9.   (*c*) Ib.

κỳ τὸν ἀέρα πολὺ διαφέρει τῶν ἄλλων (a). 'Corsica
'therefore, whether in respect of its temperate
'climate (b); or in respect of its soil, or of its air,
'greatly excelleth other countries.'

The different kinds of grain in Corsica, are
wheat, barley, rye, and millet; all of which grow
extremely well in several parts of the country. 
There are no oats here, as indeed hardly ever in
any of the southern countries. They give their
horses and mules barley. The millet is excellent
in Corsica, and when mixed with rye, makes a
wholesome bread, of which the peasants are very
fond. Chestnuts may be reckoned a sort of grain
in Corsica; for they answer all the purposes of
it. The Corsicans eat them when roasted by way of
bread. They even have them grinded into flour,
and of that they make very good cakes.

There is a vast quantity of honey produced in
Corsica; for the island has from the earliest times
been remarkable for its swarms of bees. When
it was subject to the Romans, a tribute was imposed upon it of no less than two hundred thou-

---

(a) Theophrast. Hist. lib. v. cap. 9.
(b) I follow Scaliger's interpretation of ἄιωσις. He translates it
Temperies.

sand pounds of wax yearly (*a*). Indeed the laurel, the almon tree, and the myrtle, in the flowers of which, the bees find so much sweetness, are very common here; and the hills are all covered with wild thyme, and other fragrant herbs. Yet its honey hath always been accounted bitter, by reason of the boxwood and yew, as Diodorus (*b*) and Pliny (*c*) observe; which make Virgil's Lycidas wish

>Sic tua Cyrnaeas fugiant examina taxos.
>
>         VIRG. Eclog. ix. 30.
>————————So may thy bees refuse
>The baneful juices of Cyrnaean yews.
>         WARTON.

and Martial write

>Audet facundo qui carmina mittere Nervae,
>Hyblaeis apibus Corsica mella dabit.
>         MARTIAL. lib. ix. Epig. 27.
>To tuneful Nerva, who would verses send,
>May Corsick honey give to Hybla's bees.

Many people think the bitterness which is in the Corsican honey very agreeable. The reason which Pliny assigns for the bitterness of the honey, he also assigns for the excellence of the wax.

(*a*) Liv. lib. xlii. cap. 7.   (*b*) Diodor. Sicul. lib. v. cap. 295.   (*c*) Plin. lib. xvi. cap. 16.

Having mentioned the Punick, the Pontick, and the Cretan, he says, 'Post has Corsica (cera) quo-
'niam ex buxo fit habere quandam vim medicami-
'nis putatur (*a*). After these, the Corsican wax;
'because it is made from the box tree, is reckon-
'ed to have a certain medicinal virtue.'

There are in Corsica, a great many mines of lead, copper, iron, and silver. Near to San Fiorenzo is a very rich silver mine, yielding above the value of 5 l. sterling out of every 100 lib. weight of ore. The Corsican iron is remarkably good, having a toughness nearly equal to that of the prepared iron of Spain, famous over all the world. It is said that the true Spanish barrels are made of iron which has been worn and beat for a long time in heads of nails in the shoes of the mules, who travel with a slow and incessant pace along the hard roads. But a very small proportion of the great quantity of Spanish barrels, which are sold in all parts of Europe, can have this advantage. The metal of the Corsican barrels is little inferiour to that of the generality of Spanish ones, and they begin to make them very well.

An allusion has been drawn from the iron mines, and the name of Corsica, to the charac-

(*a*) Plin. Nat. Hist. lib. xvi. cap. 16.

ter of its inhabitants. Hieronymus de Marinis, a Genoese, who writes on the dominion and government of the republick, says of this island, 'Terrae viscera ferri fodinis affluunt, naturae cum ipso Corsicae nomine in uno conspirantis praejudicio, Corsi enim corde sunt ferreo, adeoque ad sicam armaque prono (*a*). The bowels of the earth abound in mines of iron; nature conspiring, by a sort of prejudice, to form a similarity between the name (*b*) of Corsica and the temper of the people; for the Corsicans have hearts of iron, and are therefore prone to arms and the sword.' The Marquis D'Argens (*c*) applies to Corsica these lines of Crebillon,

La nature maratre en ces afreux climats,
Produisoit au lieu d'or du fer et des soldats.

In that rude isle, instead of golden ore,
   Nature, to aid the genius of the place,
On her high hills the massy iron bore,
   And bade her sons still rise a hardy race.
JOHN HOME.

I may add

And virtue springing from the iron soil.

(*a*) Graev. Thesaur. Antiq. vol. I. p 1410.    (*b*) Corsica, Cor-sica. Cor, the heart; Sica, a stiletto, heart of steel. (*c*) Lettres Juives. let. 55.

There are also mines of allum, and of saltpetre, in several parts of Corsica.

There is here a kind of granite, extremely hard, some of it approaching in quality to the oriental granite, which was so famous at Rome, and of which such noble columns are still remaining, said to have been brought from Egypt. I fear it would be extravagant to conjecture, that some of these columns may have been the produce of Corsica; for, besides the perfection of the hieroglyphicks, which prove them to have been in Egypt, I question if such large pieces of granite could be raised in Corsica. There is here likewise porphyry, and a great variety of jasper. The magnificent chapel of the grand duke of Tuscany, at Florence, is finished with Corsican jasper, with which its inside is elegantly incrusted, and has a most beautiful appearance.

On the borders of the lake of Ino, they find pieces of rock chrystal, very clear, and with five sides, as if they had been cut by a lapidary. They find some of it too in the mountains of Istria. It is so hard, that it strikes fire; and the Corsicans frequently use it for flint to their fusils.

Near to Bastia, there is found a sort of mineral, called by the country people, petra quadrata, because it is always found in little square bits. It has much about the hardness of marble, has a colour like iron-ore, and weighs like lead. The Corsicans ascribe certain mystical virtues to this stone, as appears from an odd monkish distich made in its praise.

> Petrae quadratae duro de marmore natae,
> Innumeras dotes quis numerare potest!
>
> Of the square stone of marble grown,
> The virtues fell, what man can tell!

From the description of Corsica, which I have now given, it will appear to be a country of considerable importance. According to Mr. Templeman's Tables, in his New Survey of the Globe, the island contains 2520 square miles. It hath a number of good harbours. Its air is excellent, and its productions rich and various.

I shall conclude this chapter with Homer's description of Ithaca, which, in general, may be well applied to Corsica.

> Εἰ δὴ τήνδε τε γαῖαν ἀνείρεαι· οὐδέ τι λίην
> Οὕτω νώνυμός ἐστιν· ἴσασι δέ μιν μάλα πολλοὶ,
> Η μὲν ὅσοι ναίουσι πρὸς ἠῶ τ' ἠέλιόν τε,
> Η δ' ὅσοι μετόπισθε ποτὶ ζόφον ἠερόεντα.
> Η τοι μὲν τρηχεῖα καὶ οὐχ, ἱππήλατός ἐστιν,

Οὐδὲ λίην λυπρὴ, ἀτὰρ ὐδ' εὐρεῖα τέτυκται.
Ἐν μὲν γάρ οἱ σῖτος ἀθέσφατος, ἐν δέ τε οἶνος
Γίγνεται· αἰεὶ δ' ὄμβρος ἔχει, τεθαλυῖά τε ἔρση·
Αἰγίβοτος δ' ἀγαθὴ καὶ βύβοτος· ἔςι μὲν ὕλη
Παντοίη, ἐν δ' ἀρδμοὶ ἐπηετανοὶ παρέασιν.
Τῶ τοι, ξεῖν, Ἰθάκης γε καὶ ἐς Τροίην ὄνομ' ἵκοι,
Τήν περ τηλοῦ φασὶν Ἀχαιΐδος ἔμμεναι αἴης.

Odyſſ. lib. xiii. l. 238.

Thou ſeeſt an iſland, not to thoſe unknown,
Whoſe hills are brighten'd by the riſing ſun,
Nor thoſe that plac'd beneath his utmoſt reign,
Behold him ſinking in the weſtern main.
The rugged ſoil allows no level ſpace,
For flying chariots, or the rapid race;
Yet, not ungrateful to the peaſant's pain,
Suffices fulneſs to the ſwelling grain.
The loaded trees their various fruits produce,
And cluſtring grapes afford a generous juice:
Woods crown our mountains, and in every grove
The bounding goats and friſking heifers rove:
Soft rains and kindly dews refreſh the field,
And riſing ſprings eternal verdure yield.
Ev'n to thoſe ſhores is Ithaca renown'd,
Where Troy's majeſtick ruins ſtrow the ground.

POPE.

## CHAPTER II.

*A concise View of the* REVOLUTIONS *which* CORSICA *has undergone from the earliest times.*

ALTHOUGH many distinguished authours have, in conformity with the taste of the age, rejected every inquiry into the origin of nations, and presented their readers with nothing but what can be clearly attested; I confess, I am not for humouring an inordinate avidity for positive evidence. By being accustomed to demonstration, or what approaches near to it, and at no time giving any credit to what we do not fully comprehend, we are apt to form a pride and insolence of understanding; the mind acquires a hardness and obstinacy, inconsistent with the true intention of our faculties in this imperfect state, and is rendered unfit for the reception of many important truths.

But not to deviate into metaphysical speculation, I have always thought, that even the dark and fabulous periods are worthy of some attention.

The foundest heads among the ancients thought so; and their works are therefore more agreeable, than if they had confined themselves to strict authenticity. The origin of every nation is, as Livy says, 'Poeticis decora fabulis (*a*), Adorned with poetical fables.' These are always amusing to the imagination, when neither tedious, nor too extravagant. We love to be led on in a gradual progress, and to behold truth emerging from obscurity, like the sun breaking through the clouds. Such a progress makes a part of our own nature, which advances from the dawnings of being in our infancy, to greater and greater intelligence.

They, whose genius is directed to the study of antiquities, besides the immediate delight which such traditions afford them, are often able, from hints seemingly detached and unimportant, to trace the fundamental truth, and extend the bounds of reality. Few indeed have that peculiar turn for inquiry, to deserve the name of antiquarians. But there is an universal principle of curiosity, with respect to times past, which makes even conjectures be received with a kind of pleasing veneration; and although the great end of history is in-

(*a*) Liv. Prooem.

struction, I think it is also valuable, when it serves to gratify this curiosity.

I shall therefore, in treating of the revolutions of Corsica, go as far back as books will serve me; though at the same time, I intend to give no more than a concise recital, and am rather to shew my readers what is to be seen, than to detain them till I exhibit a full view of it.

The earliest accounts that we have of Corsica, are to be found in Herodotus. He tells us, that its first inhabitants were Phenicians; for, that Cadmus, the son of Agenor, when wandering in quest of Europa, fell upon this island, which was named Callista, and left there some of his countrymen, with his own cousin Memblearéus (*a*). He tells us, that eight generations after this, Theras brought a colony to the island, from Lacedaemon. This Theras (*b*) was originally of the race of Cadmus,

(*a*) Ησαν δὲ ἐν τῇ νῦν Θήρῃ καλεομένῃ νήσῳ, πρότερον δὲ Καλλίςῃ τῇ αὐτῇ ταύτῃ, ἀπόγονοι Μεμβλιάρεω τοῦ Ποικίλεω, ἀνδρὸς Φοίνικος. Κάδμος γὰρ ὁ Αγήνορος, Εὐρώπην διζήμενος, προσέχε ἐς τὴν νῦν Θήρην καλεομένην· προχόντι δὲ, εἴτε δή οἱ ἡ χώρη ἤρεσε, εἴτε καὶ ἄλλως ἠθέλησε ποιῆσαι τῦτο, καταλείπει γὰρ ἐν τῇ νήσῳ ταύτῃ ἄλλυς τε τῶν Φοινίκων, καὶ δὴ καὶ τῶ: ἑωυτῦ συγγενέων Μεμβλίαρον.  Herodot. lib. iv. cap. 147.

(*b*) Ην δὲ ὁ Θήρας οὗτος γένος ἐὼν Καδμεῖος, τῆς μητρὸς ἀδελφεὸς τοῖσι παισὶ Αριστοδήμυ, Εὐρυσθένεϊ καὶ Προκλέϊ. Εόντων

but, being uncle by the motherside to Eurysthenes and Procles, the two sons of Aristodemus, and, on that account, having governed the kingdom as their tutor; when they grew up, and became kings of Sparta, Theras scorning to live a private life, and to be under the government of his pupils, determined not to remain at Lacedaemon, but to go and join his kindred in the island of Corsica, then called Callista. Accordingly, (*b*) he went thither with some chosen companions, not with any intention to drive out the former inha-

δ' ἔτι τῶν παίδων τύτων νηπίων, ἐπιτροπαίην εἶχε ὁ Θήρας τὴν ἐν Σπάρτῃ βασιληίην. Αὐξηθέντων δὲ τῶν ἀδελφιδέων, καὶ παραλαβόντων τὴν ἀρχὴν, ὕτω δὴ ὁ Θήρας δεινὸν ποιεύμενος ἄρχεσθαι ὑπ' ἄλλων, ἐπεί τε ἐγεύσατο ἀρχῆς, οὐκ ἔφη μενεῖν ἐν τῇ Λακεδαίμονι, ἀλλ' ἀποπλεύσεσθαι ἐς τοὺς συγγενέας.

Herodot. lib. iv. cap. 147.

(*b*) Οὗτοι ἐνέμοντο τὴν Καλλίσην καλεομένην ἐπὶ γενεὰς, πρὶν ἢ Θήραν ἐλθεῖν ἐκ Λακεδαίμονος, ὀκτὼ ἀνδρῶν. Ἐπὶ τύτοις δὴ ὦν ὁ Θήρας λαὸν ἔχων ἀπὸ τῶν φυλέων, ἔστελλε συνοικίσων τύτοισι· ἐδαμῶς ἐξελῶν αὐτὺς, ἀλλὰ κάρτα οἰκηϊεύμενος. Ἐπεί τε δὲ καὶ οἱ Μινύαι ἐκδράντες ἐκ τῆς ἐρκτῆς ἵζοντο ἐς τὸ Τηΰγετον, τῶν Λακεδαιμονίων βυλευομένων σφέας ἀπολλύναι, παραιτέεται ὁ Θήρας ὅκως μήτε φόνος γένηται, αὐτός τε ὑπεδέκετό σφεας ἐξάξειν ἐκ τῆς χώρης. Συγχωρησάντων δὲ τῇ γνώμῃ τῶν Λακεδαιμονίων, τρισὶ τριηκοντέροισι ἐς τοὺς Μεμβλιάρεω ἀπογόνυς ἔπλωσε. * * * *
* * * * Τῇ δὲ νήσῳ ἐπὶ τοῦ οἰκιστέω Θήρα ἡ ἐπωνυμίη ἐγένετο.

Ibid. et cap. 148.

bitants, but, on the contrary, with most friendly dispositions towards them.

Sometime after this, the Minyae, a wandering tribe, who had taken refuge among the Lacedaemonians, having become obnoxious, on account of their aspiring views, were thrown into prison, and condemned to die; but Theras persuaded the Spartans to spare them, promising, that he would carry them out of the country; and accordingly, he carried them to the island of Callista, to join the new colony which he had settled there; and from him, the island was called Thera.

These Minyae, though but a wandering tribe among the Lacedaemonians, were, in reality, of illustrious descent, being the posterity of the heroick Argonauts (a).

(a) Τῶν ἐκ τῆς Ἀργῆς ἐπιβατέων παίδων παῖδες, ἐξελαθέντες ὑπὸ Πελασγῶν τῶν ἐκ Βραυρῶνος λητσαμένων τὰς Ἀθηναίων γυναῖκας ὑπὸ τύτων δὲ ἐξελαθέντες ἐκ Λήμνε, οἴχοντο πλέοντες ἐς Λακεδαίμονα. Ἱζόμενοι δὲ ἐν τῷ Τηϋγέτῳ, πυρὴν ἔκαιον. Λακεδαιμόνιοι δὲ ἰδόντες, ἄγγελον ἔπεμπον, πευσόμενοι τίνες τε ᾖ ὁκόθεν εἰσί. Οἱ δὲ τῷ ἀγγέλῳ εἰρωτέοντι ἔλεξον, ὡς εἴησαν μὲν Μινύαι, παῖδες δὲ εἶεν τῶν ἐν τῇ Ἀργοῖ πλεόντων ἡρώων· προχόντας γὰρ τύτες ἐς Λήμνον, φυτεῦσαι σφέας. Οἱ δὲ Λακεδαιμόνιοι ἀκηκοότες τὸν λόγον τῆς γενεῆς τῶν Μινυέων, πέμψαντες τὸ δεύτερον, ἠρώτεον τί θέλοντες ἥκοιέν τε ἐς τὴν χώρην, ᾖ πῦρ αἴθοιεν. Οἱ δὲ ἔφασαν, ὑπ᾽ ὁ Πελασγῶν ἐκβληθέντες, ἥκειν ἐς τὺς πατέρας· δικαιότατον γὰρ εἶναι ὕτω τῦτο γίνεσθαι· δέεσθαί τε οἰκέειν ἅμα τύτοισι, μοῖράν τε

This account of the first peopling of Corsica, is a very curious piece of ancient history. It is indeed very probable, that the Phenicians, or the Phoceans, were its original inhabitants; seeing they were the first great navigatours in the western part of the world, and sent out colonies to many distant countries.

It afterwards got the name of Κύρνος, Cyrnus, from the number of its promontories; and Isidorus (*a*) relates the manner in which it got the name of Corsica. According to him, Corsa, a Ligurian woman, having often observed a bull swim over to the island, and return much fatter, she had the curiosity to follow him in a little vessel; and so discovered the island, with all its beauty and fertility. Upon which the Ligurians sent thither a colony; and from Corsa, who had made the discovery, they called the island Corsica. This is ludicrous enough; but we may trace what has given rise to so extraordinary a fiction, when we consider, that very probably, a people from the opposite coast of Italy, either

τιμέων μετέχοντες, ᾗ τῆς γῆς ἀπολαχόντες. Λακεδαιμονίοισι δὲ ἕαδε δέκεϑαι τοὺς Μινύας ἐπ' οἷσι ϑέλωσι αὐτοί.

Herodot. lib. iv. cap. 145.

(*a*) Isidor. Origin. lib. 13. cap. 6.

the Ligurians, or the Etruscans, have taken possession of Corsica.

Whatever may be in this conjecture, it is certain, that its next masters were the Carthaginians, who extended their conquests over all the islands of the Mediterranean. Aristotle relates a most extraordinary piece of Punick policy, with respect to Corsica. Finding that it was difficult to keep the inhabitants in subjection, they ordered the whole of the vines and olives in the island to be pulled up, and forbid the Corsicans, under the pain of death, to sow their fields with any kind of grain, so that they might be kept in the most absolute dependance; and, though possessed of a very fertile territory, be obliged to resort to Africa, to seek the bare necessaries of life. So early was the cowardly and barbarous policy of a trading republick exercised against this people.

Corsica next passed under the dominion o Rome. In the first Punick war, and about the 493 year from the building of the city, Lucius Cornelius Scipio conquered the island (*a*),

(*a*) Liv. Epit. lib. xvii. Flor. lib. ii. cap. 2.

being opposed by an army of Sardinians and Corsicans, headed by Hanno, a Carthaginian general.

It appears however, that the Corsicans could not bear subjection with patience, for they were continually attempting to get free. Of this, we have an instance in the epitome of the twentieth book of Livy. We next find them engaged against M. Pinarius the praetor, who slew 2000 of them, obliged them to give hostages, and took them bound to pay a tribute of 100000 lib. of wax, every year (*a*). Afterwards C. Cicereius the praetor, was obliged to give them battle, when 1700 of them were killed, and upwards of 1070 taken prisoners, and upon this occasion, their annual tribute was increased to 200000 lib. weight of wax (*b*). From these instances, we may see that Corsica was formerly much more populous than it is now, and that it hath been able to furnish amazing quantities of honey. We are told by Pliny, that Papyrius Naso first triumphed over the Corsicans, on the Alban mount (*c*).

(*a*) Liv. lib. xl. cap. 34.     (*b*) Ib. lib. xlii. cap. 7.
(*c*) Plin. lib. v. cap. 29.

It has already been said, that the Romans founded two colonies in Corsica. The island was, like their other provinces, governed by a praetor. It was also made to serve for a place of exile; and was very proper for what they called ' Relegatio in insulam, banishment to an island.' But the Romans never had a firm hold of this country, where that spirit of liberty, which tyrants call rebellion, was ever breaking forth.

On the irruption of the barbarous nations, Corsica shared the same fate with the other dominions of the ruined empire. It fell a prey to the Goths, who established there the feudal system, as they did in every other country to which their arms penetrated. Some authours say, that Corsica was conquered by Alarick, the first king of the Goths; but according to Procopius, it was conquered by a detachment sent out by Totilas (*a*).

From this period, the history of Corsica is for many ages a continued series of wars, ravage and destruction, by a variety of contending powers. We are here very much in the dark, without any sufficient clew to guide us. We find in many authours detached remarks concerning the island;

(*a*) Procop. de Bell. Goth. lib. iii. cap. 24.

but it is difficult to arrange them in tolerable order, since the dates are almost always uncertain.

I shall however give a short view of what seems to have been the progress of events.

When the power of the Saracens rose to that height, of which we read with amazement, they drove the Goths from Corsica, and maintained the dominion there for a considerable time.

It is believed, that they first gave the title of kingdom to Corsica; and, to this day, the coat armorial of the island bears a Moor's head on its shield.

There are Moorish coins frequently dug up in Corsica; and near to Ajaccio, are Saracen tombs, which appear to have had some magnificence. They are subterraneous vaults, supported by stone pillars; and in them are found sepulchral urns of an earthen composition, similar to brick.

It would appear, that the Pope has always had a view towards the annexation of Corsica to his territories. And, that he at different times instigated the kings of Arragon, as well as the sovereigns of France, to make against it, what in the stile of those times was called a holy war, which kind of wars were always calculated to serve the political views of the holy father.

At last, Corsica was actually conquered by one of the kings of France; some say, by Pepin, and others, by Charles Martel. The Corsicans shew to this day, a fountain, called by the name of Charles, in the pieve of Alesani, and, as they say, on the spot where this gallant prince vanquished the Moors.

By the kings of France, Corsica was resigned, in a perpetual gift, to the holy see. The Saracens however, from time to time returned; so that the pope had but a very feeble and uncertain sway.

The Genoese availing themselves of the distracted state of the island, had very early contrived to settle a colony at Bonifaccio; and emboldened by degrees, they landed troops on other parts of the country, and began to bear a formidable appearance.

This could not fail to incense the court of Rome, and to draw down upon them the thunders of the Vatican, from whence the holy father used, in those ages, to fulminate with serious effect against the greatest powers in Europe. Ac-

E

cordingly, the Genoese were excommunicated by pope Gregory the seventh, which made them at that time desist from their project.

In this fluctuating situation Corsica continued, till one of the popes, but which of them, historians are not agreed, sent thither Hugo Colonna, a nobleman of Rome, accompanied by several others of the Roman nobility, with a good force under his command, in order to expel the infidels from the island. When Colonna landed, he was joined by many of the inhabitants, who, during the struggle which had been subsisting so long, and with such violence, had again and again endeavoured to maintain themselves in a state of freedom, and had elected a certain number of chiefs, to whom they gave the title of caporali.

These caporali gave all the aid in their power to Colonna; and, by their influence over the people, they soon brought together such a body of men, that Colonna was enabled totally to rout the Saracens, and to dispossess them for ever.

The Moors being rendered desperate by this unexpected blow, were forced to quit the island; but before they went, they burnt all that they possibly could; and to this we must greatly impute the defolation which is yet to be feen in Corfica, and the deftruction of their ancient monuments and publick archives.

Hugo Colonna fettled in Corfica, having obtained from the Pope, diftinguifhed honours and extenfive grants. The family of Colonna is one of the moft illuftrious, and moft ancient in the world. So early as the 1200, mention is made of Pietro Colonna, the eight of the name. The branch which fettled in Corfica, continued long in great fplendour, enjoying the noble fief of Iftria; but, by the confufions and troubles which the ifland has been thrown into, by the bloody contefts between the Genoefe and the patriotrick Corficans, that family hath fuffered prodigioufly, and its poffeffions are reduced to a very narrow compafs. The prefent head of the family, is a worthy, fenfible man, and very zealous in the great caufe. I was lodged in his houfe at Sollacarò, where I found Pafcal Paoli.

It is probable, that the Corfican counts, marquiffes and barons, derive their origin from this period; for I can fee no time fo proper for their firft taking place here.

The ifland remained for fome time in tolerable

quiet. But partly from the diffensions of different parties among themselves, ever impatient of contradiction, and partly from the repeated attacks of the Genoese, whose hankering after this little kingdom still continued, there were such disorders, and such a defect of good government, that the Pope thought proper to make it over to the Pisans, who were then in great power.

This grant was upon advantageous terms for the holy father, like the many grants of fiefs which he was in use to give to various princes, to be held of the see of Rome. A learned Professour of the univerfity of Pifa, has composed a very curious dissertation concerning the ancient dominion of his countrymen over Corsica. It is to be found in the VII. volume of the Essays of the Academy of Cortona.

The Pisans, while their republick flourished, and their force was considerable, maintained their authority over Corsica to very good purpose; and, as far as we can gather from different authours, the island enjoyed more repose and tranquillity during this period, than it has ever been known to enjoy.

But this calm was of short endurance; for the

Genoese, irritated to find themselves now effectually excluded from an island on which they had long set their hearts; and being, over and above, the determined rivals of Pisa, a keen and obstinate war was carried on between these states; at last, the Genoese prevailed, in the famous sea-fight at Malora, near the mouth of the Arno; after which, they got entirely the mastery of Pisa, and so were at length enabled to seize upon Corsica, about the beginning of the fourteenth century.

Thus were the Corsicans, for the first time, brought under the power of the Genoese; with whom they have since had such struggles for that freedom, which they appear to have at all times attempted to recover.

If I have erred in any part of this recital, I am sure it is without any intention. I know some Genoese writers have maintained, that a signor Ademar, of their nation, was employed in the first conquest of the island by the kings of France. I confess I do not see sufficient authority for this. But supposing it had been so, Ademar could only be an officer under the French king. We are certain, that the French king made the conquest, because he afterwards gave a gift of the island to the pope.

But I would not dwell long upon such disquisitions. There are many pieces lately published, both by the Corsicans and the Genoese; in which the authours, with great labour, endeavour to refute each others hypotheses with regard to many ancient facts in the history of Corsica. Here indeed, there is full scope for all parties; since those periods are so obscure, that every writer may fill them up according to the turn of his imagination. Just as people who are abroad in a dark night, may with equal keenness, and equal appearance of reason affirm, that they see objects totally different.

Let Corsica have been the property of the Phenicians, the Etruscans, the Carthaginians, the Romans, the Goths, the Saracens: let it have been a conquest of France; a gift from that kingdom to the pope; a gift again from the pope to the Pisans, and at length a conquest of Genoa; still we must have recourse to the plain and fundamental principle, that the Corsicans are men, and have a right to liberty; which, if usurped by any power whatever, they have at all times a just title to vindicate.

In reviewing these strange and rapid revolutions, which this island has undergone, we may join with Seneca (*a*) in reflecting on the mutability of human affairs, and be silent on the changes which happen to individuals, when we contemplate the vicissitudes of a whole nation.

The Genoese having obtained the undoubted possession of Corsica, they were eager to enjoy their power, and thought they could not fully enjoy it, but by exercising the most severe dominion. What we have long anxiously desired, acquires in our minds an imaginary and extravagant value; and when we actually become possessed of it, a moderate and reasonable fruition, seems insipid and unsatisfactory to our heightned expectations. We are even, as it were, uncertain if we really have it. And generally, we never rest, till by abusing our powers, we destroy what we esteemed so highly.

An individual, who acquires a large fortune, and a state, which acquires an increase of dominion, may be very properly compared. He who gets a large fortune, thinks he cannot shew his

(*a*) Seneca de consolatione.

command of riches, but by such acts of profusion, as must quickly dissipate them. And a state, which has acquired an increase of dominion, thinks its sovereignty is not sufficiently manifested, but by such acts of arbitrary oppression, as must tend to force its subjects to throw off their allegiance. For however a people may, from indolence, from timidity, or from other motives, submit for a season to a certain degree of tyranny; if it is long continued, and pushed to an exorbitant length, nature will revolt, and the original rights of men will call for redress.

The Genoese were the worst nation to whom Corsica could have fallen. The Corsicans were a people, impetuous, violent and brave; who had weathered many a storm; and who could not have been governed, but by a state of which they stood somewhat in awe, and which, by humanity and proper encouragement, might have conciliated their affections. Whereas, the Genoese were a nation of republicans just in the neighbourhood of the islanders; who had long been their enemies; who had made so many cunning, and impotent attempts to seize upon the island; that although, by the unexpected course of events, they were now masters of it, the Corsicans could not look upon them with any respect. And as it has been always remarked that the foreign subjects of a little republick, are much worse used, than those of a great kingdom; they had reason to expect nothing but avowed tyranny from Genoa.

Accordingly the Genoese, who were themselves in an unstable, and perilous condition, seeking the protection sometimes of one powerful state, and sometimes of another; did not treat the Corsicans with that gentleness and confidence, which alone could have secured their attachment and obedience; by insensibly leading them to a participation of the culture and felicity of civil life, and accustoming them to consider the Genoese as their fellow subjects, and friends.

They took a direct contrary course; and, although they did not use so desperate a measure, as that of the Carthaginians, their oppression was heavy; their system was not to render the Corsicans happier and better, but by keeping them in ignorance, and under the most abject submission, to prevent their endeavouring to get free; while Genoa drained the island of all she could possibly get, choosing rather even to have less advantage by tyranny, than to have a much greater advantage, and risque the consequences of permitting to the inhabitants the blessings of freedom.

In this unhappy situation was Corsica. Often did the natives rise in arms; but having no head to direct them, they were immediately quelled. So apprehensive however were the Genoese, that, according to their own historian Filippini, they burnt 120 of the best villages in Corsica, while 4000 people left the island.

What shewed the Genoese policy in the worst light, and could not but be very galling to the Corsicans who remained at home, was, that many of these islanders, who had gone over to the continent, made a distinguished figure in most of the European states, both in learning, and in arms.

About the 1550, Corsica revived under the conduct of a great hero, who arose for the deliverance of his country. This was Sampiero di Castelica. He early discovered extraordinary parts and spirit; and had the advantage of being educated in the house of cardinal Hypolitus de Medicis, the nephew of pope Clement the seventh. He was created colonel of the Corsicans in France, and distinguished himself in almost every one of the great actions of that nation in his time.

After the death of Francis the first, he went home to his native country; where he married Vannina, heiress of the house of Ornano, of the most ancient and rich of the Corsican nobility; and from this time, he was generally called Sampiero di Ornano.

Being moved with the miserable state of his countrymen, he resolved to procure them relief; and for this, a very favourable opportunity then presented itself.

Here history begins again to open upon us. The clouds of antiquity, and barbarism are dispersed, and we proceed clearly, under the guidance of the illustrious Thuanus (*a*).

France had of a long time claimed a right over Genoa; but after the battle of Pavia, when the French were forced entirely to abandon Italy, that claim had become of no effect. Henry the second however, having commenced a new war in Ita-

(*a*) Thuan. Hist. lib. xii. cap. 2.

ly, againſt the emperour Charles the fifth, reſolved to aſſert his power in Corſica; Sampiero di Ornano encouraged this diſpoſition, that he might avail himſelf of it, to free the iſland from a yoke which galled it ſo much.

He repreſented to Henry, that as the Genoeſe had taken part with the emperour, his majeſty was debarred from all entrance to Italy by ſea; whereas, by putting himſelf in poſſeſſion of Corſica, he might have a free paſſage through the Mediterranean, and might, at the ſame time, employ that iſland as a commodious garriſon, where troops and warlike ſtores might be lodged, to be from thence thrown in upon Naples or Tuſcany, as the ſituation of affairs ſhould require.

An expedition was therefore ordered to Corſica, in the year 1553, under the command of general Paul de Thermes, accompanied by Sampiero di Ornano, Jourdain des Urſins, and ſeveral other able commanders. Henry had alſo the Turks joined with him in this expedition, having prevailed with their fourth Emperour, Solyman, ſtyled the magnificent, to ſend out a large fleet to the Tuſcan ſea (a).

This expedition was powerfully oppoſed by

(a) Knolles's hiſtory of the Turks, p. 757.

the Genoese; who had given Corsica in charge to their celebrated bank of St. George. The great Andrew Doria, though then in his eighty seventh year, bid defiance to age and infirmities, and, since Corsica was an object of importance to his country, the gallant Veteran embarked with all the spirit of his glorious youth, having a formidable armament under his command.

The war was carried on with vigour on both sides. At first however, several of the best towns were taken by the French and Turks, particularly Ajaccio, where were a number of merchants, whose riches afforded good pillage to the enemy, and helped to make the enterprise go on with more spirit. The Corsicans joined in the common cause, and the greatest part of the island was once fairly delivered from the tyrant.

But the Genoese were so well commanded by the intrepid Doria, and had besides such assistance from Charles the fifth, who sent strong reinforcements, both of Spanish and German troops, that the expedition was not entirely effectual.

In the course of this war, so many valourous actions were performed, that, fired with the contemplation of them, I am almost tempted to forget the limited bounds of my plan, and of my abilities, and to assume the province of an historian; I hope a Livy, or a Clarendon, shall one day arise, and display to succeeding ages, the Corsican bravery, with the lustre which it deserves.

The Corsicans were now so violent against the Genoese, that they resolved with one accord, that rather than return under the dominion of the republick, they would throw themselves into the arms of the great Turk. At length however, a treaty was concluded between the Corsicans and Genoese, advantageous and honourable for the former, having for guarantee, his most Christian Majesty.

But, as there was an inveterate, and implacable hatred between those two nations, this treaty did not long subsist; and upon Henry's death, the same oppression as formerly, became flagrant in Corsica.

Sampiero di Ornano, who had been again for sometime in France, having lost his royal master, went himself to the Ottoman Porte, and earnestly solicited fresh assistance to his unhappy nation. But the face of affairs was changed. The same political views no longer existed; and it must be a miracle indeed, when states are moved by virtuous principles of generosity. This brave man, being unsuccesful at Constantinople, returned to Corsica, where his presence inspired the islanders with fortitude, and occasioned a very general revolt.

He carried on his glorious enterprise with considerable effect; and the more so, that, as he had now no foreign assistance, he was not looked upon as very formidable; and the republick made little preparation against him. But he was stopped in his career by the treachery of the Genoese, who had him basely assassinated, by a wretch of the name of Vitolli (*a*), in the year 1567.

Thus fell Sampiero di Bastelica di Ornano, a Corsican worthy of being ranked with the most distinguished heroes. He displayed great bravery and fidelity in foreign service; and with unremitting constancy endeavoured to restore the liber-

(*a*) Michael Metello, who writes a particular history of the Corsican revolt under Sampiero, gives a different account of his death. He will have him to have been killed from motives of private revenge, by his brother in law, Michael Ang lo di Ornano. But, besides the improbability that Vannina, the spouse of Sampiero, had a brother when it is certain she inherited the family domains; I own, that the assassination, as related by several other authours, appears to me so much of a piece with the oppressions of Genoa, both before and since, that I give it the preference.

ties of his country. Thuanus calls him ' Vir bello impiger et animo invictus (*a*). A man active in war, and of a spirit invincible.' The shades which were in his private conduct, are to be forgotten in the admiration of his publick virtues. His son Alphonso, and his grandson John Baptist, both arrived at the dignity of mareschal of France, after which his posterity failed.

Alphonso di Ornano, who had been brought up in the court of Henry the second, kept alive the patriotick struggle for a short while; but unable to make head against the republick, he retired from the island and settled in France.

The Genoese were thus again put in possession of Corsica. Enraged at what they had suffered from a daring rebellion, as they termed it; and still dreading a new insurrection, they thought only of avenging themselves on the Corsicans; and plunging that people still lower than ever, in ignorance and slavery.

Their oppression became now, if possible, worse than before. They were inflamed with hotter resentment, and their tyranny formed itself into something of a regular system. Forgetful of

(*a*) Thuani Hist. lib. xli. cap. 31.

every equitable convention that France had established, they exercised, without controul, the utmost rigours of arbitrary power. They permitted nothing to be exported from the island, but to Genoa, where, of necessity, the Corsicans were obliged to sell their merchandise at a very low rate; and in years of scarcity, the island was drained of provisions by a sort of legal plunder. For the inhabitants were forced to bring them to Genoa, so that actual famine was often occasioned in Corsica.

The Genoese did every thing in their power to foment internal dissensions in Corsica, to which the people were naturally too much inclined. These dissentions occasioned the most horrid bloodshed. They reckon that no less than 1700 Corsicans were assassinated in the space of two years. Assassinations were, in the first place, a certain cause of hatred among the Corsicans, and often between the best families, so that they would not unite in any scheme for the general liberty. And in the second place, they could be turned to very good account, either by confiscating the estates of the assassins, or by making the criminals pay heavy compensations to the judge.

The judge could wave the pursuit of justice by saying, 'Non procedatur, Let there be no process;' which could easily be cloaked under the pretence of some defect in point of form; or could even acquit the deepest offenders from his own will alone, by what was called ' Ex informata conscientia, The information of his own conscience;' of which he was not obliged to give any account.

It was not till the year 1738, that Genoa made an edict against this most dreadful abuse.

M. De Montesquieu thus writes concerning it, with that calm dignity which becomes so great a master; ' Une république d'Italie tenoit des insu-
' laires sous son obéissance; mais son droit politique
' et civil a leur égard étoit vicieux. On se souvient
' de cet acte d'amnistie, qui porte qu'on ne les con-
'. damneroit plus à des peines afflictives sur la con-
' science informée du gouverneur. On a vu sou-
' vent des peuples demander des privileges; ici le
' souverain accorde le droit de toutes les nations (a).
' A republick in Italy held a nation of islanders
' under her obedience. But her political, and ci-
' vil constitution among them, was bad. We re-
' ember that act of amnesty, which bears, that

(a) Esprit des Loix. edit. Edin. Liv. x. cap. 8.

'they should no more be condemned to afflic-
'tive pains, upon the informed conscience of
'the governour. We have often seen people
'asking privileges. Here, the sovereign is pleased
'to grant the common right of all nations.'

During this oppression, it was common to condemn multitudes to the galleys, for frivolous offences, that they might purchase their liberty at a high price; and it is hardly possible to conceive greater barbarity, than what these islanders now endured.

The Genoese sent to Corsica a commissary general, or governour over the whole island; whose office continued for two years. He was generally a nobleman of desperate fortune, who by shameful extortions, returned home in opulence; and by his interest in the senate, prevented any inquiry being made into his conduct. For although the unhappy Corsicans offered many complaints to the republick, they were instantly stifled; which was not difficult to do, as the Corsicans were considered to be so turbulent and mutinous, that no administration could please them; and as every senatour who was to give his vote, did not know, but by extravagance, he himself might one day be obliged to have recourse to the same expedient.

The commissary general had his residence at Bastia. There were also other commissaries at Calvi, Ajaccio and Bonifaccio; and Lieutenants, and inferiour officers, dispersed over the island; who all in their several stations, contributed to rob, and to ruin the country; while they triumphed in a mean security, that as Corsica was overlooked, and, as it were, hid in a corner of Europe, their injurious proceedings were not known to the world.

During this period of secret, and cruel oppression, there happened a curious enough event, which was the establishment of a colony of Greeks in Corsica; of which I shall now give an account.

After Mahomet and his successuors, had subdued almost the whole of ancient Greece, and Scanderbeg, who so gloriously defended his country, was dead; there still remained a few brave souls who inhabited a part of Peloponnesus of old, now the kingdom of Morea. This part was, what is called a branch of the Maina, the very spot where Lacedemon stood.

Here, covered by impassable mountains, with only a small entrance, they resisted the Ottoman empire, as Leonidas formerly resisted the millions of Xerxes.

But when the Turks got possession of the isle of Candia, in 1669, they came by sea, and made a descent upon Maina, penetrated into the heart of the territory, and soon became masters of it; and then, the unfortunate posterity of the Spartans, were reduced to a state, little better than slavery. Exorbitant taxes were imposed upon them; their finest women were forced away to the seraglios; and towers were built in different parts of the country, where troops were garrisoned, to keep them in awe; so that they had no hope of deliverance. Their spirits gradually sunk, and many of them embraced the faith of the Koran.

Still, however, a spark of the ancient fire was preserved amongst those, who dwelt at Porto Vitilo; who, despairing to see any change in their dejected country, came to the resolution of abandoning it altogether, and of seeking an establishment somewhere else.

With this view, they sent to Italy, deputies who had some acquaintance with the different states, and who were intrusted by the community to look out for a convenient settlement, and to conclude the terms of a convention.

The Genoese sent them over to Corsica, where

they were shewn a tract of ground, belonging to the chamber of the state, on the western side of the island, about three miles from the sea. The deputies were very well pleased with it; and, on their return to Genoa, they entered into an agreement with the republick.

They then went home to Greece, and having made a report to their countrymen, the plan was approved of; and, in the month of October, 1676, these 'Tristes reliquiae Danaûm, Sad remains of the Greeks,' embarked, in all about 1000 souls. The family of Stefanopoli was the most distinguished among them, and conducted the whole enterprise.

They arrived at Genoa, in the month of January, 1677, where they remained, till the month of March. The republick paid all the expence of their freight, and afforded them lodging and subsistence, till they were safely landed in Corsica.

The conventions entered into, were, that the Genoese granted to the Greeks, the territories of Paomia, Ruvida and Salogna, in perpetual fief. They furnished them with houses, with grain, and with cattle; and engaged to maintain a body of Genoese soldiers to defend them against all insults, for the first years of their residence. They also appointed a Genoese gentleman, with the title of Directour, as judge over them, whose office was to be biennial, so that it should go by rotation, among the Genoese nobility; and they agreed to support, at the expence of the republick, a vicar, skilled in the Greek language, who should instruct their children in different studies; and, at the same time, celebrate mass, and preach in the chapel of the directour.

On the other hand, the Greeks obliged themselves to labour the lands, and with all expedition, to discharge the debts they should incur to the republick, for supplying them with every necessary, in the infancy of their colony. They also obliged themselves, to pay to the republick, a tax of five livres, for every family, besides a tenth of all their productions, and to be ready to serve the republick, either by sea, or land, whenever their service should be required.

Thus, was this colony settled. They enjoyed the free exercise of their own rites of religion, according to the Greek church, having brought with them the bishop of Porto Vitilo.

They had also brought with them, some religious, of the order of St. Basil, the only order in their church; who established a convent in a wild and romantick valley. But the Genoese did not approve of these fathers; and, in a short time, their convent was shut up.

The Greeks found themselves very easy and happy, for a good many years. By their industry and activity, they beautified and enriched their possessions, and built very good houses, doing every thing with a taste, altogether new in Corsica.

But their neighbours, the natives of the island, did not live in great harmony with them. Perhaps, in this, envy may have had some share; for their vines and their olives, their herds and their flocks, were, by care and skill, much superiour to those of the Corsicans. But besides, the islanders looked upon the Greeks as auxiliaries of the Genoese, to whom they, from time to time, swore fidelity; and were ever ready to give their assistance. They also knew, that the Greeks were well supplied with arms; and therefore, there were frequent skirmishes between them and the peasants of the province of Vico, of which their territories had formerly made a part; and in the year 1729, when the nation rose against the the Genoese, the Greeks were seriously attacked; and many a desperate action they fought with great bravery. The Genoese formed three regular companies of them, to whom they gave pay; and they were always employed in the most difficult einterprises. In particular, they were detached to attempt taking the castle of Corte from the patriots, on which occasion, they were sorely defeated, and a great number of them were killed.

After various struggles, which the plan of this work does not allow me to relate, the Greeks were forced to leave their possessions, and retire to Ajaccio, where they now support themselves tolerably by their labour: and being convinced of the tyranny of the Genoese, wait with impatience for their total expulsion from the island; and hope from the generosity of Paoli and the Corsicans, that protection and encouragement which they deserve.

This colony has been sober, virtuous and industrious; and if they have acted in a hostile manner against the nation, it was from a good principle; from the fidelity which they owed to the republick that had granted them an afylum; which fidelity they would ever have preferved, had not the republick included them in the general oppreffion. I muft obferve of this colony, that that it hath had the honour of producing an excellent phyfician, Signor Giovanni Stefanopoli, the firft who hath had the wifdom and the fpirit to bring inoculation into practice in Corfica, by which he preferves multitudes of lives; and may therefore be juftly reckoned a diftinguifhed benefactor to the ftate.

Long defpifed, plundered and oppreffed, the Corficans again revived in 1729, when the war commenced, which, with fome intervals, has continued till now; and after fo many changes, misfortunes and ftruggles, will probably fix on a folid bafis the Corfican liberty.

It is wonderful to fee how great events are produced by little caufes. A late authour (*a*) hath given us an entertaining felection of fuch inftances, from the hiftories of different nations. The rife of the Corficans in 1729, was occafioned by a fingle paolo, a piece worth about five pence Englifh. A Genoefe collector, went to the houfe

(*a*) Monfieur Richer.

of a poor old woman, and demanded this trifling sum, as the money for which she was assessed. Being in extreme penury, she had not wherewithal to satisfy the demand. Upon which, the collector began to abuse her, and to seize some of her furniture. She begged him to have patience, and said, she hoped in a few days to be able to pay him. He persisted in his severity, and the poor woman made a great lamentation. Two or three people hearing the noise, entered the house, took the part of the woman, and exclaimed against the barbarity of the collector. He threatened them with punishment, for having hindered him in the execution of his office. This provoked the villagers, and they drove him away with stones. The Genoese sent troops to support their collector, and the Corsicans assembled in large bodies to defend themselves. The tumult encreased. A spark was sufficient to kindle the generous flame, in a people, who had so often glowed with the enthusiasm of liberty; and in a very short time, the whole island was in motion.

The Corsicans immediately rushed upon the capital, which they took almost without resistance; and they would have been masters of the castle of Corte, had they been a little better regulated.

They saw it was neceffary to put themfelves under the direction of certain chiefs. They therefore chofe Signor Andrea Ceccaldi, one of the higheft nobility in the kingdom; and Signor Luiggi Giafferi, not indeed of the firft rank, but who had a numerous parentage; a fpirit, warm to a degree of fanaticifm, againft the republick; and the moft fteady and undaunted refolution. To thefe was joined, Signor Domenico Raffalli, a worthy and learned ecclefiaftick, as a fort of prefident of juftice, whofe wifdom might preferve order in their adminiftration, and whofe religion might temper the violence of their meafures, by principles of confcience.

The Genoefe at firft endeavoured to overcome the Corficans by the fole force of the republick; but finding themfelves altogether unable for it, while the Corficans were every day growing ftronger, cutting to pieces the poor reinforcements of Genoefe troops, and thereby fupplying themfelves with more arms; the republick was under the neceffity of feeking foreign affiftance.

They applied to the emperour, Charles the fixth, who fent to Corfica, a body of auxiliaries;

under the command of General Wachtendonck. These harrassed the island, without being powerful enough to overawe it. They had continual rencounters with the Corsicans, who, in one action, killed 1200 of them. The emperour then sent a strong army of Germans, with the prince fo Wirtemberg at their head. The Corsicans were not in condition to resist such a force. They laid down their arms upon condition, that a treaty should be made between them and the Genoese, having for guarantee the emperour.

To this the republick having acceded, the Corsicans consented that their three chiefs, together with Signor Aitelli, a pievano of great influence, should go to Genoa as hostages.

These were accordingly conducted thither, dreading no violation of the promise of safety, which had been made to them. The Ligurians however, inclined to put them to death; and their minister at Vienna, had almost obtained the emperour's consent; but the prince of Wirtemberg, who was afterwards killed at the battle of Guastalla, a prince of a brave and gallant spirit, sent an express to the emperour, with a very strong letter, representing how much the honour of

Caesar would suffer, should he consent to the death of those who had surrendered themselves upon the faith of his sacred protection. This was seconded by the generous interposition of the great prince Eugene of Savoy; and instructions were sent to Genoa, that the hostages should be released.

Giafferi and Aitelli went home to Corsica. Ceccaldi went to Spain, where he died with the rank of colonel; and Raffalli went to Rome, where he remained till he became very old. He then returned to end his days in his native country, where he still lives, regarded with veneration.

The treaty which had been formally concluded between the Corsicans and the Genoese, having been broken by the latter, there was a very short suspension of hostilities; and in 1734, the Corsicans rose anew.

Giafferi was again elected a general, and got for his collegue Signor Giacinto Paoli, father of the present general.

Giacinto Paoli, was a Corsican gentleman of a good family. But his merit distinguished him more than his rank. He was a man of learning, religion and bravery; well qualified to serve his country, either in politicks, or in war. These chiefs were assisted by a variety of presidents of justice, elected one after another.

The Genoese had paid very dear for their victory, in the former struggles. It was computed, that it had cost them above thirty millions of livres, besides costly presents to the prince of Wirtemberg, and to the other general officers.

The Marquis d'Argens very pleasantly applies to the Genoese, the French fable of a gardener, who complained to a gentleman in the neighbourhood, that a hare came every day into his garden, and eat his cabbages; and begged the gentleman would be so good, as drive her out for him. The Gentleman comes with a pack of hounds, and half-a-dozen huntsmen, and does more mischief in five minutes, than the hare could have done in seven years. After a prodigious chace, the hare made her escape through a hole in the wall. Upon which the gentleman congratulated the gardener on getting rid of his enemy, and advised him to stop up the hole (*a*). So the Genoese, after hav-

(*a*) Lettres Juiv. lett. 34.

ing expended a great deal more upon foreign auxiliaries, than any advantage they can ever derive from Corsica; upon the departure of these auxiliaries, have the mortification to find themselves just as they were.

Genoa again tried her force against Corsica; but she only shewed her weakness, and bad politicks. So much fallen was she from that adventurous state, which had formerly extended her influence so far. Genoa indeed, was unhappily administrated. They relate, that the city of Savona having rebelled several times, it was deliberated in the senate, whether they ought not to destroy it altogether. When a witty senator of the Doria family, rose, and said, 'If that be your intention, gentlemen, you need only send them such another governour, as the two last were; you cannot fall on a better expedient.'

The Corsicans on this occasion, displayed their resolution afresh, in the cause of liberty. They were well conducted, and had many successful engagements with the Genoese.

Their noble enthusiasm always continued, and, notwithstanding many unlucky divisions among themselves, there were still, in different parts of the island, intrepid bands, animated by the example of distinguished leaders.

I must here take notice of count Domenico Rivarola. His family was a branch of the house of Rossi, at Parma, one of the most ancient and conspicuous of the Italian nobility. His ancestor had left his fief of Rivarola, in the territory of Mantua, on account of the wars between the emperour, and the countess Matilda, and had settled in the Genoese state, where he quitted the name of Rossi, and took that of Rivarola. This family of Rivalora, greatly increased. In the fifteenth century, Francis Rivarola was, on account of long services, raised to the dignity of a count Palatine, by the emperour Maximilian; from which period, the title has since been in the family. Several descendants of Rivarola were established in Spain, Sicily, and the dominions of Sardinia, and three were established in Corsica, one in Calvi, one in Ajaccio, and one in Bastia; of which last, count Domenico Rivarola was the representative.

This gentleman had the lands of Chiaveri, on the river of Genoa; was considered as a friend of the republick, and was intrusted by

G

her, with the office of commiffary in Balagna; a fingular honour for a Corfican.

He endeavoured, at this time, to make a reafonable accommodation between the Corficans and Genoefe, which having proved ineffectual, he was convinced, that the republick was determined to perfevere in tyranny; he therefore embraced the patriotick party, and was ever after, moft firm and zealous, in the great caufe of liberty. He quitted the ifland, and went over to Leghorn, that he might be at full liberty to negotiate upon the continent, in behalf of his country.

The Genoefe immediately confifcated his lands of Chiaveri. He had ftill the lands of Oletta, in Corfica; to which, he made his family remove from Baftia. But, he had foon a very fevere trial of his conftancy. For, the fame year, his fon Antonio, who was ftudying at the academy of Siena, went home, to bring with him his brother Nicholas; and, as they were croffing over to Leghorn, in a little Tufcan veffel, with a Britifh paffport, they were taken by the Republick, and carried to Genoa, where they were thrown into prifon.

The republick thought this would certainly

prevent count Domenico, the father, from continuing with the patriots. They offered to restore him his possessions, to release his sons, and to make him general of the Corsican troops in their service, if he would return to their side. But he answered with resolution and magnanimity, 'I miei figliuoli me li daranno a lor
' dispetto; e tutte le altre offerte le stimo un
' nulla a paragone del giusto impegno che ho
' preso e che seguiterò fin che ho vita. My sons
' they shall be obliged to give me, whether they
' will or no; and all their other offers I con-
' sider as nothing, in comparison of the just en-
' terprise in which I am engaged, and in which
' I will persevere while I have life.' Such instances of patriotick spirit deserve to be recorded. The annals of Corsica will furnish many of them.

When the Austrian troops entered Genoa, the young counts Rivarola were set at liberty. Count Antonio, the eldest, my very good friend, is a major, in the service of the king of Sardinia, and consul general for that sovereign in Tuscany. Count Nicholas, the other, lives at Oletta in Corsica, but is of so delicate a constitution, that he cannot serve his country as he would wish to do. Both the brothers have the spirit of their father.

Count Domenico Rivarola obtained a Regiment in the Sardinian service, and by his influence at Turin, procured such assistance, that he would have been able to free his country, had it not been for the house of Matra in Corsica, which stood by the republick, and had interest enough to make a strong party in the island.

In the mean time, the Corsican war went on with spirit. Sometimes it was expected, that the king of Spain would strike in on one side or other. But that prince did not choose to interfere. Probably he foresaw, that it would involve him in a quarrel with France.

While the Genoese and the Corsicans were thus keenly engaged, and the politicians of Europe were forming various conjectures, a most extraordinary circumstance occurred, to the amazement of every body. This was the appearance of Theodore, whose singular story has made so much noise.

As many inconsistent reports have been circulated, with regard to this man, I have been at great pains to obtain authentick accounts concerning him, which, I am perfuaded, will be very acceptable to my readers.

Theodore Baron Newhoff, in the county of La Marc in Weftphalia, was the perfonage who afpired to the fovereignty of Corfica. He had his education in the French fervice. He afterwards went to Spain, where he received fome marks of regard from the duke of Riperda and cardinal Alberoni. But being of a ftrange unfettled projecting difpofition, he quitted Spain, and went and travelled into Italy, England and Holland; ever in fearch of fome new adventure. He at laft fixed his attention on Corfica, and formed a fcheme of making himfelf a king.

He was a man of abilities and addrefs; and, after having fully informed himfelf of every thing relating to the ifland, he went to Tunis, where he fell upon means to procure fome money and arms; and then came to Leghorn, from whence he wrote a letter to the Corfican chiefs, Giafferi and Paoli, offering confiderable affiftance to the nation, if they would elect him as their fovereign.

This letter was configned to count Domenico Rivarola, who acted as Corfican plenipotentiary, in Tuscany; and he gave for answer, that if Theodore brought the assistance he promised to the Corsicans, they would very willingly make him king.

Upon this he, without loss of time set sail, and landed at Tavagna in spring, 1736. He was a man of a very stately appearance; and the Turkish dress which he wore, added to the dignity of his mien. He had a few attendants with him. His manners were so engaging, and his offers so plausible, that he was proclaimed king of Corsica, before count Rivarola's dispatches arrived to inform the chiefs of the terms upon which he had agreed. He brought with him about a thousand zechins of Tunis, besides some arms and ammunition, and made magnificent promises of foreign assistance; so that the Corsicans, who were glad of any support, willingly gave into his schemes; and it must be considered, that there could be no great harm in allowing a man the name of king, since they had always the power of restraining his authority.

Theodore assumed every mark of royal dignity. He had his guards, and his officers of state. He conferred titles of honour, and he struck money, both of silver and copper. The silver pieces were few in number, and can now hardly be met with. I have one of his copper coins, on one side of it is 'T. R. (Theodorus Rex) King Theodore,' with a double branch crossed, and round it this inscription, ' Pro bono publico Re. Co. (Regni Corsicae) For the publick good of the kingdom of Corsica.' On the other side, is the value of the piece, ' cinque soldi, five sous.' There was such a curiosity over all Europe to have king Theodore's coins, that his silver pieces were sold at four zechins each; and when the genuine ones were exhausted, imitations of them were made at Naples, and, like the imitations of antiques, were bought up at a high price, and carefully preserved in the cabinets of the virtuosi.

Theodore immediately blocked up the Genoese fortified towns; and he used to be sometimes at one siege, sometimes at another, standing with a telescope in his hand, as if he spied the assistance which he said he expected. He used also the artifice of making large packets be continually brought to him from the continent, which he gave out to be from the different sovereigns of Europe, acknowledging his authority, and promising to befriend him.

The Genoese were not a little confounded with this unexpected adventurer. They published a violent manifesto against Theodore, treating him with great contempt, but at the same time shewing, that they were alarmed at his appearance. Theodore replied, in a manifesto, with all the calmness and dignity of a monarch, expressed his indifference as to the injurious treatment of the republick, and appeared firm in the hopes of victory.

The Genoese minister at London, made strong interest against the Corsicans; and on the 24 of July, 1736, her majesty, the queen regent of Great Britain, issued out her royal proclamation, prohibiting any of his majesty's subjects from furnishing provisions or assistance to the malecontents of Corsica.

After having been about eight months in Corsica, Theodore perceived, that the people began to cool in their affections towards him, and did not act with the same resolution as before. He therefore wisely determined, to leave them for a little, and try his fortune again upon the continent. So, after having laid down a plan of administration, to be observed in his absence, he quitted the island, in the month of November.

He went to Holland, and there he was successful enough to get credit to a great extent, from several rich merchants, particularly Jews, who trusted him with cannon, and other warlike stores, to a great value, under the charge of a supercargo. With these, he returned to Corsica, in 1739; and, on his arrival, he put to death the supercargo, that he might not have any trouble from demands being made upon him.

By this time, as shall be afterwards shewn, the French had become so powerful in the island, that, although Theodore threw in his supply of warlike stores, he did not incline to venture his person, the Genoese having set a high price upon his head.

He therefore chose to relinquish his throne, and give up his views of ambition for safety, furnishing a remarkable example, how far a daring and desperate spirit may go; for, had Theodore had a little more prudence, and some better fortune, he, and his posterity, might have worn the crown of Corsica, upon the generous title, of having delivered the island from oppression.

It has often been said, that Theodore was secretly supported by some of the European powers. But, from all that I can learn, there is no foundation whatever, for this conjecture. It is, indeed, a rare thing, to find a private gentleman embarking on his own bottom, in an enterprise of such a nature. But the truth is, Theodore was a most singular man, and had been so beaten about, by change of fortune, that he had lost the common sentiments of mankind, and viewed things as one who is mad, or drunk, or in a fever. He had nothing to lose, and a great deal to win. His scheme was, to amuse the Corsicans with hopes of foreign aid; and, by the force of hope, to carry them foreward. This might have succeeded, in which case, he could very easily have said, that the foreign aid would have come, had there been occasion for it; but they had behaved with such spirit, as to require no help. And, had he been fortunate, it is probable, some of the powers of Europe might have, in reality, stood by him.

The Corsicans now, talk differently of king Theodore. Some of them, who had most faith in his fine speeches, still extoll him to the skies, to support their own judgment; others, who looked upon him as an impostour, and never joined heartily in his measures, represent him as a kind of

Wat Tyler, a king of a rabble; but the moſt knowing and judicious, and the General himſelf, conſider him in the moderate light in which he has now been repreſented, and own, that he was of great ſervice in reviving the ſpirit of the nation, which, after a good many years of conſtant war, was beginning to droop, but which, Theodore reſtored, while he rekindled the ſacred fire of liberty.

They, indeed, are ſenſible, that his wretched fate has thrown a ſort of ridicule on the nation, ſince their king was confined in a jail at London, which was actually the caſe of poor Theodore; who, after experiencing the moſt extraordinary viciſſitudes of fortune, choſe to end his days in our iſland of liberty; but was reduced to the wretched ſtate of a priſoner, for debt.

Mr. Horace Walpole generouſly exerted himſelf for Theodore. He wrote a paper in the World, with great elegance and humour, ſoliciting a contribution for the monarch in diſtreſs, to be paid to Mr. Robert Dodſley, bookſeller, as lord high treaſurer. This brought him a very handſome ſum. He was allowed to get out of priſon. Mr. Walpole has the original deed, by which Theodore made over the kingdom of Corſica, in security to his Creditors. He has also the great seal of the kingdom.

Mr. Walpole has told me, that he had the curiosity to see king Theodore, and was accordingly in company with him, at a lady's of his acquaintance. But whether from dullness, or from pride, he did not open his mouth.

I suppose he has been so much dejected, and so much hurt by his misfortunes, that he was become sullen and indifferent. He died very soon after he got out of prison, and was buried in St. Anne's church-yard, Westminster; where a simple, unadorned monument is erected to him, with the following inscription.

>    Near this place, is interred
>    Theodore, king of Corsica;
>  Who died in this parish, Dec. 11,
>                1756,
>         Immediately after leaving
>         The king's bench prison,
>  By the benefit of the act of insolvency:
>          In consequence of which,
>      He registered his kingdom of Corsica
>          For the use of his creditors.

The grave, great teacher, to a level brings,
Heroes, and beggars, galley-slaves, and kings;
But Theodore, this moral learn'd, e'er dead;
Fate pour'd its lesson on his living head,
Bestow'd a kingdom, and deny'd him bread.

To return to the affairs of the island. The Genoese, eager to repress the rise in 1734, hired some Swifs and Grifons, who from being accustomed to such a country at home, might scour the mountains of Corsica. But these soldiers found it no easy matter to scour mountains, where the natives were continually firing upon them, and had numberless ways of escaping. They soon saw that they had made a bad bargain, and that they gave the Genoese too much blood for their money.

Genoa had also recourse to the desperate expedient of Marius and Sylla. She published an indemnity to all her assassins, and outlaws of every sort, on condition that they should fight for the republick, in Corsica. The robbers and assassins of Genoa, are no inconsiderable proportion of her people. These wretches flocked together, from all quarters, and were formed into twelve companies, who were joined with the Swifs and Grifons.

It may well be believed, that venal stipendiaries, and abandoned criminals, could not oppose an army of brave men, who were fighting in the great cause of liberty, and had every thing that was dear to them, at stake.

But France, who has ever had an eye to this island, now began to be apprehensive that the Corsicans might entirely throw off the yoke of Genoa, in which case, they would either become a free state, which the powers of Europe would, from a mutual jealousy, protect, or perhaps, would put themselves under the sovereignty of some great nation. She resolved then to force them back under the dominion of Genoa; for, by constant negotiations with that republick, France has such an ascendancy, that she may command, when she pleases, whatever belongs to it.

A treaty was therefore made at Versailles, by which, his most Christian Majesty engaged to reduce the Corsicans to obedience; and it was contrived with such address, as to appear done at the earnest desire of Genoa; though in reality, the republick had too recently experienced the danger of calling in the aid of a great state, to wish for a repetition of the same expedient.

In the month of March, 1738, the count de Boisseux was sent with a detachment of French troops to Corsica. This general was a good officer, but of no great enterprise. He was attended on this expedition, by M. de Contades, since, mareschal of France, who commanded the French army, at the battle of Minden. After several conferences with the chiefs of the Corsicans, Giafferi and Paoli, with whom we may also mention Luca di Ornano, a collateral branch of the great family, which Sampiero di Bastelica formerly represented, M. de Boisseux finding that the Corsicans would not submit to their old oppressors, began his hostilities.

The people of Corsica remonstrated to his most Christian Majesty in a very affecting memorial, in which they enumerated at great length their grievances, and as France had formerly afforded them protection, they hoped she would not now compel them to yield to the worst of tyranny. To the memorial were subjoined articles of accomodation, which they submitted to the French king.

These articles were thought too bold, for a people in the situation of the Corsicans; and articles formed by the Genoese were approved by France: so that no accommodation could be brought about. Giafferi and Paoli published a spirited manifesto to their countrymen, concluding it with the noble sentiment of Judas Maccabeus;

' Melius est mori in bello quam videre mala gen-
' tis nostrae (*a*). It is better for us to die in bat-
' tle, than to behold the calamities of our people.'

M. de Boisseux did considerable hurt to the Corsicans; for, although his operations were slow, they were well conducted. He had even recourse to art; for he had a part of his troops drest exactly like the people of the country, and, by that device, they destroyed multitudes, and occasioned a strange confusion and dismay among the Corsicans, in so much, that till they came very near parties, who appeared upon the mountains and in the woods, they could not be certain whether they were friends or enemies. Meanwhile, more troops being sent from France, the transports were overtaken with a terrible storm, and some of them wrecked on the Corsican coasts; where the patriots took the soldiers prisoners, and seized their arms. M. de Boisseux did not live to see the success of his operations. He was taken ill, and died at Bastia, on February 1739.

The Genoese, much elated with the success that the monarchy of France had against the Corsicans, published a long memorial. The be-

(*a*) 1 Maccabees chap. iii. ver. 59.

ginning of it, is truly pleasant. 'All the world
'knows so well, the mildness and love, with
'which the republick of Genoa governs her
'people; and above all, with what goodness and
'affection she hath ever regarded those of Corsi-
'ca, &c. (*a*).' They really intended this should
pass in Europe, as a serious truth.

Still supported by the goodness of their cause, the Corsicans remained inflexible, nor would they ever have given way, but to such a superiority of force, as it was impossible for them to withstand.

In March, 1739, the French sent to Corsica, the marquis de Maillebois, a commander every way fitted for such an expedition, being an officer of great penetration, and uncommon fire. He saw, that the Corsicans had long been trifled with by Genoa, and that even the French had not acted against them with sufficient vigour. He saw, that it was necessary to strike a bold stroke, if he wanted to make any impression on the valiant islanders, so long accustomed to scenes of blood; and since his sovereign had committed to him the charge of conquering this people, he resolved to do it effectually.

(*a*) Jauffin, tom. 1. p. 358.

Every thing therefore, was provided for the enterprise. He had 16 battallions of the best troops of France, besides some Arquebusiers and Bearnois, expert in climbing the mountains. Having formed two great corps, and several small parties, all compleatly furnished with ammunition, and whatever else was necessary, or convenient; he pierced into the innermost parts of the country, while his grenadiers carried heavy cannon acrofs the rudest passes. He cut down the standing corn, the vines, the olives, set fire to the villages, and spread terrour and desolation in every quarter. He hanged numbers of monks, and others, who were keenest in the revolt, and at the same time, published, wherever he went, his terms of capitulation, which had the best chance to be accepted, amidst so general a destruction. Notwithstanding the ungenerous cause, in which they were displayed, one cannot but admire the martial abilities of M. de Maillebois.

We have seen, that Theodore durst not land. The succours which he left, were not of much avail. Such unprecedented, and terrible slaughter, as now took place, with the dread of still greater vengeance, from so formidable a nation as France, obliged the Corsicans to lay down their arms, at the end of the campaign, 1739, which was indeed a hot one. Of these arms, a thousand were found to have the Genoese mark. The republick demanded to have them restored, a circumstance little to their honour.

The Generals, Giafferi and Paoli, left the island, and went to Naples; where they were both made colonels, which character, they enjoyed till their death.

There were still some few enthusiastick patriots, who skulked in the wildest parts of the island; but these were all reduced before the end of the year 1740, as was also the young baron Newhoff, the nephew of Theodore, who with a small party of desperadoes, had long escaped the utmost diligence of the French commander. He surrendered, on condition, that he and his attendants, should be landed in safety on the continent, which was faithfully performed.

In this manner was Corsica totally vanquished by France, of which the Genoese were as proud, as if it had been their own achievement. They gave in proposals to M. de Maillebois, for keeping the island in perpetual quiet. These proposals are preserved by M. Jauffin (*a*); and they are such, as any state should be ashamed of. Amongst many other barbarous schemes, one was, to transport a considerable number of the inhabitants, and make them over to the king of France, to people his distant colonies. Could there be a more harsh, or a more absurd measure, than this? Jauffin is much on the side of Genoa, and through the whole of his two volumes, does not seem to have felt one spark of true liberty, or at all to have entered into the spirit of what the Corsicans were fighting for; yet when he recites this proposal, he cannot help saying, 'Il sembloit par là qu'ils auroient 'été contens d'etre sovcrains des seuls rochers 'de Corse sans sujets (*b*). It would thence appear, that the Genoese would have been satisfied to be sovereigns of the bare rocks of 'Corsica, without subjects.'

France being engaged with more important objects than Corsica, or any thing concerning the Genoese, was no longer at leisure to employ her

(*a*) Jauffin, tom. 1. p. 468.  (*b*) Ib. p. 481.

attention on that island. All Europe being now in agitation, she thought proper to recall her troops from Corsica. They accordingly quitted the island, in the end of the year 1741, leaving it in perfect submission and quietness; as was said of the Romans by Galgacus, the ancient Scottish chief, in his famous speech, upon the Grampian mountains; 'Ubi solitudinem faciunt, pacem appellant (a). Where they make a desart, they call it peace.'

The French, indeed, knew the Corsicans too well, to believe, that they would submit to Genoa, when left to themselves. The event happened accordingly; for the French were hardly gone, before the Corsicans were again as much in motion as ever. Several of their countrymen, who were settled in different towns in Italy, furnished them with arms; and, as they had formerly done, they took a good many arms from the Genoese. From having been long depressed, like a strong bow recovering its elasticity, they rose with renewed vigour. Man, woman and child, may be said to have engaged; for very young boys took the field; and even

(a) Tacit. de vit. Agric. cap. 30.

some of their women, like those of Sparta, shewed their valour in battle. Many of the religious also carried arms; and, as if actuated by a kind of universal inspiration, every soul was ardent against the tyrant.

Gaffori and Matra, now obtained the government of Corsica, under the title of Protectours of the kingdom. Gaffori was a man of distinguished talents. His eloquence was most remarkable; and the Corsicans still talk with admiration of his harangues to them. He heard once, that a band of assassins were coming against him. He went out, and met them with a serene dignity, which astonished them. He begged they would only hear him a little; and he gave them so pathetick a picture of the distresses of Corsica, and roused their spirits to such a degree against those, who caused the oppression, that the assassins threw themselves at his feet, intreated his forgiveness, and instantly joined his banners.

The Genoese being in possession of the castle of Corte, it was besieged with great vigour by the Corsicans, commanded by Gaffori. By a strange want of thought, the nurse, who took care of Gaffori's eldest son, then an infant, wandered away, at a little distance from the camp. The Genoese perceived it, and making a sudden sally, they got hold of the nurse and the child, and carried them into the castle. The General shewed a decent concern at this unhappy accident, which struck a damp into the whole army. The Genoese thought they could have Gaffori upon their own terms, since they were possessed of so dear a pledge. When he advanced to make some cannon play, they held up his son, directly over that part of the wall, against which his artillery was levelled. The Corsicans stopt, and began to draw back; but Gaffori, with the resolution of a Roman, stood at their head, and ordered them to continue the fire. Luckily, his firmness was not broken by losing his child, who escaped unhurt. I had the pleasure of knowing the young gentleman, who inherits his father's estate. He related to me himself, from the best authority, this story, which does so much honour to his father. I had it also vouched, by such as had no particular interest in it.

Matra, the other general or protectour, was always suspected, as secretly favouring the views of Genoa, and was rather a promoter of division, than a patron of liberty. Indeed, the great misfortune of the Corsicans, was their want of union; which made particular animosities take up their attention, and divert their zeal from the great cause.

In 1745, Count Domenico Rivarola, arrived at Bastia, along with some English ships of war. Great Britain had forbidden her subjects to give any assistance to the Corsicans; but, by the changeful schemes of political connections, she consented to send some ships against the Genoese; not, as if from herself, but, as complying with the request of her ally, the king of Sardinia, who had taken the cause of Corsica much to heart. These ships bombarded Bastia, and San Fiorenzo, both of which they delivered into the hands of the Corsicans. The force of the British men of war, and the great service done by us, to their cause, are never forgotten, by the brave islanders.

Count Rivarola, was proclaimed generalissimo of the kingdom. Gaffori and Matra, were not present at this election, and did every thing in their power to oppose it; so that there was nothing but heart-burnings, and miserable dissensions; and the British went away with an idea of this people, as if they had been a parcel of half-barbarians.

As our information, with regard to Corsica, has been very imperfect, these unhappy impressions have continued ever since, and have had too much influence in Great Britain.

Rivarola, Gaffori and Matra, having at length come to a tolerable agreement, matters went on a little better, though the Genoese were not long of recovering Bastia and San Fiorenzo.

In 1746, the Corsicans sent two envoys, with proposals to the Earl of Bristol, then his Britannic Majesty's ambassadour, at the court of Turin. The intention of these proposals was, that Corsica should put herself entirely under the protection of Great Britain. The envoys waited at Turin, till My Lord Bristol had a return from the ministry at London, signifying their satisfaction at what had been communicated, hoping the Corsicans would preserve the same obliging sentiments; but that it was not then the time to enter into any treaty with them.

Count Domenico Rivarola, finding that he could be of most service to his country, when at a distance, returned to Turin, where he constantly improved the benevolent intentions of his Sardinian Majesty towards Corsica. He died with the rank of colonel, in April 1748, and left behind him the character of an honest man, and a gallant patriot.

In the same month and year, the British ship, the Nassau, commanded by captain Holcomb, together with some transports, carried over to Corsica, two battallions, one of the king of Sardinia's troops, and one of Austrians, in order to aid the Corsicans; but the general peace being concluded, at Aix la Chapelle, no foreign states could any longer interfere, and the Corsicans and Genoese, were again left to themselves.

My Lord Hailes has, among his valuable collection of historical manuscripts, two pieces relating to Corsica. The one entitled, 'Information de l'état dans lequel se trouve presentement la Corse, et de ce qu'il faudroit pour la delivrer de l'esclavage du gouvernement Genois, traduit de l'Italien,' is written by Count Domenico Rivarola. The other, is an account of the state of Corsica, in the original Italian; drawn up by one, who appears to have been well acquainted with the subject. Both of these papers set forth, the advantages to be derived to a maritime power, from an alliance with Corsica. They were communicated by M. Carlet de Gorregne, the Sardinian minister, to General Wentworth, the British ambassadour, at the court of Turin; and, I believe, they had considerable influence, in procuring the interposition of Sardinia and Great Britain, in favour of the Corsicans.

Matra, in the end of the year 1748, went to the service of Piedmont, and left Gaffori sole general of the island. A repetition of the same desperate actions continued, till on the 3d of October, 1753, Gaffori was assassinated by a band of murderers, set on by the republick. At least, it is a fact that some of these wretches have still a miserable pension to support them, in the territory of Genoa. There is a pillar of infamy erected at Corte, on the place, where stood the house of the principal actor in this bloody villainy. The house was burnt, and razed from the foundation.

The Corsicans, from their family connections, and violent parties, differ in their accounts of Gaffori. Some of them would have it believed, that he was too much engrossed by selfish views, and in order to promote his own interest, endeavoured to bring about unworthy schemes of reconciliation with Genoa. But, besides the reluctance which every generous mind must feel, to give credit to injurious reports of a hero, whose greatness of soul shone forth, in the manner I have related, what I heard of Gaffori from those, in whose judgement and impartiality I could confide, joined with the regard with which he is had in remembrance by the majority of his countrymen, determine me to a persuasion of the reality of his virtues.

The administrators of the island had been so well instituted by General Gaffori, that Corsica was able to continue for two years without any chief; while the war was still carried on with various success.

The patriots did not however, swear a solemn oath, that, rather than submit to the republick, they would throw themselves into the fire, like the Saguntines of old. This oath, which is conceived in terms of strength and violence, not unlike the Corsican stile, but somewhat exaggerated, was circulated over Europe, and generally believed to be genuine. Doctor Smollet, who displays a generous warmth in favour of the

Corsicans, hath given this oath a place in his history (a); but Paoli assures me, that it was a fiction.

I come now, to a remarkable event in the annals of Corsica, an event, from which the happiness and glory of that island will principally be dated. I mean, the election of Pascal Paoli, to be general of the kingdom.

Pascal Paoli*, was second son to the old chief Giacinto Paoli. He had been educated with great care by his father, who formed his taste for letters, and inspired him with every worthy and noble sentiment. He was born in Corsica, where he remained long enough, to contract a love and attachment to his country, and to feel the oppression under which it groaned.

When the patriots were totally crushed by the marquis de Maillebois, his father took young Pa-

(a) Smoll. hist. vol. 16. p. 384.
* His name, in Italian, is Pasquale de' Paoli. I write Pascal, as more agreeable to an English ear. I also avoid giving him any title. I owe this thought to My Lord Hailes. When I asked him, Whether I should call Paoli, Signor, or General? his answer was, 'Signor is better than General, but plain Pascal is better than either. 'You do not say, King Alexander, but Alexander of Macedon; no 'title adds to the dignity of Judas Maccabeus.'

oli to Naples, where he had the advantage of attending the academy, got a commission as an officer in that service, and was much about court.

Here he lived twelve or thirteen years, cultivating the great powers with which nature had endowed him, and laying the foundation of those grand designs, which he had early formed, for the deliverance of his country.

His reputation became so great among the Corsicans, that he received the strongest invitations to come over and take the command. He embarked in the glorious enterprise, stimulated by generous ambition, and undismayed by a consideration of the dangers, the cares, and the uncertainty which he was about to encounter.

There was something particularly affecting, in his parting from his father; the old man, hoary and gray with years, fell on his neck, and kissed him, gave him his blessing, and with a broken feeble voice, encouraged him in the undertaking, on which he was entering; 'My son,' said he, ' I may, possibly, never see you more; but in my ' mind, I shall ever be present with you. Your ' design is a great, and a noble one; and I doubt ' not, but GOD will bless you in it. The little

' which remains to me of life, I will allot to
' your cause, in offering up my prayers and sup-
' plications to heaven, for your protection and
' prosperity.' Having again embraced him, they
parted.

Pascal Paoli no sooner appeared in the island, than he attracted the attention of every body. His carriage and deportement prejudiced them in his favour, and his superiour judgment, and patriotick spirit, displayed with all the force of eloquence, charmed their understandings. All this, heightened with condescension, affability and modesty, entirely won him their hearts. A way was open for him to the supreme command, and he was called to it by the unanimous voice of his countrymen; upon which occasion, was issued the following manifesto.

*The Supreme, and General Council of the Kingdom of* CORSICA, *to the Beloved people of that* NATION.

BELOVED PEOPLE AND COUNTRYMEN,

' THE discords and divisions, that have begun
' to infect the publick, as well as private tranqui-

'lity of our country, by the revival of ancient, and
' personal enmities amongst those, who have very
' little fear of God, and are little interested and
' zealous, for the good of the publick, have oblig-
' ed our principal chiefs to call us together, to
' this general Consulta, in order to deliberate on
' such necessary measures, as may effectually con-
' tribute to the establishment of a common union,
' and to cause the most rigid laws to be put in
' execution, against such as shall dare to disturb
' it by their private piques, or unruly disposi-
' tions.

' The most proper and effectual means, to suc-
' ceed in this our desireable end, are by us seri-
' ously thought to be, the electing of one oeco-
' nomical, political and general chief, of enlight-
' ened faculties, to command over this kingdom
' with full power, except when there shall be oc-
' casion to consult upon matters concerning the
' state, which he cannot treat of, without the con-
' currence of the people, or their respective repre-
' sentatives.

' By the general voice is elected for that trust,
' Pascal Paoli; a man, whose virtues and abilities,
' render him every way worthy thereof.

' After so general an election, by the chiefs of the council of war, the deputies of the provinces, and the respective representatives of the parishes assembled, this gentleman was invited, by a letter, to come; and a large committee of the principal members of the assembly, was sent to his house, to desire him to accept of the charge, and to repair hither to be acknowledged as our chief; and to take the solemn oath, to exercise the office, with which he is invested, with the utmost zeal, affection and disinterestedness; and to receive the oath of fidelity and obedience from the commons.

' Besides, having given many reasons against this, he has shewn much reluctance to take upon him so great a charge; but having been informed of our resolutions and determinations, in case of any obstacle or refusal, he was obliged to acquiesce, being necessitated so to do. He was conducted hither last night, and hath plighted and received the oaths abovementioned.

' He is to take the government upon himself, assisted by two counsellors of state, and one of the most reputable persons from each province, who shall be changed every month.

'The third day of August shall be fixed on, 'for a general circuit, in order to punish the au- 'thours of many crimes, particularly murders, 'committed lately in different parts. This circuit, 'to be directed by the aforesaid General, with the 'deputies. The number of armed men, as he 'shall think fitting.

'We hope, that these our resolutions and de- 'liberations, will be to the general satisfaction, as 'it concerns the common good: and we charge 'all the chiefs and commissaries over the parish- 'es, to co-operate, as far as lies in their power, 'to promote the publick tranquillity.'

Dated at St. Antonio of the White House, this 15th of July, 1755.

Though Paoli had long meditated on the importance of the charge he was to enter upon, its near approach struck him with awe; for his ideas were enlarged, his resolves were magnanimous, and the office appeared more momentous to him, than it could appear to one of more confined views, and more moderate plans.

His hesitation and diffidence, when called to the supreme command, was not affected. He balanced the confequences, and he could not but be ſerioufly moved. For he could not divine with certainty, the aftoniſhing influence which his government was to have, on the happineſs of his country. But the repreſentations made to him, were ſo earneſt, and, in ſome meaſure, ſo peremptory, that he thought himſelf bound in duty to accept of the arduous taſk.

When he enquired into the ſituation of the affairs of Corſica, he found the utmoſt diſorder and confuſion. There was no ſubordination, no diſcipline, no money, hardly any arms and ammunition; and, what was worſe than all, little union among the people. He immediately began to remedy theſe defects. His perſuaſion and example, had wonderful force; all ranks exerted themſelves, in providing what was neceſſary for carrying on the war with ſpirit; whereby, in a ſhort time, the Genoeſe were driven to the remoteſt corners of the iſland.

Having thus expelled the foe, from the boſom of his country, he had leiſure to attend to the civil part of the adminiſtration, in which he diſcovered abilities and conſtancy, hardly to be paralleled. He rectified innumerable abuſes, which had insinuated themselves, during the late times of trouble and confusion. He, in a manner, new-modelled the government, upon the soundest principles of democratical rule, which was always his favourite idea.

The Corsicans having been long denied legal justice, had assumed the right of private revenge, and had been in use to assassinate each other upon the most trivial occasions. He found it extremely difficult to break them of this practice, by which it was computed, that the state lost 800 subjects every year. The disease was become so violent, that it seemed almost incurable. However, by seasonable admonition, by representing to them the ruin of this practice to the cause of liberty, at a time when they had occasion for all the assistance they could lend to each other, joined to a strict exercise of criminal justice; he gradually brought them to be convinced, that the power of dispensing punishment belonged to the publick; and that, without a proper submission, and a regular system of administration, they never could make head against an enemy, or, indeed, be properly speaking, a state. So effectual were the measures he took, that a law was paffed, making affaffination capital, let it be committed on any pretence whatever.

The Corficans are naturally humane; but, like the Italians, and moft fouthern nations, are extremely violent in their tempers. This is certainly the effect of a warm climate, which forms the human frame to an exquifite degree of fenfibility. Whatever advantages this fenfibility may produce, by cherifhing the finer feelings and more exalted affections; it is at the fame time productive of fome difadvantages, being equally the occafion of impatience, fudden paffion, and a fpirit of revenge, tending to the diforder of fociety.

Paoli, by his mafterly knowledge of human nature, guided the Corficans to glory, and rendered the impetuofity of their difpofitions, and their paffion for revenge, fubfervient to the noble objects of liberty, and of vindicating their country. His wife inftitutions had fo good an effect, that notwithftanding of their frequent loffes in action, it was found, that in a few years, the number of inhabitants was increafed 16000.

When a proper fyftem of government was formed, and fome of the moft glaring abufes rectified, Paoli proceeded to improve and civilize the manners of the Corsicans. This was a very delicate task. They had been brought up in anarchy, and their constant virtue had been resistance. It therefore, required the nicest conduct, to make them discern the difference between salutary restraint and tyrannick oppression. He was no monarch, born to rule, and who received a nation as a patrimonial inheritance. It was, therefore, in vain to think of acting with force, like the Czar Peter towards the Russians. It was not, indeed, consistent with his views of forming a free nation; but, had he been inclined to it, he could not have followed out such a plan. He was intirely dependant upon the people, elected by them, and answerable to them for his conduct. It was no easy matter to restrain those of whom he held his power. But this, Paoli acccomplished.

He gradually prepared the Corsicans for the reception of laws, by cultivating their minds, and leading them, of their own accord, to desire the enactment of regulations, of which he shewed them the benefit. He established an university at Corte; and he was at great pains to have proper schools, for the instruction of children, in every village of the kingdom.

The laſt ſtep he took was, to induce the Corſicans to apply themſelves to agriculture, commerce, and other civil occupations. War had entirely ruined induſtry in the iſland. It had given the Corſicans a contempt for the arts of peace; ſo that they thought nothing worthy of their attention, but arms and military achievments. The great and valorous actions, which many of them had performed, gave them a certain pride; which diſdained all meaner and more inglorious occupation. Heroes could not ſubmit to ſink down into plain peaſants. Their virtue was not ſo perfect, as that of the ancient Romans, who could return from the triumphs of victory, to follow their ploughs.

From theſe cauſes, the country was in danger of being entirely uncultivated, and the people of becoming, a lawleſs and ungovernable rabble of banditti.

Paoli therefore, ſet himſelf ſeriouſly to guard againſt this; and by degrees, brought the Corſicans to look upon labour with leſs averſion, ſo as at leaſt to provide themſelves ſufficiently in food and cloathing, and to carry on a little commerce.

His adminiſtration, in every reſpect was ſuch,

that, from being rent into factions, the nation became firm and united; and had not France again interposed, the Corsican heroes would long e'er now have totally driven the Genoese from the island.

Feeling its own importance, the Corsican nation resolved to give the Genoese no quarter at sea, which they had hitherto done, out of indulgence to the individuals of the republick; lamenting their unhappy situation, which obliged them to live under a tyrannical government. But finding that the Genoese continually attacked, and made booty of the Corsican vessels, it was thought highly equitable to retaliate; preserving at the same time, all due respect for the other maritime powers. To this effect, a manifesto was issued in 1760 *(a)*.

These firm and rapid advances of the Corsican nation, filled the Genoese with serious concern; and in 1761, they published a manifesto, in very mild and insinuating terms, to try if they could allure the Corsicans to a pacifick submission *(b)*.

Immediately upon this, a general council was assembled at Vescovato in Casinca, where

---

*(a)* Appendix. N° I.   *(b)* Appendix. N° II.

the strongest resolutions were taken, never to make any agreement with the republick, but on condition of having Corsica secured in its liberties and independency (*a*).

A memorial was also published by the Corsicans, to the sovereigns of Europe (*b*), calling upon them, by the rights of humanity, to interpose and give peace to a nation which had done so much for freedom.

In these various writings, there is a spirit of eloquence, a feeling, and a resolution, which does honour to the character of this people.

But the politicks of Versailles did not favour the Corsican cause; France has been alternately, the scourge and the shield of Genoa. Paoli had well nigh compleatly finished his great scheme of freeing every part of the island from the Genoese, when a treaty was concluded between France and the republick, by which the former engaged to send six battalions of troops to garrison the fortified towns in Corsica, for the space of four years.

When this treaty was first known in Europe, every noble heart was afflicted; for

(*a*) Appendix. N° III.   (*b*) Appendix. N° IV.

every body believed, that France was again determined to carry fire and sword into Corsica, and blast the hopes of the brave islanders. Mr. Rousseau wrote of it, with his usual energy, to his friend and mine, M. De Leyre, at Parma; one of the authours of the Encyclopedie, a man who unites with science and genius the most amiable heart and most generous soul. ' Il
' faut avouer que vos François, sont un peuple
' bien servile, bien vendu à la tyrannie, bien cruel,
' et bien acharné sur les malheureux. S'ils sa-
' voient un homme libre à l'autre bout du mon-
' de, je crois qu'ils iroient pour le seul plaisir
' de l'exterminer. It must be owned that your
' countrymen, the French, are a very servile
' nation, wholly sold to tyranny, exceedingly cru-
' el and relentless in persecuting the unhappy.
' If they knew of a freeman at the other end
' of the world, I believe they would go thither
' for the mere pleasure of extirpating him *.

But it turned out to be a prudent and politick scheme on the part of France. She was ow-

* It is difficult to give a good translation of a sentence so original and forcible. I am indebted for the above, to a friend who does not choose to have his name mentioned as a translator.

ing the Genoese some millions of livres. Her finances were not such as made it very convenient for her to pay. But the French Ministers are never at a lose to conclude an advantageous treaty for their monarch. They told the Genoese, 'We cannot yet let you have your money. 'But we will send you six battalions of auxilia-'ries to Corsica, and let that be a sinking fund 'for the discharge of our debt.' The Genoese, who recalled with barbarous satisfaction what France had formerly done against the Corsicans, never doubted, that if French soldiers were again in the island, continual skirmishes would ensue; France would be provoked, and a bloody war would be the consequence, by which the Corsicans would again be reduced to a state of slavery. They were therefore extremely pleased with the scheme.

The French, however, took care to engage to act only in the defensive, and to fix the treaty for four years, that they might be sure of having time to sink their debt. They sent the troops as stipulated in the end of the year 1764; and the Count De Marboeuf was appointed commander in chief.

M. de Marbeuf was an officer of experience and temper; and, no doubt, had his inſtructions to conduct himſelf mildly towards the Corſicans. All his duty was, to take care that things ſhould not become worſe for Genoa; but, that ſhe ſhould ſtill retain the garriſon towns of Baſtia, San Fiorenzo, Calvi, Algagliola and Ajaccio.

The Corſicans conducted themſelves, upon this occaſion, with the greateſt propriety. A general council was held, and determinations (*a*) publiſhed; from which it appears, that they ſhewed no diſtruſt of the French, who, they truſted, would not begin hoſtilities againſt them. But, for greater ſecurity, it was provided, that a council of war ſhould be appointed by the government, to be ever vigilant againſt any infractions of what they ſuppoſed France had tacitly promiſed to them, and was bound by the law of nations to obſerve; that the French troops ſhould not be allowed to have acceſs to the territories of the nation; that the General ſhould poſt ſufficient guards upon the frontiers; and if any French officer deſired a paſsport, he might grant him it; but ſhould be obliged

(*a*) Appendix. N° V.

to give an account, in the first general consulta thereafter, of what passports he had granted; of his motives for granting them; and of every treaty he should have with the French. That, as it was reported, some new proposals of peace with the republick would be offered, they should reject all such, if they did not first grant to the nation, the preliminaries resolved upon in the general council of Casinca. That the General should make a respectful remonstrance, in name of the nation, to his most Christian Majesty, with regard to the loss it must sustain by the arrival of his troops; by which, the Genoese would be relieved of the great expences they had been obliged to lay out upon the Corsican war, and the patriots be prevented from following out their successful enterprises, and totally expelling their enemies from the island. That this remonstrance might be more effectual, his excellency should, at the same time, apply to the powers favourable to Corsica, that they might employ their mediation with the French king, in order to preserve to the nation its rights, prerogatives, liberty and independency. And they further ordered, that as every body had, without controul, cut timber in the woods of Corsica, they should be prohibited so to do, without the permission of the government.

These determinations were wise and moderate. Without giving umbrage to the French, they secured the patriots from sudden attacks, or insidious wiles. The article relating to the cutting of timber, was essentially requisite to prevent the French from carrying it away to Marseilles and Toulon; which they, probably, would have done, had it not been for this edict, which preserved to the Corsicans a noble supply of wood, to be ready, either for their own service, or for the service of any maritime power, with whom they might make an alliance.

The warlike operations of Corsica were now suspended. But Paoli improved the season of tranquillity to the best purpose, in preparing for future schemes of victory, and in giving perfection and stability to the civil constitution of his country; effectuating what ages had not been able to produce, and exhibiting an illustrious instance of what was said of Epaminondas; ' Unum

'hominem pluris fuisse quam civitatem (*a*). That
'one man has been of more consequence than a
'whole nation.'

(*a*) Corn. Nep. Vit. Epam. in fin.

## CHAPTER III.

*The Present State of* CORSICA, *with respect to Government, Religion, Arms, Commerce, Learning, the Genius and Character of its* INHABITANTS.

AFTER running over the revolutions of an island, which has experienced so many vicissitudes, it will be agreeable to consider the result of these vigorous exertions in the cause of liberty. I shall, therefore, with much pleasure, present my readers with the state of Corsica as it now is.

The government of Corsica is, as follows. Every paese or village, elects, by majority of votes, a Podestà and other two magistrates, who have the respectable name of ' Padri del Commune; Fathers of the Community.' These magistrates are chosen annually. They may be continued in office for several years, at the will of the community; but there must be a new election every year.

The Podestà, by himself, may determine causes to the value of ten livres; and united with the Padri del Commune, may finally determine causes to the value of thirty livres. The Podestà is the representative of the government, and to him are addressed all the orders of the supreme council. The Padri del Commune superintend the oeconomy and police of the village, call the people together, and consult with them on every thing that concerns their interest. In some villages, the inhabitants join with the Podestà and Padri del Commune, twelve honest men, in whom they can confide, and to whom they can delegate their power of settling the affairs of the publick. These are called counsellors, and sit as assessors with the three magistrates of the village. The names of these magistrates, as soon as elected, must be transmitted to the magistrates of the province, who have it in their power to oppose the choice, and order a new election; but this never happens when the people have been unanimous. Sometimes they choose two Podestàs and one Padre del Commune, and sometimes more and sometimes fewer counsellors. These irregularities are permitted to humour the caprices of different villages in an infant state, and are of no consequence;

for the same degree of power remains to each office, whether it be held by a lesser or a greater number; as in the states of Holland, those who send two or three representatives, have but an equal voice with those who send only one. In some of the more considerable towns, the Podestà is not subject to the provincial magistrates, but is considered as having equal authority with them.

Once a year, all the inhabitants of each village assemble themselves and choose a Procuratour, to represent them in the general consulta or parliament of the nation, which is held annually in the month of May, at the city of Corte. This procuratour is elected by the majority of the voices. He must have a mandate, attested by a notary publick, which, on his arrival at Corte, he presents to the great chancellor of the kingdom, by whom it is registered. Each procuratour has, from his community, a livre a day, to bear his charges from the time of his setting out till his return home. This allowance is too small, and must soon be increased.

Sometimes the procuratours of all the villages, contained in the same pieve, choose from among themselves one who goes as representative of the pieve, which saves some expence to the villages. But this is an abuse, and when matters of any consequence are deliberating, it renders the number of those who are to consult greatly too small. A little expence should be despised, in comparison of having a voice in making the laws, and settling the most serious affairs of the country; and the greater the number of voices, the more does the assembly approach to the idea of a Roman comitia.

The general consulta is, indeed, a great and numerous assembly; for, besides the ordinary procuratours, it is usual to call in several of those who have formerly been members of the supreme council, and several of those who have lost their fathers or near relations in the service of their country, that the blood of heroes may be distinguished by publick honours.

The magistrates of each province also send a procuratour to the general consulta; and when all the procuratours are assembled at Corte, in presence of the General and the supreme council of state, it is recommended to the procuratours of each province, to choose two of their number, who, together with the procuratour of their magistrates, may proceed to the election of the President and oratour of the general consulta. The procuratours of each province accordingly choose two of their number by votes viva voce, if they are unanimous; and if not unanimous, by ballot.

These two, with the procuratour of the magistrates of each province, come before the supreme council, to whom every one of them gives in a sealed note, containing the name of the person who, he thinks, should be president: these notes are considered by the supreme council, and the three who have most notes inscribed with their names, are put to a ballot; and he who carries two thirds of the votes in his favour, is made president.

In the schedule or note, a procuratour may insert the name of his relation, or of one who has been strongly recommended to him; but by ballot, he can freely give his vote for the person whom he thinks most deserving; so that it often happens, that the person among the three, who had the fewest notes for him, will be made president by a great majority. This appears to me another abuse; for a procuratour, by inserting in the schedule the name of one of whom he does not approve, runs a rifque of having the man whom he thinks moſt deſerving, thrown out altogether. Beſides, he ought not to be moved by conſiderations of connection or of recommendation. The members of the ſupreme council have alſo their votes in this ballot for the preſident. The oratour is choſen exactly in the ſame manner.

The preſident governs during the ſitting of the general conſulta. The oratour reads the different papers ſubjected to deliberation. Propoſitions from the government are addreſſed to the preſident. Thoſe from the people are addreſſed to the oratour. If a propoſition from the government is approved of by a majority of voices, it is immediately paſſed into a law. But a propoſition from the people, though approved of, may be ſuſpended by the government, without aſſigning their reaſons; which, however, they are ſtrictly obliged to do at the next general conſulta.

This ſuſpending power was greatly agitated in the Corſican parliament; and the people oppoſed it ſo much, that it was thought it would not take place. But Paoli, ever ready to enlighten his countrymen, shewed them, that in the present state of affairs, the government may have many designs, not mature enough for being communicated to the publick, but of essential advantage to the nation; so that it is highly proper they should have the privilege of delaying for a while, any proposition which might interfere with these designs. Besides, the supreme council, as the grand procuratours of the nation, and possessed of their greatest confidence, ought to be specially heard; and if they think a proposition important and critical, may well be allowed to put it off, till it shall be fully considered by all the subjects of the state. And this can be attended with no bad consequences; since the people may, at an after period, pass their proposition into a law.

The procuratours of each province next assemble themselves, in presence of the president of the general consulta, or a president deputed by him; and each province appoints its representative in the supreme council, for the ensuing year; and one of these is elected into the office of Great Chancellor. The supreme council, for the time being, may remonstrate against this election; and the election of each province must be confirmed by a majority of the other provinces; becaufe thefe counfellors, with the General of the kingdom, are to form the executive power of the whole nation; the general confulta or legiflative power devolving upon them that high commiffion.

The General holds his office for life. He is perpetual prefident of the fupreme council of nine. He votes in all queftions; and in cafe of an equality, he has a cafting vote. He is abfolute commander of the troops or militia of the ifland. His office much refembles that of the ftadtholder of Holland.

The procuratours of each province alfo choofe the provincial magiftrates for the enfuing year. This magiftracy is regularly compofed of a prefident, two counfultors, an auditour and a chancellor: but the number is varied in different provinces, in the fame manner as the magiftracy in different villages. The auditour and chancellor have fmall falaries; and the magiftracy have their table kept at the publick expence, with a guard of foldiers in pay. The provincial magiftrates can try criminals, and pronounce fentence againft them; but a fentence for capital punifhment cannot be put in execution, till it is approved by the fupreme council. In civil causes, they can determine finally to the extent of fifty livres; in causes exceeding that sum, parties may appeal to the Rota Civile, which is a tribunal consisting of three doctours of laws, chosen by the supreme council, and continued at their pleasure. This tribunal judges according to the civil and canon laws, and according to the particular laws of Corsica. These last were partly formed in old times, and afterwards augmented and improved by the Genoese, who published them under the title of, 'Statuti Civili et Criminali del Isola di Corsica.' They are become very scarce. I have a copy of them, a thin folio, printed at Bastia, in 1694. It is a very good little code, and does credit to Genoa. 'Felix si sic omnia. Happy would it have been 'had she shewn the same equity in all respects.' There are also a few modern laws. Although the judgment, both of the magistrates of the villages, and of the provincial magistrates, be final to the extent of the values I have mentioned, yet if any person is manifestly aggrieved, he may obtain redress by applying to the supreme council, or to the court of syndicato, another excellent institution, which is conducted in the following manner,

In the general consulta, besides the elections of which I have given an account, the procuratours also choose some persons of high credit and respect, as syndicatori. These make a tour through the different provinces, as our judges in Britain go the circuits. They hear complaints against the different magistrates; and if any of them have transgressed their duty, they are properly censured. These syndicators are exceedingly beneficial. The General himself is for the most part one of them. They save poor people the trouble and expence of going to Corte to lay their grievances before the supreme council. They examine into every thing concerning the provinces, reconcile the people to the wholesome severity of law, encourage industry and every good undertaking, and diffuse a spirit of order and civilization in all corners of the island.

Such is the government of Corsica; which exhibits a compleat and well ordered democracy. From the Podestà and Padri del Commune, up to the supreme council, there is a gradual progression of power, flowing from the people, which they can resume, and dispose of at their pleasure, at the end of every year; so that no magistrate or servant of the publick, of whatever degree, will venture, for so short a time, to encroach upon his conſtituents; knowing that he muſt ſoon give an account of his adminiſtration; and if he ſhould augment the authority of his office, he is only wreathing a yoke for his own neck, as he is immediately to return to the ſituation of an ordinary ſubject. Nay, if a magiſtrate is not totally loſt to every manly feeling, he will not even allow himſelf to reſt in ſupine negligence; but will exert his powers for the good of the country, that he may recommend himſelf to his fellow citizens, and be honoured with farther marks of their confidence.

In the general conſulta held in the year 1764, ſeveral wiſe regulations were made with regard to the government, of which I ſhall give the ſubſtance.

No propoſitions made to the general conſulta, ſhall acquire the force of laws, if they be not approved by two thirds of the voices.

Propoſitions approved by one half of the voices, may be propoſed in the ſame ſeſſion, a ſecond or third time: thoſe which are not approved by one half of the voices, cannot be propoſed again, in the ſame ſeſſion; but may be brought in, with consent of the government, in some future session.

The supreme council of state shall consist of nine counsellors, six of this side, and three of the other side of the mountains, one for each province. Three of them shall reside at Corte, during the first four months; three during the second, and three during the third: that is to say, during each space, there shall be two of this side, and one of the other side of the mountains; and the three in residence shall have the authority of all the nine. But it shall be lawful for the General, to call the whole nine to the residence, whenever he shall think it necessary on account of any important affair.

None of the three residing counsellors of state shall be absent from the residence, for any cause whatever, without having first obtained leave in writing, from the General; and this leave shall not be granted for a longer time than eight days, and but upon the weightiest motives. In case of the General's absence from the residence, at the same time that one of the three counsellors is also absent, all judicial proceedings shall be suspended.

No man shall be elected a counsellor of state,

who is not above thirty five years of age, and who has not held with approbation, the office of president in a provincial magistracy, or the office of Podestà in some principal town. Notwithstanding which, however, any person of singular merit, who has sustained with approbation, other respectable charges, in the service of his country, though he hath not borne the offices abovementioned, may be elected a counsellor, provided he be of the age prescribed by law.

No man shall be appointed to the office of president of a provincial magistracy, who is under thirty years of age, and who has not twice held the office of consultor in the said magistracy, or some other respectable employment in the service of his country; and who has not the proper knowledge necessary for that office.

The office of Podestà, in the towns not subject to the provincial magistracy, shall be conferred by the same regulations.

The charge of General of the kingdom, being vacated by death, by resignation, or by any other means, the whole of the supreme authority shall then remain in the actual counsellors of state, the eldest of whom shall preside at the council, by which in the space of a month after the vacancy intimation must be made for a Confulta to be held, for electing a new general.

The counsellors of state, the presidents of magistracies, and other officers and judges, shall remain in their respective charges, and have the full exercise of their authority, till they are relieved by their lawful successours.

The counsellors of state, the presidents of provincial magistracies, and the Podestàs of the larger towns shall not be re-elected to the same charge, without having been two years out of office, and without producing credentials from the supreme syndicators, attesting their good and laudable conduct in the employment which they have exercised.

Paoli has succeded wonderfully in settling the claims of the feudal signors. These signors made several applications to the government, praying for the restitution of their ancient rights. This was a very delicate question. To allow to these signors the ample privileges which they enjoyed of old, would have been to establish independent principalities in Corsica, and must have tended to subvert the enlarged and free constitution, which Paoli had formed, for the permanent felicity of the state.

The signors had not been foremost in the glorious war. They had much to lose; and hesitated at taking arms against the republick of Genoa, lest they should forfeit their domains.

The peasants, on the contrary, had plunged at once into danger. These had nothing to lose but their lives; and a life of slavery is not to be prized. If they should be successful, they were fired with the hopes of a double deliverance, from the distant tyranny of the republick, and from the more intimate oppression of their feudal lords. This was become so grievous, that a very sensible Corsican owned to me, that supposing the republick had abandoned its pretensions over Corsica, so that the peasants should not have been obliged to rise against the Genoese, they would have risen against the signors.

The peasants therefore, would not now consent, to return under the arbitrary power, from which they had freed themselves, in consequence of their bravery. To propose such a measure to them, would have been enough to excite a revolt, to break the nation anew into parties, and give their enemies an opportunity, of again fomenting discord, and hatred, and assassinations; till the Corsicans should themselves do, what all the stratagem and force of Genoa had attempted in vain.

On the other hand, the signors were not to be offended, so as to make them become malecontents, and disturb the operations of the government. The motto of the sagacious Hollanders, 'Frangimur si collidimur, We shall go to pieces, if we dash against each other,' should be impressed on the minds of the different orders of men, in every nation; but is doubly important in an infant state.

Paoli indulged the signors so far, that they themselves should not be personally amenable before the magistrates of the provinces in which their respective jurisdictions lie. That they should have the power of determining causes between the peasants upon their fiefs, without being responsible for their sentences, to the provincial magistrates; but that they should be subject to the review of the supreme council, and of the court of the syndicato.

In this manner, the fignors have the flattering diftinction of a certain degree of authority, while, in reality, they are difcharging the united duties of fathers of the community, Podeftàs, and provincial magiftrates. And as they are, like them, fubject to the rectification of higher judicatories, they cannot abufe their powers; but while they enjoy a preeminence over the other nobles, they juft afford the ftate, at no expence, an additional number of judges to promote civilization among a rude and unpolifhed people.

Thus have the hereditary feudal jurifdictions been moderated in Corfica, by a fortunate concurrence of accident and wifdom; partly by the tumults of a fpirited war, partly by the prudent difpofitions of an able legiflatour. And a fyftem tranfplanted from the north, by robuft Barbarians, into moft countries of Europe; where having taken deep root, and fpread wide its branches, the utmoft violence has been required to extirpate it, has, by a ftorm falutary to the ifland, and by fkilful management, been brought under command, and even rendered ufeful in Corfica.

When the government fhall have arrived at greater maturity, and time fhall have abated the ardour of rule, the signors will be disposed to resign a distinction attended with more trouble than advantage.

In this manner is the Corsican government carried on, and, no doubt, they will be able to render it still more perfect; though as it now is, I look upon it as the best model that hath ever existed in the democratical form.

Sparta, indeed, was a nervous constitution; but, with reverence to the memory of immortal Lycurgus, Sparta was deficient in gentleness and humanity. That total inversion of the human affections, that extinction of every finer feeling, was a situation so forced, and so void of pleasure, that it is not to be envied. We must indeed admire the astonishing influence of their Legislatour. But we may be allowed to think that all he obtained by it, was only the preservation of a state; and preservation is nothing, without happiness. Sir James Steuart is of opinion, that, ' had the Lacedemonians adhered to the principles of their government, and spirit of their constitution, they might have perhaps subsisted to this very day (*a*).' I believe

---

(*a*) Inquiry into the Principles of Political Oeconomy, book II. chap. 14.

it might have been so. But, could Lycurgus have changed his Spartans into men of stone, they would have lasted still longer.

In the constitution of Corsica, while proper measures are taken for the continuation of the state, individuals have the full enjoyment of all the comforts of life. They are men, as well as citizens; and when once they shall have intirely freed themselves from the Genoese, I cannot imagine a country more happy. Animated with this prospect, Paoli sways the hearts of his countrymen. Their love for him is such, that although the power of the general is properly limited, the power of Paoli knows no bounds. It is high Treason so much as to speak against, or calumniate him; a species of despotism, founded, contrary to the principles of Montesquieu, on the affection of love. I shall finish my account of the government of this island, with a very remarkable anecdote.

A Corsican who had been formerly in the service of the French king, and had obtained the cross of St. Louis, upon his return to his native country, had entered into some practices which were contrary to the liberty of it. He was also suspected to have a design against the general's life. Upon this he was sent to prison, from whence, however, after some time, he was, at the intercession of the French general then in the island, set at liberty. Not long after, he was a second time caught in other secret and treasonable practices, and was again sent to prison. His life was again asked, together with his freedom, by the French commander; who being refused this request, desired to know of Paoli what he intended to do with the prisoner? 'Sir,' said Paoli, 'I will tell you, when I shall have perfected the 'liberty of my country, and shall have fixed it 'upon that establishment which I think most 'likely to maintain it; I will then call together 'the states of the island, and will produce the 'man. I will shew him that liberty, that form 'of government, that happiness which he wanted 'to destroy. After which, I will banish him 'from the island, for ever.' Such is the manner of thinking of this illustrious chief.

The religion of Corsica is the Roman Catholick faith, in which these islanders are very zealous. Perhaps they have a degree of superstition; which is the best extreme. No nation can prosper without piety; for when that fails, publick spirit and every noble sentiment will decay. The doctrine of looking up to an all-ruling Providence, and that of a future state of rewards and punishments, rendered the Roman people virtuous and great. In proportion as these doctrines were weakened, by the false philosophy of Epicurus, the minds of the Romans were impoverished, and their manly patriotism was succeeded by effeminate selfishness, which quickly brought them to contempt and ruin.

Although firmly attached to their religion, as the revelation sent from GOD, the Corsicans preserve in ecclesiastical matters, the same spirit of boldness and freedom, for which they are distinguished in civil affairs. They are sworn enemies to the temporal power of the church. Indeed the late violent differences between the national government and the bishops, has pretty well diminished their prejudices with respect to the persons of the clergy.

The Corsican bishops, who are five in number, and suffragans of the archbishop of Pisa, were warmly attached to Genoa; for on Genoa they depended for promotion. They thought fit to preach up the most slavish doctrines of submission, and stigmatized the patriots as rebels. The government desired that they might reside in the territories of the nation, and promised them a guard, to protect them from any insult. But the bishops knew well, that in the territories of the nation, they could not preach the doctrines of tyranny, and therefore refused to reside there. Upon which, the government prohibited the patriots from having any intercourse with the bishops; with which they most readily complied.

The Pope, sorry to see the Corsicans like sheep without a shepherd, resolved to send them an apostolick Visiter, to officiate in place of the bishops.

The Genoese, considering this as in some measure taking part with the malecontents, gave in a long remonstrance to the Pope, setting forth, ‘ That they were sensible of the rectitude of the ‘ intentions of his holiness, and were ever ready ‘ to shew their unalterable devotion towards the ‘ holy see: but they begged leave to say, that no ‘ provision he should make against the spiritual ‘ evils of Corsica, could be effectual, without the ‘ concurrence of the republick.’

The Corsicans, happy to receive such counte-

nance from the church, laughed at this laboured and artful remonstrance. 'Ecco la statua di Na-
'bucco, il capo d'oro e piedi di creta. Si comin-
'cia dal complimento, e si termina nella minaccia.
'Behold the statue of Nebuchadnezar! the head
'of gold, and the feet of clay. It begins with a
'compliment, and ends with a threatening.'

The court of Naples thought proper to interpose, in behalf of Genoa. Cardinal Orsini, the Neapolitan minister at the court of Rome, gave also in remonstrances; and some very plodding and heavy Genoese Canon, published a very long Discorso Theologico-Canonico-Politico, full of quotations from innumerable authorities, and no doubt assured himself, that his performance was unanswerable. But the Pope adhered to his resolution, and sent Monsignore Cesare Crescenzio de Angelis, bishop of Segni, as apostolick Visiter over all Corsica.

The Corsicans accepted of his mission, with the greatest cordiality and joy. Signor Barbaggi, who is married to the niece of Paoli, welcomed him to the island, in a polite oration. He was not only to perform the functions of the bishops, but was to be general of all the Religious in Corfica, appointing under him a provincial vicar. He was a man of so much piety, good sense, and engaging conduct, that the people conceived an universal love and regard for him.

The Genoese no longer continued their Ligurian deceit, but threw off the mask. They published a manifesto, prohibiting all their subjects in Corsica, under the heaviest penalties, to comply with the orders of the apostolick Visiter, and offering six thousand Roman crowns, to any person who should bring him prisoner to any of their fortresses.

This audacious edict the Pope very gravely annulled, with great solemnity. Some ages ago, he would have performed a more dreadful ceremony. The government of Corsica again, publickly proclaimed their displeasure, at the scandalous temerity of the republick of Genoa, ' who,' said they, ' have sent forth an edict, by which they
' have not only offended against the respect due
' to the holy see; but have presumed to meddle
' in the affairs of this kingdom, which no longer
' acknowledges them as sovereign. Therefore we
' declare the said edict, to be destructive of religion, and of the apostolick authority; offensive

'to the majesty of the vicar of Christ; seditious,
'and contrary to the security and tranquillity of
'our state, and tending to corrupt our laws and
'good customs. And we have condemned it to
'be publickly torn, and burnt, by the hands of
'the common hangman: and this to prevent such
'unworthy memorials from Genoa, in time com-
'ing.'

This sentence was put in execution, by beat of drum, below the gallows, in the city of Corte, upon the spot where stood the house of the wretch who assassinated Gaffori.

It was a most political step in the Corsicans. They recommended themselves to the Pope; they appeared firm, and authoritative; and they put contempt upon their enemies.

Having thus got rid of their tyrannical bishops, the Corsicans very wisely began to consider, that, as these dignified churchmen refused to reside and perform the duties of their offices, there was no occasion for sending them considerable sums, to enable them to live in idleness and luxury, when the money might be much better employed. They therefore thought it highly reasonable, that the bishops tithes should go to the publick chamber of the state; and accordingly it was so decreed.

A prodigious outcry was raised against this. But the Corsicans defended their conduct with great force and spirit.

‘ Hanno usurpate le decime, ed occupati I be-
‘ ni dei vescovi. They have usurped the tithes,
‘ and seized upon the goods of the bishops,’ said
the Genoese.

Replied the Corsicans, ‘ Usurpate è mal detto.
‘ Noi confesseremo la verità senza corda; perchè
‘ qui ambulat simpliciter ambulat confidenter. Il
‘ governo ha preso una porzione delle decime, e
‘ dei beni de' vescovi; ed ecco perchè. Primo,
‘ perchè ne ha avuta necessita; e questo è un di-
‘ ritto superiore ad ogni altro. Nello stato in cui
‘ siamo, per noi non vi è mezzo. O libertà, o
‘ schiavitù la più orribile. Per non cadere nella
‘ schiavitù, è necessaria la guerra: per sostenere la
‘ guerra, è necessaria la truppa; ma per pagarla,
‘ non bastando le tasse dei secolari, fu stabilito in
‘ una consulta, di prendere un sussidio dagli eccle-
‘ siastici; sull' esempio di S. Pietro, e di tutti I
‘ principi. Ma i principi, si dice, non alimentano
‘ una truppa ribelle. Una truppa che difende la

' libertà, la vita, l'onore, e la patria, dalla più ini-
' qua di tutti le oppressioni, è più sacra, venerabi-
' le, e pia, di quella di una Crociata. Secondo,
' perchè appunto per discacciare i Genovesi da
' questo regno, Benedetto XI. concesse a Giacomo
' rè di Arragona, per tre anni, le decime. Ora,
' se il caso è lo stesso, il bisogno maggiore, più
' pressanti le circonstanze, perchè non sarà lecito
' adesso quel che fu conceduto allora? Terzo,
' perchè niuno è più obligato dei nostri vescovi,
' di contribuire alle spese di questa guerra, da cui,
' essi soli finora hanno ricavato profitto; ottenen-
' do una sacra mitra, che non avrebber ottenuta,
' in mille anni di pace. Come? I secolari hanno
' versato un fiume di sangue, per procurar loro un
' sì bel capitale, ed essi faranno sentire per par-
' ticiparne qualche frutto; tanto più dovendo im-
' piegarsi, per conservare alla nazione lo stesso
' vantaggio, e procurargliene dei maggiori? Quar-
' to, perchè i nostri vescovi, in vece di farla da
' pastori e da padri, si portan da nemici. Han
' disertato dalle loro diocesi; si son ritirati presso
' à nemici; hanno loro imprestate grán somme,
' perchè ci facciano guerra; cela fanno eglino
' stessi orribilmente, colle armi spirituali, e si sono

' ostinati a non volersi restituire al suo gregge. Il
' nostro governo, per obligarli al ritorno, si è ser-
' vito del ripiego, di cui si valse Assalonne, per
' ridurre al dovere Gioab. Or se essi sono di Gi-
' oab più caparbii, chi li compatirà? chi del nostro
' governo riprenderà la condotta? Si aggiunga, che
' i frutti di chi non risiede, di chi non serve l'Al-
' tare, e molto più di chi lo tradisce, son devoluti
' a' poveri. Ora, chi più povera della nostra trup-
' pa, della nostra finanza?

' Usurped is ill said. We will confess the truth,
' without disguise; since he who walketh simply,
' walketh surely. The government hath taken a
' portion of the tithes, and of the goods of the
' bishops. And the reasons for it, are these, first,
' because we are under a necessity to do so, which
' is a right superiour to every other. In the situ-
' ation in which we are, there is no medium; or
' liberty, or the most horrible slavery. Not to fall
' into slavery, it is necessary for us to make war.
' To sustain the war it is necessary for us to have
' troops. And when we found, that the taxes of
' the seculars were not sufficient to pay the troops,
' it was decreed in a Consulta, that we should
' take a subsidy from the ecclesiasticks, after the

' example of S. Peter, and of all princes. **But,**
' say the Genoese, ' Princes do not support a
' rebel army.' An army which defends their
' liberty, their life, their honour and their coun-
' try, from the most unjust of all oppressions,
' is more sacred, more venerable, more pious
' than that of a croisade. Secondly, because Be-
' nedict the XI. granted the tithes, for three years,
' to James king of Arragon, on purpose tha the
' might drive the Genoese from this kingdom.
' And if the case is the same, the necessity still
' greater, and the circumstances more pressing,
' shall not what was lawful then, be granted
' now? Thirdly, because nobody is under a
' greater obligation to contribute to the expence
' of this war, than our bishops; as they alone
' have hitherto derived any profit from it; hav-
' ing obtained the sacred mitre, which they
' would not have obtained in a thousand years
' of peace. How? The seculars have shed a
' river of blood, to procure them so noble a ca-
' pital, of which they have enjoyed the fruits,
' and are they not in duty bound, to do every
' thing to preserve to the patriots, what advan-
' tage they have gained, and to aid them in get-

' ting more? Fourthly, because our bishops, in-
' stead of being grateful, instead of acting like
' pastours and fathers, have behaved themselves
' as enemies. They have deserted their dioce-
' ses, and retired into the territory of our foes.
' They have lent large sums of money, to car-
' ry on the war: nay they have themselves
' shewn a dreadful hostility by their spiritual
' arms, and have obstinately refused to return
' to their flocks. To oblige them to return, our
' government hath tried the same remedy which
' Absalom employed, to bring Joab back to his
' duty. If they are more froward than Joab,
' who will feel for them? who will find fault
' with the conduct of our government? To
' conclude, the tithes of those who do not re-
' side, who do not serve at the altar, and much
' more of those who betray it, fall to the poor.
' Now what can be poorer than our troops,
' than our finances?'

The tithes in Corsica are, in general, about a twentieth part of every production. The government has at present a pretty good share of them; as it not only takes the revenues of the bishops, but also those of nominal benefices, where there is no care of souls, and all the pensions which the Pope used to grant to foreign ecclesiasticks, out of the rich livings. When the affairs of the island shall be settled, no doubt the government will restore the bishops rents. But application will be made to the Pope, to have the number of bishops increased; in order that the episcopal functions may be better administred, and that the spirit of equality may be more preserved; for the bishops, when in possession of their large revenues, would be like princes in the island.

Several of the inhabitants of Corsica, have made a composition with the church, for their tithes; and the descendants of the Caporali, who were of such service to Hugo Colonna, in expelling the Saracens, are, by special privilege, exempted from paying any tithes. This privilege is supposed to have been granted to them, very anciently by the Pope, in whose cause it was, that they shewed their zeal. The clergy of Corsica, in general, are not as yet very learned; as the barbarous policy of Genoa to keep the island in ignorance, and the many years of confusion and war, have prevented the cultivation of letters. There are, however, here and there, some priests, who have had an education upon the continent, and are very well instructed, and they are all very pious, and of irreproachable morals.

There are in Corsica, 65 convents of Mendicant Friars; viz. 34 of Observants, and 14 of Reformed, of the order of St. Francis, and 17 of Capuchins. Every one of these convents, has only a wood for retired walks, a garden and a small vineyard. They depend altogether on the charity of the people. There are two colleges of Jesuits, two convents of Dominicans, five of Servites, and one of Missionaries; all of whom have very good possessions. There are also some lands belonging to other religious orders, particularly to the Carthusians of Pisa, the severe sanctity of whom, must secure them the veneration of every body, and preserve their rights inviolated even in times of the greatest distraction.

It would be expected, that in this island, the monasteries for women should bear some proportion to the convents for men; yet, in fact, there is not a single nunnery in all Corsica. To account for this, it must be considered that the monastick institution has been frequently perverted to secular purposes; so that the nobility in catholick countries, who are desirous to aggrandize their families, make their daughters take the veil, solely that their portions may be saved for the eldest son. The Genoese, who wanted to keep the Corsicans in continual subjection, devised every method to prevent any of the nobles in the island from becoming considerable. They therefore prohibited monasteries, in order to cut them off from one method of growing richer. Friars they rather encouraged, in order to lessen population, and to leave upon families, a number of unmarried women, than which nothing can be a greater burden, as is sadly experienced in protestant countries.

Convents should be laid under such restrictions, that what is intended as a solemn religious institution, may not become so common as to lose its effect, and be reckoned a profession for the dull or the indolent.

Under proper restrictions, it must be for the advantage of religion, to have a few venerable sanctuaries, for the reception of those, who having done their duty to society, are so much raised above the world, that they would choose entirely to devote the evening of life, to pious contemplation and prayer; not to mention those, whose passions have hurried them into offences, for which they sincerely resolve, by a course of abstraction, of penitence, and of voluntary austerities (a), to make expiation to the eternal justice of the DIVINITY.

From Paoli's care and attention to the good of his country, it is probable the number of convents in Corsica will be reduced. The present fathers indeed, are well entitled to a peaceable possession, during their lives; but regulations may be made to prevent many noviciates, especially of very young persons.

The Corsican clergy, and particularly the monks, have been warmly interested for the patriots. Padre Leonardo, a Franciscan, and one of the professours of the university of Corte, hath published a little tract, a 'Discorso Sacro-Civile,' teaching that those who fall in battle for their country, are to be considered as martyrs. This

(a) See that majestick teacher of moral and religious wisdom, the Rambler, number 110.

M

discourse hath had great effect. We know what force of mind that doctrine hath given to the Turks and to the Russians. Indeed, that patriotism is a virtue which merits heaven, was held by Cicero. 'Omnibus qui patriam conservaverint, adjuverint, auxerint, certus est in coelo et definitus locus, ubi beati ævo sempiterno fruantur (*a*).' For those who have preserved, assisted and aggrandized their country, there is a certain and fixed place in heaven, where they are blest with the enjoyment of eternal life.'

The warlike force of Corsica principally consists in a bold and resolute militia: every Corsican has a musket put into his hand, as soon as he is able to carry it; and as there is a constant emulation in shooting, they become excellent marksmen, and will hit with a single bullet a very small mark at a great distance.

There is in every village a Capitano d'arme; and in every pieve, a Commissario d'arme, who has the command over all the Capitani d'arme of his district. These officers are chosen by the General, with the approbation of the people. They are ever ready to receive his orders, and to call out such a

(*a*) Cic. Somn. Scip.

number of men, as he shall at any time require for the publick service.

There are in Corsica, but 500 soldiers who have pay; 300 for a guard to the General, and 200 to furnish guards for the magistrates of the several provinces, and to garrison a few small forts at particular places in the island.

A militia is indeed the true strength of a free nation. Rome had no soldiers in pay till the 347 year after the building of the city; and then they were introduced by the patricians, to ingratiate themselves with the people, at a time when the senate was embarrassed with the great influence of the Tribunes (*a*).

Paoli devised a singular and excellent method of promoting bravery among his countrymen. He wrote a circular letter to the priests of every parish in the island, desiring a list to be made out of all those who have fallen in battle for their country. The letter was in these terms.

(*a*) Liv. lib. iv. cap. 59.

## PASQUALE DE' PAOLI

*Generale del Regno di* CORSICA.

MOLTO REVERENDO SIGNOR RETTORE,

'PER rendere al publico nota, la virtù e la pietà
' di coloro, che hanno sparso il sangue per difen-
' dere i diritte e la libertà della patria, e per con-
' tradistinguere il loro merito, e farne provare la
' benigna influenza alle loro famiglie, abbiamo
' stabilito farne un esatto e compito catalogo, da
' darsi alle stampe, quale siccome potrà giovare
' ancora alla storia della nazione. Ella come ret-
' tore dovendo più d'ogni altro essere al fatto delle
' cose della sua parrocchia, si prenderà volentieri
' l'incommodo di coadiuvarci in questo disegno, e
' sarà contenta informandosi dai più vecchi assen-
' nati del paese, segnarci i nomi e la famiglia di
' coloro che vi sono morti, o restati feriti in ser-
' vizio della patria, dal 1729 a questa parte, no-
' tando colla maggior precisione il luogo, il mese
' e l'anno &c.

## PASCAL PAOLI

*General of the Kingdom of* CORSICA.

### VERY REVEREND RECTOUR,

' TO 'make known to the publick, the bra-
' very and piety of those, who have shed their
' blood in defending the rights and the liberty
' of our country, and to distinguish their merit,
' and make their families prove its benign in-
' fluence, we have resolved to make an exact
' and compleat catalogue of those heroes, and
' have it printed, so that it may also be of use
' towards composing a history of our nation.
' You, Sir, as Rectour, being better acquainted
' than any body else, with the affairs of your
' own parish, it is expected that you will wil-
' lingly take the trouble to assist us in this de-
' sign; and for that purpose you will inform
' yourself of the oldest and most judicious in the
' village, and get them to tell you the names
' and families of such as have been killed or
' wounded in the service of their country, from
' 1729 to the present time; and you will mark
' with the greatest precision, the place, the month
' and the year, &c.'

The priests have been very regular in making returns in consequence of this letter. No institution was ever better contrived. It might be adopted by every nation, as it would give double courage to soldiers, who would have their fame preserved, and at the same time leave to their relations the valuable legacy of a claim to the kindness of the state.

I have often wondered how the love of fame carries the common soldiers of our armies, into the midst of the greatest dangers; when all that they do is hardly known even to their relations, and never heard of in any publick manner.

The Corsicans are not yet much trained, as they have been acting chiefly upon the defensive, and carrying on a sort of irregular war. But now that they are advancing fast to a total victory over their enemies, a certain degree of discipline becomes necessary.

A Corsican is armed with a gun, a pistol and a stiletto. He wears a short coat, of a very coarse dark cloth, made in the island, with waistcoat and breeches of the same, or of French or Italian cloth, especially scarlet. He has a cartridge-box or pouch for his ammunition, fixed round his middle, by a belt. Into this pouch his ftiletto is ftuck; and on the left fide of his belt he hangs his piftol. His gun is flung acrofs his fhoulder. He wears black leather fpatterdafhes, and a fort of bonnet of black cloth, lined with red frieze, and ornamented on the front, with a piece of fome finer ftuff neatly fewed about. This bonnet is peculiar to the Corficans, and is a very ancient piece of drefs: it is doubled up on every fide, and when let down, is precifely the figure of a helmet, like thofe we fee on Trajan's pillar. The Corfican drefs is very convenient for traverfing the woods and mountains; and gives a man an active and warlike appearance.

The foldiers have no uniform; nor have the Corficans any drums, trumpets, fifes, or any inftrument of warlike mufick, except a large Triton fhell pierced in the end, with which they make a found loud enough to be heard at a great diftance. The fhell would more properly be ufed at fea. Virgil reprefents Triton.

Exterrens freta.

coerula concha

Æneid. lib. x. l. 209.

Frowning he seems his crooked shell to sound,
And at the blast the billows dance around.

DRYDEN.

Colonel Montgomery has told me, that the shell is used in America, particularly in Carolina. Its sound is not shrill, but rather flat like that of a large horn. It has however some resemblance to that of the Roman Lituus. Sir John Cuninghame of Caprinton has shewn me a Lituus in his possession, of which mention is made in Blaeu's Atlas (*a*). It was dug up in an ancient field of battle at Coilsfield in Ayrshire, and served the old barons of Caprinton to call together their followers.

As the Corsicans advance in improvement, they will certainly adopt the practice of having warlike instruments of musick, the effects of which have been very great in ancient times, as we are assured by Polybius, a judicious and grave historian, a careful observer of human nature, and a man not too much given to credulity. Even in modern armies we find considerable effects produced by them.

The Corsicans make a good many guns and pistols, most of which are of excellent workman-

(*a*) Blaeu's Atlas, p. 71. Province de Aire.

ship. They also make great quantities of pouder; but they have as yet no foundery for cannon. These they have either taken from their enemies, or purchased from abroad, or fished from the wrecks of vessels lost in their seas. Neither do they yet make their own bullets; they bring them from the continent, or take them from the Genoese, at whose expence they have contrived to carry on the war. A Corsican told me that they did not use a great many bullets, because, said he, ' Il Corso non tira, se non è sicuro del suo colpo. A Corsican does not fire, if he is not sure of his aim.'

They are certainly designed by nature to be strong at sea, having so many good harbours, and so much excellent timber: but they are not yet sufficiently skilled in the art of shipbuilding; nor have they money sufficient to defray the expence of employing proper artificers. They have however a number of small ships, and some of a tolerable size; and their naval affairs are conducted with great prudence and spirit, by Count Peres, who may be stiled High Admiral of Corsica.

We have seen how rich Corsica naturally is in many productions; so that there is no question, but this island might carry on a pretty extensive commerce, in oil, wine, honey, bees-wax, salt, chestnuts, silk, rosin, boxwood, oak, pine, porphyry, marble of various kinds, lead, iron, copper, silver and coral. At present, commerce is but beginning to flourish among them. They find in their seas considerable quantities of coral, of all the three kinds, red, white and black. The Jews of Leghorn, who have established there a coral manufactory, have a sort of exclusive privilege, from the Corsicans, to this trade; and in return are very serviceable to the nation, by advancing them money, and supplying them with cannon.

The Corsicans may make plenty of admirable wines, for their grapes are excellent. They make in Capo Corso two very good white wines; one of them has a great resemblance to Malaga. A deal of it is annually exported to Germany, and sold as such; and some of it is bought up at Leghorn, and carried to England, where it passes equally well for the production of Spain. The other of these white wines is something like Frontignac.

At Furiani they make a white wine very like Syracuse, not quite so luscious, and upon the whole, preferable to it. Furiani is famous in the Corsican annals, for a violent siege, where 500 Genoese were repulsed and defeated by 300 Corsicans.

In some villages, they make a rich sweet wine much resembling Tokay. At Vescovato and at Campoloro, they make wine very like Burgundy; and over the whole island there are wines of different sorts. It is indeed wonderful, what a difference a little variation of soil or exposure, even in the same vineyard, will make in the taste of wine. The juice of the Corsican grapes is so generous, that although unskilfully manufactured, it will always please by its natural flavour.

I think there might be a wine made in Corsica of a good sound moderate quality, something between Claret and Burgundy, which would be very proper for this country. But the Corsicans have been so harrassed for a number of years, that they have had no leisure to improve themselves in any art or manufacture. I am however assured, that the exportation of oil has amounted in one year to 2,500,000 French livres, and that of chestnuts to 100000 crowns of the same money.

We may expect to see the Corsicans distinguish themselves as a commercial nation. Trade has always flourished most in republican governments, as in Tyre, Sydon and Carthage, in ancient times; Venice, Genoa, Lucca and the United Provinces, in modern times. This is fully illustrated by the great John de Witt, pensioner of Holland (*a*), whose reflections were the result of the soundest sense and a long experience.

Nothing has cast a greater damp upon the improvements of Corsica, than the King of Great Britain's proclamation after the late peace, forbidding his subjects to have any intercourse with that nation. What may have been the reasons of state for such a proclamation, I cannot take upon me to say. It does not become me to look behind the veil, and pry into the secrets of government. This much I may venture to assert, that a good correspondence with Corsica would be of no small advantage to the commercial interest of this country, were it only on account of our fish trade and our woolen manufactures; not to mention the various other articles of traffick which would turn out to our mutual profit.

(*a*) De Witt's Interest of Holland, part III. chap. 3.

I know that if it had not been for this proclamation, the Corsicans would, at the close of the last war, have had several of our stoutest privateers in their service, which would have effectually overawed the Genoese, and given the brave islanders an authority at sea, which could not have failed to make them very respectable. And surely it would be worthy of a people whom the felicity of freedom has rendered generous, to afford their countenance to a race of heroes, who have done so much to secure to themselves the same blessings, especially when our shewing this generosity would greatly coincide with the commercial interests of these kingdoms.

It has been said, that it was the Duke de Nivernois, who had interest enough with our ministers, to obtain the proclamation in favour of the Genoese. Some politicians have exprest their surprise, that Great Britain should have favoured Genoa, which is always attached to the French; and when it is notorious, that without its assistance, the French could not have fitted out that fleet at Toulon, which enabled them to take Minorca; that the Genoese continued building ships for them, during the whole of the last war, and constantly supplied them with seamen: whereas the Corsicans, as lovers of liberty, must naturally have a respect for the British, as indeed is the case.

We may hope that other views will prevail in the councils of this nation. A Sovereign possessed of every virtue, who is animated with genuine sentiments of liberty, and who feels the joy of making his own people happy, would naturally wish to extend his beneficence.

Agriculture is as yet in a very imperfect state in Corsica. Their instruments of husbandry are ill made; and they do not make the best use of what they have. Their plowing is but scratching the surface of the earth; and they hardly know any thing of the advantages of manure, though they can be at no loss for sufficient quantities of it. This general observation is not incompatible with the large produce of several parts of the island, where a greater degree of fertility, and some more industry and attention to culture than usual are to be found.

The supreme council appoints two or more persons in each province, to superintend the cultivation of the lands, and to take the most effectual measures for promoting it; and in particular, to encourage the planting of mulberry trees, as it is certain, that Corsica may be made to produce a great deal of silk. As gardening has been almost totally neglected, there is a late ordinance by which every man who possesses a garden, or other enclosure, is obliged to sow every year, pease, beans and all sorts of garden-stuff, and not less than a pound of each, under the penalty of four livres, to be exacted by the Podestà.

The supreme council also appoints two consuls, to inspect the kind and the price of the various sorts of merchandise in the island; and to watch over every thing that can tend towards the advancement of commerce.

Provisions are not dear in Corsica. Their prices at a medium are as follows.

A labouring ox, about 80 livres.

A cow, from 20 to 30 livres.

A horse of the best quality, from 100 to 140 livres.

A mare, from 70 to 80 livres.

An ass, from 20 to 25 livres.

A sheep, about 4 livres.

A partridge, 4 sous.

Thrushes and blackbirds, 2 sous each.
Beef, 2 sous a pound.
Mutton, $\frac{2}{3}$ sous a pound.
The best fish, 2 sous a pound.
Ordinary fish, 1 sou a pound.
Wine, 4 sous a flask of 6 lib. wt.

The money of Corsica is of the same value as that of Tuscany.

Oil is sold in barrels valued from 40 to 50 livres. A barrel contains 20 pints. A pint contains 4 quarts.

Wine is sold in barrels of 12 zuchas. The zucha contains 9 large Florence flasks.

Grain is sold by the bushel. The bushel contains 12 bacini. The bacino weighs about 20 pounds. The sack or bushel sells at 18 livres.

The Corsican pound weight is also the same with that of Tuscany.

The government is gradually taking care to establish an uniformity in weights and measures.

The wages of a tradesman, or of a day-labourer, are a livre a day, and victuals and drink.

If a tradesman is particularly ingenious in his profession, he has something more.

Reapers have no wages in money; but besides

their victuals, each gets a bacino of the grain which he cuts down.

The manufactures of Corsica are as yet very rude. I have observed that their wool is exceedingly coarse, and generally black, and that of this they make but a thick heavy cloth. The pure black is the most valuable: when a little white wool is mixed with it, the cloth is not so much esteemed, being of a russet grey, or brown dusky colour. They import all their fine cloth; for besides that there is not a sufficient quantity of wool for the service of the island, the Corsicans have not learned to make any thing else of it, but the coarse cloth I have mentioned.

In Sardinia they make coverings for beds and carpets of various colours, besides many different stuffs for clothes. When the Corsicans have more leisure, they will probably imitate their neighbours, in those arts. Indeed over the greatest part of Italy, none but the very peasants wear home-made cloth; and if in some places they make cloth of a finer kind, it is made of foreign wool imported from different countries.

A good deal of flax grows in Corsica; and no doubt abundance of it might be raised. I expected to have found there, if not the fine webs of Holland, Ireland and Scotland, at least plenty of good, strong, houshold linnen. But, in reality, the Corsicans are as yet so backward, that they hardly make any linnen at all, which occasions a very expensive importation.

A Corsican gentleman observed to me, 'If we 'had in our kingdom such an institution as the 'Dublin Society, and a Doctor Samuel Madden 'to give praemiums to those who distinguish 'themselves in manufactures, as is done in the ca-'pital of Ireland, we might soon bring our linnen 'to some perfection as well as other branches.'

The Corsicans have plenty of oil for their lamps, which is the light they generally use. They also make wax candles, and a few tallow ones; for, as I have formerly remarked, their cattle do not yield much fat.

There is plenty of leather in the island. Many of the peasants just harden the hides in the air, particularly the wild-boar-skins, and have their shoes made of them without being tanned. This they are under no temptation of doing, but that of poverty and laziness, for the art of tanning is very well understood in Corsica, and the materiials for it are in such abundance, that a great deal of bark is carried over to Italy. The Corsicans have a method of tanning with the leaves of wild laurel, dried in the sun, and beaten into a powder. This gives a sort of greenish colour to the leather. Certainly various expedients may be used, to serve the purpose of tanning. In the island of St. Kilda, they tan with the tormentil root (*a*)

The state of learning in Corsica may well be imagined at a very low ebb, since it was the determined purpose of Genoa to keep the inhabitants of this island in the grossest ignorance; and the confusions and distresses of war have left them no leisure to attend to any kind of study. ' Inter arma silent leges. Laws are silent amidst ' the din of arms,' is an old observation; and it may be justly applied to the muses, whom war frightens away from every country.

Paoli and the wisest of the nation, with whom he consults, very soon considered, that to bring the people of Corsica to such a state as it might be hoped their freedom would last, and be carried down pure and generous to posterity, it would be necessary to enlarge their minds with the par-

(*a*) M'Aulay's History of St. Kilda, p. 214.

ticipation of true science, and to furnish them with sound and rational principles, by which the constitution might be held together in firmness.

Therefore, after long deliberation, it was at last resolved in the year 1764, to establish an university in the city of Corte; upon which occasion a manifesto (*a*) was published, recalling to the people of Corsica, the barbarous policy of Genoa, in keeping them in ignorance; and informing them of the establishments, which the parental care of the government had formed for their instruction.

This manifesto was no vain display of what could not be performed. Paoli had been at the greatest pains to collect the most knowing men in the island; and many learned Corsicans established in foreign states, were disinterested and patriotick enough, to accept of the small emoluments which Corte could afford. They thought themselves amply rewarded, in having an opportunity to contribute to the happiness of their native country, by rescuing it from the Genoese darkness, which was worse than that of the Goths, and enlightening those heroes whose untutored patriotism had shone with such lustre.

(*a*) Appendix. N° VI.

The professours in the university of Corte, are mostly fathers of different religious orders. They are indefatigable in their labours, and the youth of Corsica discover the same keenness of spirit in their studies, which characterises them in arms. There are at Corte, some pretty good halls, where the professours give their lectures. But it cannot be expected that they should as yet have any thing like the regular buildings of a college. The students are boarded in the town.

Under the head of learning I must observe that there is a printing-house at Corte, and a bookseller's shop, both kept by a Luccese, a man of some capacity in his business. He has very good types; but he prints nothing more than the publick manifestoes, calendars of feast days, and little practical devotional pieces, as also the Corsican Gazette, which is published by authority, from time to time, just as news are collected; for it contains nothing but the news of the island. It admits no foreign intelligence, nor private anecdotes; so that there will sometimes be an interval of three months during which no news-papers are published.

It will be long before the Corsicans arrive at the refinement in conducting a news-paper, of which London affords an unparallelled perfection; for, I do believe, an English news-paper is the most various and extraordinary composition that mankind ever produced. An English news-paper, while it informs the judicious of what is really doing in Europe, can keep pace with the wildest fancy in feigned adventures, and amuse the most desultory taste with essays on all subjects, and in every stile.

There are in Corsica, several treatises of political controversy, said in the title to be printed at Corte: but they are in reality printed at Lucca, or at Leghorn. In some of these treatises, of which I have a pretty numerous collection, the authours, with much care and thought, labour to prove to a demonstration, that the Corsicans must be free. Their writings are a good deal in the stile of the profound tracts for and against the hereditary and indefeasible right of kings, with which all the libraries in this country were filled in the last age. Authorities are heaped upon authorities, to establish the plainest propositions; and as the poet says, they

>  quote the Stagyrite
> To prove that smoke ascends and snow is white.
> MALLET.

The natural and divine prerogatives of liberty need not the aid of logick, which has been so successfully employed by the advocates for slavery, ' To darken counsel by words without knowledge.'

The genius and character of the inhabitants of Corsica deserve to be particularly considered; because some authours in ancient times, and the emissaries of Genoa in modern times, have represented them in the most unfavourable light.

In Muratori Rerum Italicarum Scriptores, vol. 24. We find ' Petrus Cyrnaeus de Rebus Corsicis, in four books.' This Petrus was a priest of the diocese of Aleria, in the fifteenth century. His family name was Filice; but he chose to take to himself, the learned designation of Cyrnaeus, from Cyrnus the Greek name of his native island. He was very poor, and sought a livelihood, in different parts of Italy, as a sort of pedagogue, and sojourned long at Venice as a corrector of the press. At last having returned to his mother country, he very piously composed its history, which he brings down to the year 1516.

The only manuscript of this little work is in the King of France's library; and Muratori pu-

blishes it in 1738, when, says he, 'Corsi fero-
'cium atque agrestium hominum genus, et in se-
'ditionem facile pronum, serenissimae Genuensi-
'um reipublicae, conversis in rebellionem animis,
'a multo tempore negotium non leve facessunt.
'The Corsicans a rustick ferocious race of men,
'and very prone to sedition, having turned their
'minds to rebellion, have now of a long time gi-
'ven no small trouble to the most serene repu-
'blick of Genoa.' And he adds, 'Qualem Pe-
'trus Cyrnaeus gentem suam describit, perpetuis
'contentionibus ac turbis fluctuantem, talem pre-
'sens quoque aetas agnoscit ac sentit. Such as
'Petrus Cyrnaeus describes his nation fluctuating
'with perpetual contests and tumults, such the
'present age sees and acknowledges them.'

Petrus stands greatly up for the honour of the island. He insists that a son of Hercules reigned there. Strabo (*a*) tells us that a son of Hercules settled in Sardinia, which I suppose has given occasion to the same report concerning Corsica. As Livy says, 'Datur haec venia antiquitati ut 'primordia urbium augustiora faciat (*b*). Anti-

(*a*) Strabo, lib v. cap. 225.
(*b*) Liv. in Proœm.

' quity is indulged with a privilege of rendering
' the beginnings of states more august.'

Petrus is a most enthusiastick patriot. He has no patience with Strabo, who notwithstanding of the favourable account given of Corsica by Diodorus Siculus, hath chosen to convey the worst idea both of the country and of its inhabitants. Petrus declares, that one principal reason for his writing is, ' quia Strabonis mendacia vulgata esse
' video, because I find Strabo's lies are gone a-
' broad.' And exclaims with all the fury of a true son of Hercules; ' Quum totam insulam lacerave-
' rit, non expostulemus? non accusemus? non
' graviter feramus? * * * Quod si ego tace-
' rem, nonne parietes domus ubi natus sum, nonne
' civitas ubi educatus sum exclamarent? When he
' hath torn to pieces the whole island, shall we
' not expostulate? Shall we not accuse? Shall
' we not be provoked? * * * But if I should
' be silent, would not the walls of the house where
' I was born, would not the city where I was edu-
' cated cry out?'

It is indeed strange to find two such authours as Strabo and Diodorus, differing so widely, and seemingly contradicting each other. Strabo says,

Ἡ δὲ Κύρνος ὑπὸ τῶν Ῥωμαίων καλεῖται Κορσίκα. Οἰκεῖται δὲ φαύλως, τραχεῖα τε οὖσα, καὶ τοῖς πλείςοις μέρεσι δύσβατος, τελέως ὥςτε τὸς κατέχοντας τὰ ὄρη κỳ ἀπὸ ληςηρίων ζῶντας, ἀγριωτέρυς εἶναι θηρίων. ὁπόταν γὸν ὁρμήσωσιν οἱ τῶν Ῥωμαίων Στρατηγοὶ καὶ προσπεσόντες τοῖς ἐρύμασι, πολὺ πλῆθος ἕλωσι τῶν ἀνδραπόδων, ὁρᾶν ἐςὶν ἐν τῇ Ῥώμῃ, κỳ θαυμάζειν ὅσον ἐμφαίνεται τὸ θηριῶδες κỳ τὸ βοσκηματῶδες ἐν αὐτοῖς. ἢ γὰρ ὐχ ὑπομένυσι ζῆν ἢ ζῶντες ἀπαθείᾳ καὶ ἀναισθησίᾳ τὸς ὠνησαμένυς ἐπιτρίβυσιν ὥςτε καίπερ τὸ τυχὸν καταβάλλουσιν ὑπὲρ αὐτῶν, ὅμως μεταμέλειν. Strabo. lib. v. cap. 224. 'But Cyrnus is by the Romans called
'Corsica. It is ill inhabited, being rugged, and in
'most places difficult of access; so that those who
'dwell on the mountains, and live by robberies,
'are wilder than even wild beasts. Therefore
'when the Roman generals make irruptions into
'their country, and falling upon their strong-
'holds, carry off numbers of these people, and
'bring them to Rome, it is wonderful to see
'what wildness and brutality the creatures dis-
'cover. For, they either are impatient of life,
'and lay violent hands on themselves; or if they
'do live, it is in such a state of stupefaction and

' infenfibility, that thofe who purchafe them for
' flaves have a very bad bargain, though they pay
' very little money for them, and forely regret
' their happening to fall into their hands.' So
far Strabo.

Diodorus on the other hand fays, Τὰ δὲ ἀνδράποδα τὰ Κύρνια διαφέρειν δοκεῖ τῶν ἄλλων δούλων εἰς τὰς κατὰ τὸν βίον χρείας, φυσικῆς ταύτης τῆς ἰδιότητος παρακολυθύσης * * * * τὰ δὲ πρὸς ἀλλήλυς βιῶσιν ἐπιεικῶς κὴ δικαίως παρὰ πάντας σχέδον τὺς ἄλλυς βαρβάρυς * * * * ἔν τε ταῖς ἄλλαις ταῖς ἐν βίω κατὰ μέρος οἰκονομίαις θαυμαςῶς προτιμῶσι τὸ δικαιοπραγεῖν. Diod. Sicul. lib. v. cap. 225. 'The Corfican flaves feem to dif-
' fer from all others, in their utility for the offi-
' ces of life, for which they are fitted by a pecu-
' liar gift of nature. * * * * Thefe iflanders
' live amongft themfelves with a humanity and
' juftice beyond all other barbarians. * * * *
' In every part of the oeconomy of life, they fhew
' a remarkable regard to equity.'

Mr. Burnaby thinks thefe very different accounts may be reconciled, by fuppofing the authours to fpeak of the Corficans, under different points of view; Strabo as of enemies, Diodorus as of friends; and then they will not only be found reconcileable, but will exactly correspond with the character of the Corsicans at present. In war, they are furious as lions. Death is esteemed nothing, nor is any power sufficient to make them yield against their inclination; they become irritated, and will not brook restraint (*a*). Whereas in peace, and in civil life, they are mild and just to the greatest degree, and have all those amiable qualities which Diodorus ascribes to them. Where their service is voluntary too, or they are attached to their masters, by kind and gentle treatment, they have the other perfections which he allows them.

My Lord Hailes thinks that there is properly no contradiction between these illustrious authours; since Strabo has not thrown any abuse upon the Corsicans in general. He has only talked in strong terms, of the barbarity of such of them, as inhabit the mountains and live by robberies, just as if

---

(*a*) What Mr. Burnaby says of the Corsicans puts me in mind of an admirable observation of Sir Thomas Blount: 'You may stroke the lion into tameness; but you shall sooner hew him into pieces, than beat him into a chain.' Sir Tho. Pope Blount's Essays, edit. Lond. 1697, p. 65.

writing concerning Scotland in former lawless times, he had said, the Highlanders there are a very wild set of men.

My Lord Monboddo thinks, there is nothing more required to reconcile these different characters of the Corsican slaves, but to suppose that those which Diodorus had occasion to observe, were well treated, and those which Strabo had occasion to observe, were ill treated. For, good or bad treatment was sufficient to make the Corsicans appear either of the one character, or of the other; as we may see in many barbarous nations at this day.

But I shall suppose an universal ferociousness in the Corsicans, and I think it may well be justified, considering the treatment which that brave people have met with from their oppressours. For, it is justly said by the philosopher of Malmsbury, ' Propter malorum pravitatem, recurrendum etiam ' bonis est, si se tueri volunt, ad virtutes bellicas, ' vim et dolum, id est ad ferinam rapacitatem (*a*). ' By reason of the wicked oppression of the bad, ' even a good people, must in self-defence, have ' recourse to the qualities of war, force and fraud, ' nay to a kind of savage rapacity.

(*a*) **Hobbes de Cive. Epist. Dedic.**

Petrus Cyrnaeus lays it down as a fixed principle, 'Universi Corsi liberi sunt, et propriis vivunt legibus. All Corsicans are free, and live by their own laws.' And he gives this noble eulogium to his country, 'Corsica semper alum-
' na paupertatis, hospes virtutis, misericors erga
' omnes, quam ascivit a severa disciplina quam
' usurpat * et paupertatem tuetur et liberali-
' tatem. Corsica ever nurtured by poverty, to
' whom virtue is a welcome guest, compassio-
' nate to all, maintains that poverty and gene-
' rosity which she hath learned from the hardy
' discipline to which she is inured.'

A FRIEND.

The fourth book of Petrus Cyrnaeus is entirely taken up with an account of his own wretched vagabond life, full of strange, whimsical anecdotes. He begins it very gravely, ' Quoniam ad hunc locum perventum est, non
' alienum videtur, de Petri qui haec scripsit, vi-
' ta et moribus proponere. Since we are come
' thus far, it will not be amiss, to say something
' of the life and manners of Petrus who writ-

---

* Muratori has it ' usurpant,' which will not make sense. The text has certainly been corrupted. I am obliged to a learned friend for correcting it to ' usurpat.'

' eth this history.' He gives a very excellent character of himself; and I dare say a very faithful one. But so minute is his narration, that he takes care to inform posterity, that he was very irregular in his method of walking, and that he preferred sweet wine to hard. In short he was a man of considerable parts, with a great simplicity and oddity of character.

I shall now take leave of honest Petrus; with whom perhaps some of my readers will choose to cultivate a farther acquaintance.

The Corsicans are naturally quick and lively, and have a particular turn for eloquence. Hieronymus de Marinis (*a*) gives them this character, ' Montes apum examinibus abundant, et
' lacte ac melle manant: apte etiam ad Corsorum
' ingenium, qui sub lingua, cùm lacte et melle,
' habent aculeum, adeoque foro nati sunt. Their
' mountains abound in swarms of bees, and
' flow with milk and honey; like the genius
' of the Corsicans, who while they have milk
' and honey under their tongues, have also a
' sting, and are therefore born for the forum.

I have in my possession two Corsican discour-

(*a*) Graev. Thesaur. Antiq. vol. 1. p. 1410.

ses, or popular harangues, which afford specimens of their eloquence. The one is entitled 'La Corsica a Suoi Figli, Corsica to her sons:' the other 'La Corsica a suoi Figli Sleali, Corsica to her Disloyal Sons.'

In the first of these harangues, the patriots are thus encouraged to proceed in the glorious cause. ' Seguitate voi dunque l'esempio dei salva-
' tori della lor patria, e siate sicuri, che la liber-
' tà sarà il premio delle vostre fatiche; e che all'
' ombra amena della libertà, racoglierete i soavi
' frutti di sicurezza, e di pace, di abondanza, e di
' contentezza; di avanzamento, e di gloria. Frutti,
' che vi riusceranno tanto più dolci, quanto più
' lungamente ne siete stati fuor di raggione privati
' dalla malignità dei vostri oppressori. Follow
' then the example of the saviours of their coun-
' try; and be assured that liberty will be the re-
' ward of your toils; and that under the pleasing
' shade of liberty, you will gather the agreeable
' fruits of security, of peace, of abundance and of
' contentment, of exaltation and of glory. Fruits
' which will be the sweeter to you, the longer you
' have been unreasonably deprived of them, by
' the malignity of your oppressours.'

In the second of these harangues, such of the nation as shewed any wavering or timidity, are thus rouſed againſt the Genoeſe. 'Ecco la po-
'tenza che ſi vorrebbe indurvi a temere. Voi
'l'avete ſprezzata, e ne avete trionfato nel tempo
'della voſtra maggior debolezza, nel tempo ch'e-
'ravate ſproveduti d'armi, di munizioni, di baſ-
'timenti, di porti, di finanze, e di truppa paga-
'ta; nel tempo che i voſtri capi erano novizii
'nel governo militare e politico, civile ed econo-
'mico, e che tutti queſti governi riuſcivano lo-
'ro gravi e diſpendioſi; nel tempo che i partiti
'alzavano arditamente la creſta, e da per tutto
'alla ſcoperta ſeminavano la zizania; che la par-
'te oltramontana era dalla ciſmontana indepen-
'dente e diviſa; che il dominio della nazione
'era mal ſicuro e mal noto. Ora poi, che con
'un cambiamento felice, ſiete proveduti a ſo-
'prabbondanza, d'armi e munizioni; a ſufficien-
'za, di baſtimenti e di porti; che avete ſtabilita
'la truppa ed i fondi per la ſua ſuſſiſtenza; li-
'beri perciò dagl'incommodi di molte ſpedizio-
'ni, e da i diſordini che la truppa collettiva por-
'tava ſeco; che avete inſtituite le voſtre finan-
'ze; che i voſtri capi ſi trovano molto meglio

' istruite; che i governi più non sono dispendi-
' osi; che i partiti sono tutti abbatuti, che il go-
' verno nazionale è ubidito da tutt' i ceti della
' nazione, è temuto dagli stessi nemici, e ci co-
' mincia a riconoscer dagli esteri; che le parti
' cismontane ed oltramontane son tutte unite
' sotto a un sol Capo; e sotto ad un Capo (lo di-
' rò ad onta della malignità e dell'invidia) che
' per saviezza e antivedimento, per zelo e disin-
' teresse, per coraggio e valore, per rettitudine
' d'intenzione, di fini, e di massime, non cede ad
' alcuno de' più celebri eroi: ora, dissi, in uno
' stato che per voi non fu mai sì forte e sì flo-
' rido, e che vi promette, se sarete nel vostro
' impegno costanti, una gloria immortale, una
' indipendenza totale, una perpetua felicita te-
' merete voi della republica la vana, la deplora-
' bile, la meschina potenza?

' Behold the power which they would have
' you to fear. You have despised, you have tri-
' umphed over it, in the time of your greatest
' weakness; in the time that you were unpro-
' vided with arms, with ammunition, with ships,
' with harbours, with finances and with troops.
' At a time when your chiefs were novices in

' government, whether military or political, and
' when all thefe branches of government were
' heavy and expenfive to them. At a time when
' factions audacioufly held high their crefts, and
' in every quarter openly fowed fedition. When
' the country beyond the mountains was inde-
' pendent, and divided from the country on this
' fide of the mountains; when the dominion of
' the nation was infecure and little known. And,
' when by a happy change in affairs, you are a-
' bundantly provided with arms and ammuniti-
' on, and are fufficiently accommodated with
' fhips and harbours; when you have eftablifh-
' ed troops, and funds for their fubfiftence;
' when you have regulated your finances, when
' your chiefs find themfelves much better in-
' ftructed, when government is no longer fo ex-
' penfive; when all the factions are quelled;
' when the national government is obeyed by
' all ranks in the kingdom, feared by our very ene-
' mies, and beginning to be acknowledged by fo-
' reign ftates: when the countries both on this,
' and on the other fide of the mountains are all
' united under one Chief, and under a Chief, (I
' will fay it to the fhame of malignity and of envy)

'who for wisdom and foresight, for zeal and dis-
'interestedness, for courage and valour, for the
'rectitude of his intentions, views and maxims,
'does not yield to any of the most famous he-
'roes. Now, I say, when you are in a situation
'more strong and flourishing than ever, and
'which if you are constant in your undertakings,
'promises you immortal glory, a total indepen-
'dence and a perpetual felicity; shall you be a-
'fraid of the vain, the pitiful, the contemptible
'power of the republick?'

The language of the Corsicans is remarkably good Italian, tinctured a little with some remains of the dialects of the barbarous nations, and with a few Genoese corruptions, but much purer than in many of the Italian states. Their pronunciation however is somewhat coarse. They give in particular a broad sound to the vowel E which displeased me a good deal. That the Corsicans write Italian in a great degree of perfection may be seen from some quotations in the course of this account, as well as from the manifestoes subjoined in the appendix.

The Corsicans have all a turn for the arts. I cannot indeed say that painting has yet flourished among them; but they succeed well in musick and poetry. There are few of them who do not play upon the citra, an old Moorish instrument, which they are pleased to think the ancient cythara. It has a sweet and romantick sound, and many of their airs are tender and beautiful.

They have not yet produced any large and finished poem. But they have many little pieces exceedingly pretty, most of them on war or on love. Old Giacinto Paoli, father to the present General, has left several sonnets composed with great spirit. I have a good many of them; and shall insert one, of which I have attempted a translation. It was composed in praise of his brother-commander General Giafferi, upon occasion of a victory obtained by him over the Genoese, at the siege of Cordone; and while it gives a specimen of the talents of the venerable Chief, it at the same time shews his generous satisfaction at the success of another engaged in the same glorious cause.

### SONETTO.

A coronar l'Eroe di Cirno invitto,
Morte discenda e se l'inchini il fato;
E li sospiri del Ligure sconfitto
Diano alla tromba della Fama il fiato.

Fatto appena di Golo il bel tragitto,
Del nemico efpugna forte fteccato;
Sprezzò perigli; e al difugual conflitto,
Virtu prevalfe, ov' ci comparve armato.

Cirno lo fcelfe, e'l fuo deftin l'arrife;
E'l gran litigio a cui l'Europa è attenta
Al fuo valor, al brando fuo, commife. -

Il brando, ch' anche il deftin fpaventa,
All' ingrata Liguria il crin recife;
E a Cirno il fcetro la fua man prefenta.

## SONNET.

To crown thy heroes, Cyrnus, from the fkies
    Lo Fate with joy inclines, defcends fierce death!
While vanquifh'd Genoa's defpairing fighs
    Give to Fame's glorious-founding trumpet breath.

Scarce was the Golo paft with courage bright,
    The pallifadoed hoftile fort to ftorm,
Dangers he reck'd not in th' unequal fight;
    Virtue prevail'd when feen in armed form.

His country chofe him, and celeftial Fate
    Pleas'd to behold the Corfick fire reftor'd,
The mighty ftrife on which the nations wait,
    Entrufted to his valour, to his fword.

That fword, at which ev'n Fate recoils with dread,
    The vaunting treffes cut with vigour brave,
From the ingrate Ligurian's faithlefs head;
    Cyrnus, to thee his hand the fceptre gave,

They have also many little ballads and madrigals, full of drollery and keen satire against the Genoese; and they have their essays of grave humour, and various allegories respecting themselves and their enemies. They have in particular a curious paraphrase of the Lord's Prayer, where all the petitions are strangely turned into severe accusations against the Genoese.

The character of the Corsicans has been already touched, in the comparison between Strabo and Diodorus Siculus. They are no doubt a people of strong passions, as well as of lively and vigorous minds. These are the materials, of which men are to be formed either good or bad in a superiour degree. I always remember an observation which M. Rousseau made to me, one day, in the Val de Travers, when we were talking of the characters of different nations; said he, ' J'aime ces caracteres ou il y a de l'etoffe.' It was well said. A poor feeble spirit is unable to support the weight of great virtues. It is only where there is strength and fire, that we can hope to form characters of worth and dignity.

These islanders have abilities for any thing: but their fortune has been such, that they have been conspicuous only for the hard and resolute qualities. Abandoned by the nations around to the oppression of a tyrannical republick, they have had no opportunity of shewing their genius for learning and the arts, their hospitality, their courteousness, and their other amiable virtues in civilized life. What they have had an opportunity to shew, they have shewn with distinguished glory.

The authours of the Encyclopedie say, 'Les 'Corses sont remuans, vindicatifs, et belliqueux. 'The Corsicans are tumultuous, vindictive and 'warlike.' Their struggles against the tyrant could shew them in no other light.

A writer of the highest class thus characterises them; 'Les Corses sont une poignée d'hommes 'aussi braves et aussi deliberès que les Anglois. 'On ne les domptera, je crois, que par la pru- 'dence et la bonte. On peut voir par leur 'exemple, quel courage et quelle vertu donne 'aux hommes l'amour de la libertè, et qu'il est 'dangereux et injuste de l'opprimer (a). The 'Corsicans are a handful of men, as brave and as 'determinate as the English. I believe they will

(a) Essai de Crit. sur le Prince de Machiavel. p. 114.

'not be subdued but by prudence and good
'treatment. We may see by their example, what
'courage and what virtue the love of liberty gives
'to men; and how dangerous as well as unjust
'it is to opprefs it.'

The manners of the Corficans have a great similarity with thofe of the ancient Germans, as defcribed by Tacitus. They have not however the fame habit of drinking; for they are extremely temperate. Their morals are ftrict and chafte to an uncommon degree, owing in part to good principles unhurt by luxury; and partly to the exercife of private revenge againft fuch as violate the honour of their women.

This laft may to fome appear rude and barbarous; but I hold it to be wife and noble. Better occafional murders than frequent adulteries. Better cut off a rotten branch now and then, than that the whole of the fociety fhould be corrupted. When morals are intimately connected with ideas of honour, and crimes of an alluring nature are not committed with impunity, we may expect that mankind will retain a proper awe, and be kept within the bounds of their duty: and if we have not the frivolous embellifhments and tranfient pleasures of licentious gallantry, we are free from its effeminate disquiets, its feverish passions, its falseness and dissimulation; while honest principles and manly and generous affections are kept in full vigour.

They who think duelling necessary to preserve the nice decorum of politeness, ought not to censure private revenge, the rough guardian of that virtue which is the support of every community.

What Tacitus says of ancient Germany we may say of Corsica; 'Nemo illic vitia ridet; nec corrumpere et corrumpi saeculum vocatur (*a*). Nobody there laughs at vice; nor is corrupting and being corrupted called the way of the world.'

The Corsicans like the Germans of old, are extremely indolent. The women do the greatest part of the drudgery work, (*b*) as is also the custom among the Scots Highlanders. Yet they are very active in war, like the same Germans, of whom Tacitus says, 'Mira diversitate naturae cum iidem homines sic ament inertiam et oderint quietem (*c*). By a wonderful variety of nature the same men are fond of indolence and

(*a*) Tacit. de Mor. Germ. (*b*) Ib. (*c*) Ib.

'impatient of rest.' Notwithstanding all that Paoli has done, the Corsicans are still indolent and averse to labour. Every year 800 or 1000 Sardinians and Luccese are employed as artificers and day-labourers in the island.

M. De Montesquieu observes, that all indolent nations are also proud. This is indeed the case of the Corsicans, to which, as I have formerly observed, their success in war has contributed.

M. De Montesquieu proposes a very good remedy for this: 'On purroit tourner l'effet contre
' la cause et detruire la paresse par l'orgueil. Dans
' le midi de l'Europe, où les peuples sont si fort
' frappés par le point d'honneur, il seroit bon de
' donner des prix aux laboureurs qui auroient
' porté plus loin leur industrie. Cette pratique
' a reussi de nos jours en Irlande; elle y a établi
' une des plus importantes manufactures de toile
' qui soit en Europe (*a*).

' One might turn the effect against the cause,
' and destroy indolence by pride. In the south
' of Europe, where the people are so much struck
' with the point of honour, it would be right to
' give premiums, to the labourers who have best

(*a*) Esprit des Loix liv. xiv. chap. 9.

'cultivated their fields, or to artificers who have
'carried their industry the greateſt length. This
'practice hath ſucceeded in our days, in Ireland;
'it hath there eſtabliſhed one of the moſt impor-
'tant linen manufactures in Europe.'

The Corſicans love much to lie round a fire.
This practice ſeems peculiar to rude nations. The
Indians in North America do it, and the ancient
Germans did it. 'Totos dies juxta focum atque ig-
nem agunt (*a*). They paſs whole days by the fire.'
The Scythians too had this cuſtom.

> Ipſi in defoſſis ſpecubus, ſecura ſub alta
> Otia agunt terra, congeſtaque robora, totaſque
> Advolvere focis ulmos, ignique dedere.
> VIRG. Georg. iii. l. 376.
>
> In caverns deep with oaks uppil'd, they raiſe,
> And many a branching elm, the crackling blaze;
> From cold ſecure, around the flaming hearth,
> Waſte the long dreary night in ſocial mirth.
> WARTON.

There have been many very ſtrange cuſtoms
in Corſica. Diodorus tells us, that after the women were brought to bed, the men immediately
took care of the children, laying themſelves down
as if they were ſick, and fondling the infants, ſo

---

(*a*) Tacit. de Mor. Germ.

that the mothers had no farther trouble than to give them suck (a). So great attention to a woman after she has suffered so much for the good of society, had really something humane in it; though we must smile at such simplicity. We may say that it has never been paralleled by all the complaisance of modern gallantry. But this equitable custom is no longer in use.

Petrus Cyrnaeus says, that in his time marriage was so much honoured among the Corsicans, that if any young woman was so poor that nobody asked her, the neighbours raised a contribution to help her to a husband. Generosity could never be more properly exercised. Epaminondas used to exercise his generosity in that way (a).

There are some extraordinary customs which still subsist in Corsica. In particular they have several strange ceremonies at the death of their relations. When a man dies, especially if he has been assassinated, his widow with all the married women in the village accompany the corpse to the grave, where after various howlings, and other expressions of sorrow, the women fall upon the widow,

(a) Diod. Sicul. Wesseling. p. 341.   (b) Corn. Nep. in vit. Epam.

and beat and tear her in a moſt miſerable manner. Having thus ſatisfied their grief and paſſion, they lead her back again, covered with blood and bruiſes, to her own habitation. This I had no opportunity of ſeeing, while I was in the iſland; but I have it from undoubted authority.

Having ſaid ſo much of the genius and character of the Corſicans, I muſt beg leave to preſent my readers with a very diſtinguiſhed Corſican character, that of Signor Clemente de' Paoli, brother of the General.

This gentleman is the eldeſt ſon of the old General Giacinto Paoli. He is about fifty years of age, of a middle ſize and dark complexion, his eyes are quick and piercing, and he has ſomething in the form of his mouth, which renders his appearance very particular. His underſtanding is of the firſt rate; and he has by no means ſuffered it to lie neglected. He was married, and has an only daughter, the wife of Signor Barbaggi one of the firſt men in the iſland.

For theſe many years paſt, Signor Clemente, being in a ſtate of widowhood, has reſided at Roſtino, from whence the family of Paoli comes.

He lives there in a very retired manner. He is of a Saturnine disposition, and his notions of religion are rather gloomy and severe. He spends his whole time in study, except what he passes at his devotions. These generally take up six or eight hours every day; during all which time he is in church, and before the altar, in a fixed posture, with his hands and eyes lifted up to heaven, with solemn fervour.

He prescribes to himself, an abstemious, rigid course of life; as if he had taken the vows of some of the religious orders. He is much with the Franciscans, who have a convent at Rostino. He wears the common coarse dress of the country, and it is difficult to distinguish him from one of the lowest of the people.

When he is in company he seldom speaks, and except upon important occasions, never goes into publick, or even to visit his brother at Corte. When danger calls, however, he is the first to appear in the defence of his country. He is then foremost in the ranks, and exposes himself to the hottest action; for religious fear is perfectly consistent with the greatest bravery;

according to the famous line of the pious Racine,

> Je crains Dieu, cher Abner; et n'ai point d'autre crainte.
>
> I fear my God; and Him alone I fear.
>
> A FRIEND.

In the beginning of an engagement, he is generally calm; and will frequently offer up a prayer to heaven, for the person at whom he is going to fire; saying he is sorry to be under the necessity of depriving him of life; but that he is an enemy to Corsica, and providence has sent him in his way, in order that he may be prevented from doing any farther mischief; that he hopes God will pardon his crimes, and take him to himself. After he has seen two or three of his countrymen fall at his side, the case alters. His eyes flame with grief and indignation, and he becomes like one furious, dealing vengeance every where around him.

His authority in the council is not less than his valour in the field. His strength of judgement and extent of knowledge, joined to the singular sanctity of his character, give him great weight in all the publick consultations; and his influence is of confiderable fervice to his brother the General.

When we thus view the Corficans glorioufly ftriving for the beft rights of humanity, and under the guidance of an illuftrious commander and able ftatefman, eftablifhing freedom, and forming a virtuous and happy nation, can we be indifferent as to their fuccefs? Can we Britons forbear to admire their bravery, and their wifdom? One Englifh Poet hath celebrated Corfica. I know not who he is. But I would thank him for the fpirit he hath fhewn; and I would beg leave to felect a few of his verfes.

> Hail CORSICA! than whofe recorded name
> None e'er ftood fairer on the rolls of fame!
> Rapt at the found, my foul new ardour fires,
> Each thought impaffions, and each ftrain infpires.
> Pity, to injur'd honour that is due,
> Pleads in my heart, and bids me pity you;
> For worth like thine, one honeft wifh receive;
> 'Tis all the mufe, and all the friend can give.

> Ye who are flaves of pow'r, or drones of peace,
> Ambition's tools, or votaries of eafe,
> If not quite abject, nor quite loft to fhame,
> Your hearts can feel one particle of fame,
> Stand forth; on CORSICA reflect, and fee
> Not what you are, but what you ought to be.

P

The general good's their aim; no slavish awe
Marks man from man, but LIBERTY is LAW;
No venal senates publick credit drain,
No king enslav'd by creatures of his reign.
Of publick honours merit is the test,
And those obtain them who deserve them best.

In this vile age, no virtue now rever'd,
No godlike patriot prodigy appear'd,
'Till one small spot, (for in th' ALMIGHTY's Book,
The smallest spot is never overlook'd)
Held forth the wonder to all Europe's shame,
Produc'd the man, and PAOLI his name.
Go on immortal man! the path pursue
Mark'd out by heav'n, and destin'd but for you;
Fix your firm hope on this, on this your trust,
Your arms must conquer as your cause is just.
By heav'n! it makes my life's best blood run cold,
Then glow to madness when thy story's told;
On those vile slaves be heav'n's choice thunder hurl'd,
Who chain'd themselves, would gladly chain a world.
PRIDE A POEM.

The Corsicans are in general of small stature, and rather hard-favoured, much like the Scots Highlanders; though as we find among these, so we also find among the Corsicans many of a good size, and comely countenances.

The number of inhabitants in Corsica has not been exactly taken of late, but they may be reckoned 220000 souls; for, previous to the rise in 1729, there were 40000 families who payed tax to Genoa, and reckoning five to each family, the inhabitants were then 200000.

Now although it may appear a paradox, it is certain that the number of inhabitants has increased during the war; as will appear from the following confiderations.

Father Cancellotti a Jefuit miffionary, who travelled over Corfica, and informed himfelf with great exactnefs, made a computation, that in thirty years of Genoefe government, the ifland loft by affaffinations and other caufes 28000 people.

Whereas in the thirty feven years of war, the ifland has not loft above 10000 people, including thofe who have fled from the confufions of their country, to follow fortune upon the continent.

And therefore this calculation of the number of inhabitants at prefent, is a juft one.

The number of Corficans is however much lefs than it was in ancient times. It is well obferved by an able writer (*a*), ' That the depopu-
' lation of many countries feems to have been
' firft occafioned by the havock the Romans
' made among the fmaller ftates and cities, before
' they could fully eftablifh their fovereign power.'

(*a*) Wallace on the Numbers of Mankind. p. 106.

In no state could this cause of depopulation take place, more than in Corsica; for in no state were the natives harder to be subdued. When to the Roman havock we add the reiterated turmoils, which during a course of ages, have shaken this island, we need be at no loss to account why the number of its inhabitants is diminished.

Of the 220000 people computed to be in Corsica, there may be 10000 in Bastia, and in all 25000 in the territories of the Genoese; so that I reckon there are about 200000 of the patriotick nation, and of these Paoli can bring 40000 armed men into the field.

It is therefore by no means probable, that the Genoese should reduce to abject submission so considerable a nation, and a nation of such men; most of whom have been born in the troublous times, and been brought up with sentiments of the most violent hatred at the republick. There is not a Corsican child who can procure a little gun-powder, but he immediately sets fire to it, huzzas at the explosion, and as if he had blown up the enemy, calls out, 'Ecco i Genovesi. 'There go the Genoese.'

I believe the wisest and best nobles of Genoa

are now of opinion, that the republick should renounce her pretensions of dominion, over a people whom long experience has proved to be unconquerable by the Genoese arms, who have baffled every attempt that the republick has made against them, and who are at last formed into a state that has a solid claim to independency. But the wisest and best of Genoa, like the wisest and best of other states, are over-ruled by the majority; and the republick has hitherto continued to drain her treasury, and sacrifice her soldiers, in fruitless attempts to recover Corsica.

The Abbé Richard (a) hath given a very just and lively account of this: ' Le royaume de
' Corse dont la republique possede quelques places
' maritimes lui coute prodigieusement; elle n'en
' retire aucun avantage réel, et elle a toujours à
' combattre un peuple indiscipliné armé pour la
' liberté.

' Mais comme les nobles Genois se regardent
' tous comme solidairement rois de Corse, cette
' raison qui est tres forte sur leur esprit, les deter-
' minera toujours à ne rien epargner pour conser-
' ver au moins ce titre. C'est l'objet d'ambition

(a) Richard Descrip. Hist. et Crit. de l'Ital. tom. I. p. 118.

' qui les touche le plus. Rien n'eſt auſſi intereſſant
' pour eux, que les nouvelles de ce païs; ſour tout
' quand la ballance paroit pancher du coté des re-
' belles.*

' Une dame Génoiſe fort inquiete de quelques
' ſuccès qui ſembloient annoncer une revolution
' totale en faveur des inſulaires, apprenant que les
' eſperances de la republique ſe retabliſſoient, dit
' dans un tranſport de joie, "DIEU merci nous
' ſommes donc encore un peu reines."

' The kingdom of Corſica, of which the re-
' publick poſſeſſes ſome maritime ſtrong places,
' coſts her a prodigious expence. She derives no
' real advantage from it, and ſhe hath always to
' combate an undiſciplined people armed for li-
' berty.

' But as the Genoeſe nobles look upon them-
' ſelves to be all joint kings of Corſica, this con-
' ſideration which is very ſtrong upon their minds,
' will ever determine them to ſpare nothing in
' order to preſerve at leaſt the title. It is the
' point of ambition which touches them the moſt.
' Nothing is ſo intereſting to them as the news

---

* He ſhould not call thoſe ' rebelles' whom he hath before repreſented as ' armés pour la liberté.'

' from that country, especially when the balance
' seems to lean to the side of the rebels (patriots.')

'A Genoese lady who was very uneasy, on
' account of some successes which seemed to an-
' nounce a total revolution in favour of the islan-
' ders, hearing that the hopes of the republick
' began to be re-established, cried in a transport
' of joy, "Thank GOD then, we are yet some-
' what queens."

While I was employed in writing this Account of Corsica, the brave islanders resolved on striking a bold stroke, and making a conquest of the island of Capraja.

Capraja or Caprara lies to the east of Corsica, about five and twenty miles off Capo Corso, over against the coast of Tuscany. This island was formerly annexed to the kingdom of Corsica, being a portion of the feudal territory of the noble family of Damari who were deprived of it by the Genoese.

Capraja is about fifteen miles in circumference. The whole of it is exceedingly mountainous, and of a dry craggy surface. It is all around so pointed with rocks, that it is inaccessible almost on every quarter, except at one harbour, which is a pretty good one; and where numbers of vessels passing the Mediterranean are in use to take shelter. It hath upwards of 3000 inhabitants, all of whom are assembled in a town at the extremity of the island just above the harbour.

The men of Capraja are strong and robust. They all go to sea, and are reckoned the hardiest and most expert sailors in that part of the world. The women employ themselves chiefly in cultivating vines, in which the island is pretty fertile. There is here a strong citadel built on a high rock, so that it commands the town and harbour. It is well furnished with artillery, and the Genoese kept there a garrison. There are also two other towers at the two extremities of the island, built rather in order to descry the Barbary Corsairs, than to defend a country so well fortified by nature*.

In the month of December 1766, Signor Paul Mattei of Centuri having gone to France to

* I know Capraja well, for I was driven into it by stress of weather in my return from Corsica. I was detained there six days, and was lodged in a Franciscan convent, where the worthy fathers entertained me very hospitably. I employed my time in writing a minute detail of every thing in the island, which I still have by me, and often amuse myself with it, at a vacant hour.

transact some private affairs, in his passage home he went ashore at Capraja, where he was at great pains to inform himself with regard to the situation of their garrison, their harbour and their coasts, the scarcity of provisions, and the little attention with which the island was defended.

On his return to Corsica, he proposed to Paoli to make a descent upon Capraja. His proposal was immediately approved, and the conduct of the enterprise was committed to Signor Achilles Murati, commandant at Erbalonga, and Signor John Baptist Ristori, commandant at Furiani, who on the evening of the 16th of February 1767, set sail from the port of Macinajo, accompanied by Signor Mattei and several gallant young gentlemen of the principal families in the provinces of Capo Corso and Nebbio, who chose to go as volunteers. They had also a few Capraese to serve as guides.

They landed on Capraja that night. The Corsican commanders signified to the Capraese, that they were come with no hostile intentions against them; but only to expell from their country, the Genoese, that the inhabitants of Capraja might participate the happy fruits of liberty; in common with their ancient friends the Corsicans: and therefore they hoped that instead of meeting with opposition, they would be received with cordiality. Upon this, a number of the inhabitants immediately joined them, and they laid siege to the citadel.

The Genoese were piqued to the greatest degree, to find that those islanders, whom they gave out to be a set of rebels under the awe of a French guard, were boldly sallying forth, and wresting from them the sovereignty of another island in the Mediterranean; an event which could not fail to blaze abroad over Europe, and equally contribute to the glory of the Corsicans and to the disgrace of the republick. They therefore spared no expence or care to defeat the enterprise.

They sent out a considerable armament under the command of Signor Augustino Pinello, a man of tried activity and valour, and an actual senatour of Genoa.

They also sent Colonel Antonio Matra, with a body of chosen men, who by the assistance of a Capraese galley-slave effectuated a landing, at a place neglected by the Corsicans as inaccessible.

While Matra attacked the Corsicans by land, Signor Pinello attacked them from the sea, on two different quarters; so that they had a very hot and difficult action to maintain. Notwithstanding all which, Pinello was beaten off, and Matra's detachment was totally routed.

I could wish to relate the various particulars of this expedition. I have materials sufficient for it; but the plan of my work does not permit me. The citadel of Capraja surrendered on the 29th of May.

The Corsicans have by this conquest added considerably to their dominion. They have acquired an increase of most useful people; and they are in condition to prevent, or at least render extremely difficult, the communication between Genoa and her garrisons in Corsica.

Sir James Steuart hath placed the Corsicans in rather an unfavourable light. His words are, ‘ The Corsicans have exported, that is, sold the ‘ best part of their island to Genoa; and now, ‘ after having spent the price in wearing damask ‘ and velvet, they want to bring it back, by con- ‘ fiscating the property of the Genoese, who ‘ have both paid for the island, and drawn back

'the price of it, by the balance of their trade
'against these islanders.' (a)

With this respectable writer's permission, it was not a balance of trade, but a balance of bad fortune, which subjected Corsica to the Genoese; and the greatest part, if not all the property of the nobles of the republick in that island, was acquired only by force or by fraud. The expensiveness of the Corsicans in wearing damask and velvet, is merely ideal. Corsica is perhaps the only country upon the face of the globe, where luxury has never once been introduced. The Genoese cannot pretend to have made themselves masters of Corsica, by commercial superiority; for those republicans have been supplied from that fertile island, with a great many of the necessaries of life, which their own narrow dominions could not furnish in sufficient quantities.

I have thought myself called upon to rectify this mistake, in a book which may afford many important lessons to free nations, and among the rest to the brave Corsicans themselves.

(a) Inquiry into the Principles of Political Oeconomy, Book II. Chap. 29.

It is in vain for the Genoese to pretend any longer that the Corsicans are to be looked upon as rebels. It is nobly opposed by a Corsican writer; with whose words I shall conclude my Account of Corsica.

'Rebelli! come non hanno vergogna di dar
' a noi questo titolo! a noi che facciamo la guer-
' ra con tanto spirito di lenità e di dolcezza, che
' non altro si studia che risparmiare il sangue, i
' beni, e l'onore de' nostri concittadini? a noi
' che non cercando se non di liberare la patria
' della più iniqua di tutte le cattività, altro tito-
' lo non conviene che quello di salvatori. E poi-
' chè lode a Dio dator d'ogni bene, abbiamo
' già conseguito l'intento; poichè abbiamo già
' formato in sequela un governo sovrano libe-
' ro, independente, assoluto, padrone della vi-
' ta e della morte di tante migliaja di sudditi,
' che lo riconoscono, ed ubidiscono con fedeltà e
' con prestezza. Avendo stabilito successivamente
' rota e tribunali; giudici e magistrati; ministri ed
' esecutori di giustizia; secreterie e cancellerie; aper-
' te stamperie; composte leggi e statuti; truppe e
' finanze; poichè sotto al nostra dominio abbiamo
' torri e presidi; castelli e carceri; armi e canno-
' ni; porti e bastimenti, poichè assolviamo e con-

' danniamo per via di processi e sentenze; impo-
' niamo tasse e contribuzioni; improntiamo i nos-
' tri sigilli; sventoliamo le nostre bandiere; con-
' cediamo tratte e licenze; creiamo notari; inti-
' miamo guerre; formiamo assedi; capitoliamo re-
' se ed armistizi; contrassegni tutti di sovranità, e
' di dominio? come posson più appellarci gente
' privata? (a)

' Rebels! are they not ashamed to give to us
' that title? to us, who make war with such a spi-
' rit of lenity and mildness, that our only study is
' to spare the blood, the effects and the honour of
' our fellow-citizens? to us, who seek for nothing
' but to free our country from the most iniqui-
' tous of all captivities, and therefore well deserve
' the title of saviours. And thanks to GOD the
' Giver of all good, we have now obtained our
' purpose: for we have now formed a government
' sovereign, free and independent, with the power
' of life and death over so many thousand sub-
' jects, who acknowledge it, and obey it with fi-
' delity and with alacrity. We have now succes-
' sively established a rota and tribunals, judges
' and magistrates, administratours and executers of

(a) Manifest. di Gen. Colle Rispost. di un Cors. p. 23.

' justice. We have secretaries offices, and publick
' archives; open printing-houses, laws and sta-
' tutes, troops and finances. We have moreover
' under our dominion towers and garrisons, castles
' and prisons, arms and cannon, harbours and
' shipping. Besides, we absolve and condemn in
' the regular form of processes and sentences; we
' impose taxes and contributions, we adhibit our
' seals, we display our colours, we declare wars,
' we form sieges, we capitulate for truces and ces-
' sations of arms. Are not all these the marks of
' sovereignty and dominion? How then can they
' any longer call us a private band?'

# APPENDIX,

## CONTAINING

## CORSICAN STATE PAPERS.

# APPENDIX.

### N° I. page 136.

# MANIFESTO

## DEL GENERALE,

## E SUPREMO CONSIGLIO DI STATO

### DEL REGNO DI CORSICA.

LA giuftizia della noftra guerra contro la repubblica di Genova è tanto nota al mondo, quanto la neceffità che ci ha indotti a prender le armi per fottrarci dalla più obbrobriofa, ed infoffribile tirannia degl'ingiufti occupatori della noftra ifola, e de nemici della noftra libertà. La moderazione, ciò non oftante, colla quale ci fiamo fempre diportati in quefto sì giufto, e lodevole impegno, avendo viepiù riempiti d'orgoglio, e fatti ogni giorno più arditi a noftro danno i Signori di Genova, rende a noi indifpenfabile il dovere nel punto che fiamo per cambiar di condotta a lor riguardo, manifeftarne al pubblico li motivi, e le ragioni, onde ognuno fia perfuafo della rettitudine delle noftre determinazioni, e di quella equità, che forma il carattere della noftra nazione.

Da trenta anni che noi fofteniamo la prefente guerra per ifnidare affatto dalla noftra ifola la repubblica di Genova, mai in alcun modo avevamo tentato fraftornare il commercio di mare a fudditi di quella fignoria, compaffionando di quelli piuttofto l'infelice fituazione, che l'obligava a vivere fotto un governo, che per la ifteffa fua coftituzione non può fe non effer tiranno. Ma vedendo ora con quanta oftinazione, ed efficacia la predetta repubblica s'affatichi per interdire, e precludere ogni ftrada al commercio marittimo nel noftro regno, prendendo non folamente co' fuoi Baftimenti armati in Corfo quelli che loro riefce incontrare di noftra bandiera, ma per anche con felice ardimento finora abbrugiando, ed infultando quelli delle altre nazioni più rifpettabili dell' Europa, che per ragion di traffico fi portino ad approdare, o partano da porti e fcali a noi foggetti della noftra ifola. E vedendo in fine, che quefta noftra lenità, e contegno niente è corrifpofto dalli fudditi Genovefi, e che anche effi inftigano il loro principe a privarci del beneficio del commercio con qualunque bandiera, lufingandofi con quefto mezzo vedere affatto la noftra nazione toffrir nelle loro mani il monopolio delle fue foftanze, colle quali fi fono obbligati provedere quei prefidi, che noi teniamo bloccati. Per non mancar quindi di riguardo a noi medefimi, per togiier gli oftacoli, e proteggere il noftro commercio, e per render fenfibile il noftro rifentimento a coloro, che ful mare impunemente finora ci hanno infultati con tanto noftro pregindizio; prevalendoci del dritto, che ci compete, e perchè è infeparabile da quella libertà, che il cielo ha conceffa al noftro valore, abbiamo deliberato conceder la facoltà a qualunque de' noftri nazionali, che voleffe armar baftimenti da Corfo contro de Genovefi noftri nemici, e lor bandiera, d'inalberare il noftro padiglione dopo aver prefo però da noi il paffaporto, e le iftruzioni opportune; la quale facoltà nell' ifteffo modo, e forma, volentieri accorderemo ancora a qualunque ftraniere, che voleffe fervirfene contro de' medefimi noftri nemici, e lor bandiera, bonificandogli, ed afficurandogli tutti que' privilegi, che in uguali circoftanze fogliono accordarfi agli armatori.

Coftretti per tanto da così preffanti motivi, e fode ragioni a far la guerra anche per mare alla repubblica noftra nemica, ci proteftiamo nondimeno voler ufare il maggior rifpetto, ed i riguardi poffibili a tutti i prencipi dell' Europa, e di voler praticare, ed offervare le leggi, e confuetudini introdotte, ed ammeffe nelle guerre marittime anche verfo de Genovefi, quando i medefimi colle folite loro irregolari, ed inumane procedure non ci coftringano ad appartarcene.

Cafinca 20. Maggio 1768.

N° II. page 136.

# DOGE

## GOVERNATORI,

## E PROCURATORI

### DELLA REPUBBLICA DI GENOVA.

NELLA determinazione, in cui fiamo di dare a' noftri popoli della Corfica i contraffegni più indubitati, ed autentici della paterna noftra amorevolezza, e del fincero defiderio che abbiamo di renderli tranquilli e felici; effendoci fatte prefenti le inftanze di una gran parte di detti popoli, abbiamo deliberato di fpedire in quel noftro regno una eccellentiffima deputazione munita di tutte le opportune facoltà, ed autorizzata in nome della fereniffima noftra repubblica a promoverri efficacemente, ed a fiffare i mezzi di quella ftabile pacificazione, che fù da tanto tempo l'oggetto delle più vive noftre premure.

Notifichiamo quindi col mezzo delle prefenti a' fopraddetti noftri popoli, che faranno effi, niuno efclufo, pienamente rimeffi nella grazia e favore della prefata noftra repubblica col generale indulto di tutto ciò che può effere accaduto in occafione de' moti trafcorfi: gli accertiamo inoltre della immancabile noftra difpofizione ad afficurare la tranquillità, e la felicità loro col mezzo di tutte quelle graziofe conceffioni, che fervano non folo a confermare, e fpiegare le precedenti, e particolarmente quelle, che furono accordate in tempo dell' illuftriffimo Pietro Maria Giuftiniano, ma ancora la ferma intenzione, in cui fiamo, di concedere alla nazione Corfa diftinzioni maggiori, ftabilire una retta, ed invariabile amminiftrazione della giuftizia civile e criminale, favorire ed ampliare il commercio, e procurare in fomma alla predetta nazione col bene della pace ogni altro poffibile vantaggio.

A quefti giuftiffimi fini la prefata eccellentiffima deputazione impiegherà ogni fua cura e penfiero; ed invitiamo perciò non meno tutti i foggetti più riguardevoli, che qualunque altro particolare del regno a contribuirvi per parte loro con quella fteffa affezione, impegno, e buona fede, che per parte noftra, e dell' eccellentiffima deputazione vi faranno certamente apportati, procurando altresì il più pronto generale concorfo di tutte le pievi, e provincie, onde poffa colla maggior follecitudine, concordia, ed unanimità perfezionarfi un' opera, che dev' effere per i fuddetti noftri popoli di fommo intereffe, ed importanza.

In vifta di quanto fopra proibiamo efpreffamente a chi avrà cara la noftra grazia il recare qualunque danno alle perfone, e bene di chiunque fiafi de' fuddetti noftri popoli; e ficcome ci promettiamo, che l'opera, e lo zelo di ognuno fi adopereranno efficacemente per un oggetto, che tanto intereffa la repubblica, e'l vero bene del regno, così avremo noi prefente il merito di quelli, che con più di attività, e d'impegno contribuiranno a promuoverlo, e ftabilirlo.

Dat. in Genova nel noftro Real Palazzo li 9. Maggio 1761.

Domenico MARIA TATIS Segretario di Stato.

N° III. page 137.

RISULTATO DEL CONGRESSO TENUTO DA' CORSI IN CASINCA, IN OCCASIONE DELLA GIUNTA SPEDITA IN CORSICA DA' GENOVESI.

# IL GENERALE,

## ED IL SUPREMO CONSIGLIO DI STATO

## DEL REGNO DI CORSICA.

La repubblica di Genova conosciute insufficienti le proprie sue forze, non che per sottometterci all' aborrito di lei dominio, ma ben anche per far più lunga resistenza a quelle, che ci fornisce la nostra unione, ed il nostro invincibile attaccamento alla libertà da qualche tempo a questa parte, ma sempre invano non ha mai cessato di tentare con tutta la maggior efficacia delle sue imposture d' indisporre contra di noi, e ricever soccorso da qualche gran Corte d' Europa.

Vedendosi ora delusa in questo suo disegno, e sapendo benissimo riputarsi da ogn' uno un dritto dell' umanità il dare una volta quiete a questa nazione, fortemente ella teme, che nel futuro congresso di pace considerata, e la giustizia della nostra causa colle nostre solenni determinazioni, e l' incompatibilità del suo governo col genio dei nostri popoli, i principi d' Europa per non lasciare accesa in seno all' Italia una scintilla di guerra non pensino a farla desistere dalle pretensioni che ostenta, e che ad altro fine non vorrebbe far valere sopra questo regno, che per riempirlo di miserie, e d', orrore. In tale stato di cose seguendo l' impulso della sua passione predominante di stragi, e di vendette, ella ha creduto non potersi meglio opporre alle nostre intraprese, che animando colla profusione di molto danaro, e coll' offerta di gradi militari, e stipendi alcuni uomini vili, e mercenari, esuli dalla lor patria per le enormità de' loro delitti, ad introdurvisi surrettiziamente per eccitarvi il tumulto, e la disunione; onde in apprensione, o distratti noi in una guerra civile, avesse più commodo di far valere il giro de' suoi artifizj, e nelle Corti, e nel congresso di pace. Ed ella tanto più volentieri ha adottato questo progetto, quanto che nel congresso di Aquisgrana, allorchè i ministri delle potenze pensarono, e metter le mani anche agli affari di Corsica, astutamente seppe eluderne la premura coll' affertiva, che in poco tempo avrebbe quietati i rumori di questo regno. Coll' istessa industria volendo ora prevenire l' attenzione dei gabinetti per mezzo de' suoi inviati, e con manifesti, impudentemente afferisce, e divulga, avere finalmente ritrovato il mezzo di ridurre alla quiete le cose di Corsica, ed avere a tale oggetto sulle richieste della maggior parte de' popoli, e de' principali della nazione destinata una giunta di sei soggetti dell' ordine senatorio munita di ample facoltà, e per attirarsi la confidenza, ed il concorso delle pievi nella città di Bastia, e per ultimarvi il trattato di pacificazione.

Noi amatissimi compatriotti quali per raggione del nostro ministero colla maggiore sollecitudine, ed indefessa attenzione siamo continuamente applicati, e vegliamo alla conservazione della vostra interna tranquillità, ed a sconcertare i progetti, e respingere i tentativi de' nemici della nostra libertà, avendo penetrato questo piano ed idea della repubblica di Genova, non credemmo poter più lungamente differire la citazione del solito annuale congresso, espediente sperimentato efficacissimo in trenta, e più anni di guerra per confondere l'orgoglio, e frastornar le misure de' Genovesi. Fu intimato, e notificato a tutti quelli, che hanno voce, ed autorità su' i pubblici affari, e fu tenuto col maggior concorso di tutti gli ordini, e rappresentanti della nazione nel convento di S. Francesco della pieve di Casinca nelle festività di pentecoste. Previddero il colpo fatale della lor macchina i nostri nemici, e fecero ogni sforzo per farlo cadere a vuoto. D. Filippo Grimaldi alla testa de' banditi, le facinorosi fatti venire appostatamente da Genova in Bastia coll' intelligenza del Martinetti, e coll' apparato di molti bastimenti féce uno scalo in Fiumorbo, e stabilissi a casa di Sardo, da dove con minuccie e lusinghe, e colla proposizione di levare un reggimento in quella commarca, si persuase spaventare i buoni patriotti, e tirare a se il concorso di molti partiti nel disegno d' interrompere, occupandoci altrove, il citato congresso, e privarci così della congiuntura più propria d' illuminare i nostri popoli, e d' essere assistiti dal loro zelo, e generosità nel commune bisogno. L' istantaneo provedimento, che s' oppose a questo primo tentativo degli avversari, e la prontezza con cui prese l' armi per difesa della propria libertà tutta quella comarca, vi sono egualmente noti alla sconfitta de' traditori della patria, e delle truppe Genovesi. Continuò dunque il congresso colla più desiderabile unanimità di sentimenti, e colla più matura ponderazione delle cose le sue sessioni, nelle quali furono prese le qui sotto notate deliberazioni, quali perchè siano a notizia d' ogn' uno, e per la loro intiera osservanza, vogliamo ed ordiniamo che siano lette, e pubblicate, ed affissata copia ne' luoghi soliti, e consueti, riserbandoci sopra alcuni punti ad emanar fuori più circostanziato dettaglio per soddisfazione, ed intelligenza de' nostri amatissimi popoli.

I. E' stato decretato che si faccia un manifesto per mezzo di cui smentire quelli della repubblica di Genova, protestando nel medesimo, che in alcun tempo mai noi non saremo per dare orecchio a veruna proposizione d'accordo con i Genovesi, se questi per preliminari non riconoscono la nostra libertà, l'indipendenza del nostro governo, e non cedano al medesimo le poche piazze che ancor tengono nel regno. Quali preliminari accordati, od eseguiti, la nazione Corsa, ed il suo governo adotterà le misure più proprie e decenti, e farà spiccare la natural sua equità, e moderazione per indennizare il decoro, e gl'interessi della repubblica di Genova.

II. Nella più probabile supposizione, che i Genovesi acciecati dal loro orgoglio non saranno per aderire a questi preliminari di pace, per metterci maggiormente in istato di fargli con più successo, e vigorosa la guerra in conseguenza del piano stabilito per l'anno corrente, è stato pensato, ed a pieni voti determinato, che si levi una contribuzione straordinaria, in virtù della quale determinazione, ciascuno che avrà beni stabili, mobili, o semoventi fruttiferi nel regno dovrà pagare una lira per ogni mille che ne possederà in detti effetti per una sol volta. Per fare questa esigenza li signori intendenti generali, o altri presidenti della camera con una particolare istruzione si metteranno in giro nel prossimo venturo mese d'Agosto.

III. Per la più pronta spedizione degli affari, e per essere nel luogo il più a portata d'invigilare all'interna tranquillità del regno è stato conchiuso, e stabilito, che il governo supremo faccia fissa la sua residenza nella città di Corte, e che vi si debba trasferire ne' primi giorni dell'entrante Giugno, col permesso però al Sig. Generale di potersene appartare quando lo giudichi a proposito, o per l'esecuzione del piano stabilito delle operazioni di guerra in quest'anno, o per mantenersi alla fronte del nemico, ed opporsi alli di lui tentativi. Nel qual caso resteranno a di lui carico, e di sua ispezione particolare il comando, e la direzione dell'armi, la guarnigione de' presidi, torri, e postamenti, ed ogni altro affare appartenente alla guerra, e nel restante delle pubbliche incombenze procederà il supremo consiglio colla solita sua suprema autorità.

IV. Inerendo al desiderio de' veri amatori della libertà, quale in ogni cosa vorrebbero che avesse uguale influenza, ed ardentemente sollecitano per l'abolimento di ogni qualunque residuo dell'antica servitù: sicome ancora per averne quel profitto che ne ritraggono gli altri stati, si è stabilito di far coniare colle armi del regno una quantità proporzionata di moneta di rame, e d'argento, per servire agli usi correnti dentro il regno. La quale moneta non potrà esser rifiutata da alcuno, e nella quale solamente la camera, ed i tribunali riceveranno i pagamenti, i dazi, le tasse ordinarie, e straordinarie, condanne, ò altro &c. Per maggior comodo de' popoli in ogni provincia, e forse anche in ogni pieve sarà deputata una persona, a cui potrà ricorrere chiunque per far qualche pagamento pubblico, per cui avrà bisogno di cambiar moneta forastiera colla corrente del regno, o di queste colla forastiera per il commercio, ed usi fuori di stato.

V. E per viepiù fare spiccare l'independenza dei nostri tribunali, e supplire in parte alle spese della loro manutenzione, è stato risoluto, che il supremo governo pensi a far bollare colle armi del regno una quantità di carta, consegnandola agl'intendenti generali delle finanze, coll'incarico ai medesimi di distribuirne per ciascuna pieve a proporzione, perchè venga comprata a soldi due, e denari, otto il foglio da chiunque ne avrà bisogno. Poichè dal momento che sarà distribuita per le pievi, questa carta così bollata, e sarà notificato a tutti per mezzo d'una circolare, non farà ricevuto come istromento, ò scrittura pubblica, ma sarà considerato ne' nostri tribunali come di niun vigore qualunque atto in avvenire non scritto sopra questa carta.

VI. E ad oggetto di far più sensibile, e manifesto il giusto nostro risentimento contro Don Filippo Grimaldi, capo e direttore de' facinorosi felloni, ed emissari, le di cui malvagie inclinazioni lo condussero al remo nella sua gioventù, ed a cui la frequenza de' più enormi delitti contro la patria ha servito di scala per arrivare al grado di colonnello della repubblica di Genova, della quale or gode la maggior confidenza, si è ordinato, che debba costruirli la figura d'un uomo di paglia rappresentante esso Don Filippo Grimaldi, per essere dal ministro di giustizia alle forche piscaine pubblicamente impiccato, affinchè venendo in qualunque tempo nelle nostre forze, si debba eseguire il medesimo supplicio nella di lui propria persona.

VII. Ed attese le presenti emergenze, si è pensato incaricare colle più efficaci premure i commissari, i capitani delle armi, ed altri pubblici uffiziali della nazione d'arrestare, e consegnare alla giustizia tutte le persone sospette, ò che terranno discorsi sediziosi, siccome d'invigilare agli andamenti, e sorprendere gli emissari dei Genovesi nelle loro respettive pievi, e parrocchie, alla qual premurosa disposizione contravenendo si eseguiranno rigorosamente contro di loro le leggi stabilite nel congresso di Santo Pietro.

VIII. Si sono prese inoltre le misure più proprie per mantenere il buon ordine nell'amministrazione della giustizia, e nella percezione, e maneggio del danaro pubblico, ciocchè noi scrupolosamente adempiremo in quanto per ragion del nostro impiego a noi spetta, ed assiduamente invigileremo, che gli altri ancora eseguiscano colla maggior diligenza, ed esattezza le loro commissioni, e incombenze.

Noi per ultimo, amatissimi compatriotti, non stimiamo nemmeno opportuno d'esortarvi ad unire alla nostra sollecitudine la vostra costanza, mentre nell'ultimo memorabile congresso si è troppo manifestamente contradistinto il vostro zelo per la commune patria, e nel concorrere in tanto numero, e con tanto ardore ad abbattere, e punire l'indegno ribelle Martinetti, avere abbastanza fatta vedere la vostra fermezza in difendere, e mantenere la nostra libertà; onde noi siamo pieni di riconoscenza, e di gratitudine per la vostra fedeltà e valore, e l'Europa tutta sarà quindi persuasa della inalterabile nostra unione, mediante la quale noi assicureremo la nostra felicità, ed aumenteremo sempre la gloria della patria.

Vescovato 24. Maggio 1761.

Giuseppe MARIA MASSESI Gran-Cancelliere.

### N° IV. page 137.

# MEMORIA
## AI SOVRANI
## DI EUROPA.

NON dovrebbe certamente lagnarsi la repubblica di Genova, se dai Corsi non si è prestato orecchio alle lusinghevoli, e generiche espressioni d'assicurare la tranquillità, e la felicità loro contenute nell'editto dei 9 Maggio, sparso artificiosamente in più mani dai Corsi medesimi. Chiunque sia per poco informato delle circostanze foriere di questo editto, sarà astretto a confessare, che o la repubblica non ebbe lumi bastevoli per ben intraprender l'impegno di piegar l'animo dei Corsi, oppure che le di lei mire erano a tutt'altro dirette, che a renderli tranquilli e felici. Lo sbarco clandestino di diversi uomini facinorosi già sbanditi dalla Corsica; la sedizione interna tentata in più parti del regno; l'aver obbligati alcuni uffiziali Corsi, che sono al soldo dei Genovesi, a girare per i luoghi, affine di ammutinar gente; il non aver fatto il minimo capitale del regno, ma soltanto del popolo meno illuminato, sono forse mezzi adattati per dar principio alla tranquillità, e felicità dei Corsi, ovvero ad eccitare fra essi lo spargimento del sangue, e tutto l'orrore di una guerra civile? Le massime presenti della repubblica niente dissimili sono da quelle che per l'avanti hanno animato il di lei governo, reso tanto odioso ai Corsi, quanto è stato il compatimento, con cui ogni sovrano ha riguardato le di loro vicende. Nè accade che più si pensi a risogettargli una nazione, la quale siccome dalla repubblica riconosce l'avvilimento di tutto il regno, e l'abiezione de' popoli; così eleggerà una morte generosa, piuttosto che sottoporre di nuovo il collo all'antica schiavitù.

Dalla violenza, e dalla forza che potesse accorrere in ajuto della repubblica, potrebbe, non vi è dubbio, abbattersi il valore dei Corsi, ma non per tanto si otterrebbe dai Genovesi l'intento, perchè il cuore di quegli non perderebbe perciò quella connaturale libertà, con cui si nasce, ed in vece di scemarsi, maggiormente si aumenterebbe quella antipatia, che dividerà per sempre le due nazioni. E non è da credersi, che verun sovrano voglia continuamente tenere in Corsica un'armata in piedi per sostenere i dritti di una repubblica, che eccetto l'invasione, non ha titolo, che possa contrapporsi a quelli che vi hanno gli altri potentati d'Europa. O sia l'impero per rapporto alla Toscana, o sia la Francia a cui altre volte fu incorporata, o sia la Spagna per i re d'Aragona, o sia la Santa Sede Apostolica di cui fu tributaria.

Intanto però neppure è da porsi in dubbio che i re moderni, ai troni de' quali già pervennero i giusti clamori dei Corsi, vogliano trasandare quel dritto d'umanità, che può istillare nei di loro animi augusti il pensiero di dare una volta la quiete alla Corsica, col lasciarle godere la sua libertà, per cui in ogni tempo ha dimostrato tanto attaccamento, e per cui ha sostenuta con tanta costanza una guerra così disastrosa, o mettendola sotto la protezione di qualche principe, che la riguardi come figlia, e che invigli ed influisca colla minor gelosia degl'altri stati nella constituzione del suo governo; oppure adattando qualche altro spediente podo meno analogo alla naturale inclinazione de' suoi popoli, e che coll'indennità de' loro privilegi, meno anche s'opponga alle mire politiche, ed alle pretenzioni delle potenze interessate.

# N° V. page 140.

## DETERMINAZIONI

### PRESE NEL CONGRESSO

### DI TUTTI I CAPI PRINCIPALI DEL REGNO

Tenuto in Corte li 23. 24. e 25. di Ottobre
dell'Anno corrente 1764.

ATTESE le continuate notizie, che si hanno da tutte le parti, sembra, che non vi sia più luogo a dubitare dell'imminente venuta in Corsica delle truppe Francesi, leggendosi persino nelle pubbliche gazzette il minuto dettaglio del numero di esse truppe, de' luoghi che dovranno occupare in Corsica, del tempo, che dovranno restarvi, ed alcuni altri articoli concernenti a questa spedizione. Quindi è che il governo si è creduto nella indispensabile necessità di convocare un particolare congresso di tutti i soggetti, che hanno occupata la carica di consiglieri di stato nel supremo governo, de' presidenti delle provincie, de' commissari delle pievi, e di tutti gli altri capi principali del regno ad oggetto di consultare intorno alle determinazioni da prendersi in rapporto a questo incidente troppo interessante per la nazione.

E sebbene vi sia luogo a credere, che le intenzioni di S. Maestà Cristianissima non tendano con questa spedizione a fare direttamente la guerra ad una nazione, che sempre si è fatta preggio del più sincero ossequioso attaccamento alla corona di Francia, e per cui altre volte si meritò la speciale protezione de' di lui gloriosi predecessori; essendo però destinate le truppe Francesi a munire, e difendere i presidi, che ancora ritengono in Corsica i Genovesi, non possono i Corsi risguardarle, che come una specie di truppe ausiliarie della repubblica, finchè specialmente non vengano loro a notizia tutti gli articoli del trattato di fresco conchiuso colla stessa repubblica relativo a questa spedizione.

Affine pertanto di usare di tutta la possibile precauzione, e di prendere le misure più convenevoli alla pubblica sicurezza, si sono prese unanimemente alcune determinazioni contenute ne' seguenti articoli.

*Primo.* Si formerà una giunta di guerra composta di vari soggetti di tutte le provincie, da nominarsi dal supremo governo, la quale sarà incaricata d'invigilare per la esatta, e rigorosa osservanza dell'articolo 34. dell'ultima generai confulta, rifguardante la proibizione di qualunque forta di commercio co' prefidi nemici, tanto in riguardo all'acceffo dei nazionali ai detti prefidi, quanto de prefidiani agli fcali della nazione, ad oggetto di garantire i popoli dalle anguftie di una vicina careftia confimile a quella dell'anno fcorfo, per mantenere, ed aumentare il commercio introdotto negli fcali della nazione, e provvedere nel tempo fteffo alla fuffiftenza delle pubbliche finanze. Daudofi perciò piena autorità a detta giunta di punire irremiffibilmente i delinquenti.

*Secondo.* Quantunque poffa crederfi, che le truppe Francefi deftinate ora in Corfica non fiano per intraprendere cofa alcuna in pregiudizio dei diritti della nazione, e rinnovarvi alcuno degli attentati altre volte commeffi con manifefto abufo della confidenza, e buona fede de' Corfi nella inafpettata forprefa della paludella, e di alziprato, e nella refa del Caftello di Sanfiorenzo in mano de' nemici; contuttociò per maggiormente abbondare in precauzioni, farà loro onninamente vietato l'acceffo ai paefi fotto qualunque pretefto. Sarà perciò ifpezione di S. Ecc. il Sig Generale di tener muniti i poftamenti di frontiera, anche per far valere la giuridizione, e il dominio della nazione fopra i territori degli fteffi prefidi confifcati a favore della pubblica camera, come è ftato praticato finora. Potrà però il fupremo governo accordare il paffaporto a qualche officiale Francefe, che lo chiedeffe, con obbligo di manifeftare nella prima generale confulta da tenerfi i motivi della richiefta, e della conceffione di tali paffaporti, e di quanto fi foffe trattato con effi Francefi.

*Terzo.* Precorrendo voce, che poffa effere fatta qualche propofizione di pace, o di accomodamento colla repubblica, dovrà quefta affolutamente rigettarfi, fe prima non fiano accordati, ed efeguiti i preliminari propofti nella general confulta di Cafinca dell'anno 1761.

*Quarto.* S'incarica S Ecc il fig. Generale di fare a nome della nazione una rifpettofa, ed efficace rimoftranza a fua Maeftà Chriftianiffima in rapporto ai danni, che viene a rifentire la nazione fuddetta per la miffione in Corfica delle fue truppe in un tempo, che profittando i Corfi della eftrema debolezza de' lor nemici, erano ful punto di efpellerli intieramente dall'ifola, reftando perciò preclufa loro la ftrada ad ulteriori progreffi, e vantaggiata al contrario la repubblica, che viene con quefto mezzo a rinfrancarfi delle graviffime fpefe, che era tenuta fare in Corfica, e a metterfi così maggiormente in iftato di continuare la guerra contro la nazione Metterà in vifta nel tempo fteffo a S Maeftà il grave torto fatto anni adietro alla nazione colla refa in mano de' Genovefi della importante piazza di Sanfiorenzo, confegnata dai Corfi alle fue truppe affine di cuftodirla, chiedendo di tutto la convenevole indennizzazione.

*Quinto.* E perchè quefta rimoftranza abbia maggiormente il fuo effetto, farà pure incombenza di effo Sig Generale d'indirizzarfi alle potenze protettrici, ed amiche della nazione, fupplicandole a volerla coadiuvare colla loro mediazione preffo fua Maeftà Chriftianiffima, e a continuare alla nazione fteffa l'altro loro Padrocinio per la confervazione de' fuoi diritti, e prerogative di libertà, e indipendenza.

*Sefto.* Effendo venuto a notizia del fupremo governo, che qualunque privato indifferentemente fi faccia lecito di devaftare i pubblici bofchi, erigendovi fabbriche a fuo talento di qualunque forta di legnami, nell'avvenire fi proibifce rigorofamente a chiunque ogni nuova erezione di dette fabbriche, ed il taglio di qualfifoglia forta di alberi ne' bofchi fuddetti, fe prima non ne avrà ottenuta la licenza in ifcritto da concederfi dal folo fupremo governo.

Giuseppe MARIA MASSEI Gran-Cancelliere.

# GENERALE,

## E SUPREMO CONSIGLIO

### DI STATO

### DEL REGNO DI CORSICA,

#### AI NOSTRI DILETTI POPOLI.

FRA le inceſſanti graviſſime occupazioni, che ſeco porta il governo de' popoli alla noſtra cura commeſſi, una delle principali noſtre applicazioni maiſempre è ſtata quella di procurare alla gioventu del noſtro regno un pubblico comodo onde poterla iſtruire negli ſtudi delle ſcienze divine ed umane, ad oggetto di renderla maggiormente utile al ſervizio di Dio, e della patria.

Il governo Genoveſe tra le maſſime della barbara deteſtabil politica con cui reggeva queſti popoli, ſopra ogni altra, ſi attenne invariabilmente a quella di mantenergli nell'incoltura, e nella ignoranza; e per quanto fioriſſero le ſcienze, e foſſero in pregio preſſo le vicine nazioni, ed anche alcuni de' noſtri nazionali dalla generoſità de' principi d' Italia foſſero preſcelti a ſoſtenere con alta riputazion di dottrina le cattedre più ragguardevoli nelle univerſità di Roma, di Piſa, e di Padova, noi però eravamo miſeramente coſtretti a vedere in Corſica i più ſublimi e perſpicaci ingegni, che la natura ha dati in ogni tempo, ed in gran numero nel noſtro clima, ò a languire ſenza cultura, e conſumarſi nella oſcurità, e nell'ozio, ò a procacciar con grave diſpendio oltremare, e per le contrade d' Europa quel comodo di coltivarſi che non era loro permeſſo di rinvenire nella lor patria.

La Provvidenza però, che in tante maniere ha manifeſtati ſopra di noi i più ſenſibili contraſſegni della ſua protezione, ha diſſipata in gran parte quella nuvola di oſcurità, che cotanto ingiurioſamente ci copriva, e noi ſiamo a portata di diſingannare il mondo, che non era la Corſica quel barbaro paeſe, che voleaſi far credere da' Genoveſi, nemico dei buoni ſtudi, e delle ſcienze.

L' oggetto pertanto di queſto noſtro editto è quello di far noto ai noſtri amatiſſimi popoli, che l' univerſità degli ſtudi ideata da gran tempo, e fraſtor-

# APPENDIX.

nata fin qui dalle circostanze inopportune dei tempi, si aprirà il giorno tre del prossimo futuro Gennajo in questa città di Corte, luogo prescelto nell'ultima general consulta dello scaduto Maggio, come il più comodo a tutta la nazione. Quest'opera tanto salutare, e generalmente bramata dai nostri popoli, non avrà per avventura nel suo comisciamento tutta quella perfezione, a cui (come tutte le altre nostre cose, che nate da piccoli principii, perchè guidate dal zelo e dalla giustizia, hanno avuti notabilissimi accrescimenti) potrà pervenire con qualche tratto di tempo, bastando ora a noi, che vi siano le scuole più necessarie, e le più proporzionate al presente bisogno de' nostri popoli.

A tale effetto abbiamo prescelti i più valenti ed accreditati professori, che oltre l'essere benemeriti della nazione per molti altri titoli, non per avidità di lucro, o per allettamenti di vanità, ma portati da un puro e sincero zelo del pubblico bene, impiegheranno ora di buon animo le loro studiose fatiche ad istruire nella maniera più desiderabile la gioventù, insegnando giornalmente nelle pubbliche scuole dell'università le seguenti facoltà, e scienze.

I. La Teologia Scolastica Dommatica, ove i principii della religione, e le dottrine della cattolica chiesa saranno spiegate con brevità e sodezza, e il professore farà altresì una lezione fra settimana di Storia Ecclesiastica.

II. La Teologia Morale, in cui si daranno i precetti, e le regole più sicure della Cristiana morale, e in un giorno della settimana si farà la conferenza di un Caso pratico relativamente alle materie insegnate.

III. Le Istituta Civile e Canonica, ove si mostrerà l'origine e il vero spirito delle leggi, per il miglior uso delle medesime.

IV. L'Etica, scienza utilissima per apprendere le regole del buon costume, e la maniera di ben guidarsi nei differenti impieghi della società civile, e comprenderà altresì la cognizione del Diritto della Natura, e delle Genti.

V. La Filosofia secondo i sistemi più plausibili dei moderni filosofanti, e il professore darà altresì i principii della Matematica.

VI. La Rettorica.

VII. Vi sarà inoltre il comodo di istruirsi in lingua volgare nella Pratica tanto Civile che Criminale.

Le ore per le differenti scuole saranno distribuite in maniera, che chi vorrà potrà intervenire lo stesso giorno a diverse lezioni, e sarà tale il metodo che terranno i professori nell'insegnare, che basterà una mediocre cognizione della lingua Latina per l'intelligenza delle materie, alle quali vorranno applicare.

Invitiamo pertanto tutti i giovani studiosi del nostro regno, tanto ecclesiastici che secolari, a profittare di una occasione sì vantaggiosa, che loro presentiamo: e sopratutto vogliamo persuaderci, che con più ardore, ed in maggior numero vorranno concorrervi i giovani delle famiglie più ragguardevoli e facoltose, alla coltura dei quali essendo principalmente dirette le nostre sollecitudini, avremo cura speciale, che vi siano per loro scuole proporzionate, ad oggetto di fornirli delle necessarie cognizioni per abilitarli alle pubbliche cariche di configlieri di stato, di presidenti, auditori, e consultori delle giurisdizioni e provincie, e agli altri ragguardevoli impieghi della nazione, ai quali avendo essi speciale diritto di aspirare, devono mostrare nel tempo stesso un maggiore impegno di contradistinguersi nella coltura de' buoni studii, per rendersi atti a sostenerli con dignità: oltredichè ritrovandosi essi in vicinanza del supremo governo, e presso sua eccellenza il Sig. Generale saranno altresì a portata di dar saggio del loro valore, e bravura in tutti gli incontri, che ne saranno loro presentati per servizio della loro patria.

Ed affine di maggiormente eccitare la loro emulazione, per viepiù aumentare e proteggere i pubblici studii, e favorire chi gli coltiva, seguendo in ciò la massima di tutti i saggi governi, si prenderanno da noi le più efficaci misure perchè alle cariche tanto civili che ecclesiastiche del nostro regno siano sempre preferiti quelli che avranno lodevolmente fatto, ò faranno attualmente il corso dei loro studii in questa nostra università. E poiche siamo rimasti gravemente commossi in vedere ogni anno uscire dal regno un numero troppo grande de' nostri ecclesiastici per passare in Terraferma a titolo di farvi i loro studii, restando ora evacuato questo pretesto, facciamo loro sapere, che in l' avvenire non si concederanno più passaporti per Terraferma.

Si daranno finalmente gli opportuni provvedimenti per agevolare ai giovani studenti tutti i maggiori comodi in questa città, ed il minor dispendio, che sia possibile tanto in riguardo agli allogiamenti, che ai viveri, ed applicheremo a rintracciare i mezzi più proprii, onde supplire in qualche parte alla sussistenza degli studenti più poveri.

E perchè questo nostro editto pervenga à notizia di tutti, vogliamo che se ne trasmetta copia a tutti i Podestà maggiori del regno, ordinando loro di pubblicarlo, ed affiggerlo ne' luoghi soliti.

Dato in Corte ai 25 Novembre 1764.

Giuseppe MARIA MASSEI Gran-Cancelliere.

# THE JOURNAL

## OF A

## TOUR

### TO

# CORSICA;

### AND

# MEMOIRS

### OF

## PASCAL PAOLI.

Olim meminisse juvabit.
VIRG.

# THE JOURNAL

## OF A

## TOUR

### TO

# CORSICA.

HAVING resolved to pass some years a-broad, for my instruction and entertainment, I conceived a design of visiting the island of Corsica. I wished for something more than just the common course of what is called the tour of Europe; and Corsica occurred to me as a place which no body else had seen, and where I should find what was to be seen no where else, a people actually fighting for liberty, and forming themselves from a poor inconsiderable oppressed nation, into a flourishing and independent state.

When I got into Switzerland, I went to see M. Rousseau. He was then living in romantick retirement, from whence, perhaps, it had been better for him never to have defcended. While he was at a diftance, his fingular eloquence filled our minds with high ideas of the wild philofopher. When he came into the walks of men, we know alas! how much thefe ideas fuffered.

He entertained me very courteoufly; for I was recommended to him by my honoured friend the Earl Marifchal, with whom I had the happinefs of travelling through a part of Germany. I had heard that M. Rouffeau had fome correfpondence with the Corficans, and had been defired to affift them in forming their laws. I told him my fcheme of going to vifit them, after I had compleated my tour of Italy; and I infifted that he fhould give me a letter of introduction. He immediately agreed to do fo, whenever I fhould acquaint him of my time of going thither; for he faw that my enthufiafm for the brave iflanders was as warm as his own.

I accordingly wrote to him from Rome, in April 1765, that I had fixed the month of September for my Corfican expedition, and therefore begged of him to fend me the letter of introduction, which if he refufed, I fhould certainly go without it, and probably be hanged as a fpy. So let him anfwer for the confequences.

The wild philosopher was a man of his word; and on my arrival at Florence in August, I received the following letter.

A MONSIEUR, MONSIEUR BOSWELL. &c.

A Motiers le 30 May, 1765.

'LA crise orageuse ou je me trouve, Monsieur,
'depuis votre depart d'ici, m'a oté le tems de re-
'pondre à votre premiére lettre, et me laisse à
'peine celui de repondre en peu de mots à la se-
'conde. Pour m'en tenir à ce qui presse pour le
'moment, savoir la recommendation que vous de-
'sirez en Corse; puisque vous avez le desir de vi-
'siter ces braves insulaires, vous pourrez vous in-
'former à Bastia, de M. Buttafoco capitaine au
'Regiment Royal Italien; il a sa maison à Ves-
'covado, ou il se tient assez souvent. C'est un
'très-galant homme, qui a des connoissances et
'de l'esprit; il suffira de lui montrer cette let-
'tre, et je suis sur qu'il vous recevra bien, et
'contribuera à vous faire voir l'isle et ses ha-
'bitans avec satisfaction. Si vous ne trouvez pas
'M. Buttafoco, et que vous vouliez aller out
'droit à M. Pascal de Paoli general de la nation,
'vous pouvez egalement lui montrer cette lettre,

' et je suis sûr, connoissant la noblesse de son ca-
' ractére, que vous serez très-content de son ac-
' cueil: vous pourrez lui dire même que vous êtes
' aimé de Mylord Mareschal d'Ecosse, et que
' Mylord Mareschal est un des plus zelés parti-
' zans de la nation Corse. Au reste vous n' avez
' besoin d'autre recommendation près de ces
' Messieurs que votre propre mérite, la nation
' Corse etant naturellement si accueillante et si
' hospitaliére, que tous les etrangers y sont bien
' venus et caressés.

  \*   \*   \*   \*   \*   \*

  ' Bons et heureux voyages, santé, gaieté et promt
' retour. Je vous embrasse, Monsieur, de tout mon
' coeur

J. J. ROUSSEAU.

TO Mr. BOSWELL &c.

MOTIERS the 30 May 1765.

' THE stormy crisis in which I have found my-
' self, since your departure from this, has not al-
' lowed me any leisure to answer your first let-
' ter, and hardly allows me leisure to reply in a
' few words to your second. To confine myself
' to what is immediately pressing, the recommen-

' dation which you ask for Corsica; since you
' have a desire to visit those brave islanders, you
' may enquire at Bastia for M. Buttafoco, captain
' of the Royal Italian Regiment; his house is at
' Vescovado, where he resides pretty often. He
' is a very worthy man, and has both knowledge
' and genius; it will be sufficient to shew him
' this letter, and I am sure he will receive you
' well, and will contribute to let you see the is-
' land and its inhabitants with satisfaction. If you
' do not find M. Buttafoco, and will go directly
' to M. Pascal Paoli General of the nation, you
' may in the same manner shew him this letter,
' and as I know the nobleness of his character,
' I am sure you will be very well pleased at your
' reception. You may even tell him that you
' are liked by My Lord Marischal of Scotland,
' and that My Lord Marischal is one of the most
' zealous partisans of the Corsican nation. You
' need no other recommendation to these gentle-
' men but your own merit, the Corsicans being
' naturally so courteous and hospitable, that all
' strangers who come among them, are made
' welcome and caressed.

\* \* \* \* - \*

'I wish you agreeable and fortunate travels,
'health, gaiety, and a speedy return. I embrace
'you Sir with all my heart

JOHN JAMES ROUSSEAU.

Furnished with these credentials, I was impatient to be with the illustrious Chief. The charms of sweet Siena detained me longer than they should have done. I required the hardy air of Corsica to brace me, after the delights of Tuscany.

I recollect with astonishment how little the real state of Corsica was known, even by those who had good access to know it. An officer of rank in the British navy, who had been in several ports of the island, told me that I run the risque of my life in going among these barbarians; for, that his surgeon's mate went ashore to take the diversion of shooting, and every moment was alarmed by some of the natives, who started from the bushes with loaded guns, and if he had not been protected by Corsican guides, would have certainly blown out his brains.

Nay at Leghorn, which is within a days sailing of Corsica, and has a constant intercourse with it, I found people who dissuaded me from going thither, because it might be dangerous.

I was however under no apprehension in going to Corsica. Count Rivarola the Sardinian consul, who is himself a Corsican, assuring me that the island was then in a very civilized state; and besides, that in the rudest times no Corsican would ever attack a stranger. The Count was so good as to give me most obliging letters to many people in the island. I had now been in several foreign countries. I had found that I was able to accommodate myself to my fellow-creatures of different languages and sentiments. I did not fear that it would be a difficult task for me to make myself easy with the plain and generous Corsicans.

The only danger I saw was, that I might be taken by some of the Barbary Corsairs, and have a tryal of slavery among the Turks at Algiers. I spoke of it to Commodore Harrison, who commanded the British squadron in the Mediterranean, and was then lying with his ship the Centurion, in the bay of Leghorn. He assured me, that if the Turks did take me, they should not keep me long; but in order to prevent it, he was so good as to grant me a very ample and particucular passport; and as it could be of no use if I did not meet the Corsairs, he said very pleasantly when he gave it me, 'I hope, Sir, it shall be of 'no use to you.'

Before I left Leghorn, I could observe, that my tour was looked upon by the Italian politicians in a very serious light, as if truly I had a commission from my Court, to negociate a treaty with the Corsicans. The more I disclaimed any such thing, the more they persevered in affirming it; and I was considered as a very close young man. I therefore just allowed them to make a minister of me, till time should undeceive them.

I sailed from Leghorn in a Tuscan vessel, which was going over to Capo Corso for wine. I preferred this to a vessel going to Bastia, because, as I did not know how the French general was affected towards the Corsicans, I was afraid that he might not permit me to go forward to Paoli. I therefore resolved to land on the territories of the nation, and after I had been with the illustrious Chief, to pay my respects to the French if I should find it safe.

Though from Leghorn to Corsica, is usually but one day's sailing, there was so dead a calm that it took us two days. The first day was the most tedious. However there were two or three Corsicans aboard, and one of them played on the Citra, which amused me a good deal. At sun-set all the people in the ship sung the Ave Maria, with great devotion and some melody. It was pleasing to enter into the spirit of their religion, and hear them offering up their evening orisons.

The second day we became better acquainted, and more lively and chearful. The worthy Corsicans thought it was proper to give a moral lesson to a young traveller just come from Italy. They told me that in their country I should be treated with the greatest hospitality; but if I attempted to debauch any of their women, I might lay my account with instant death.

I employed myself several hours in rowing, which gave me great spirits. I relished fully my approach to the island, which had acquired an unusual grandeur in my imagination. As long as I can remember any thing, I have heard of ' The ' malecontents of Corsica, with Paoli at their

' head.' It was a curious thought that I was juſt going to ſee them.

About ſeven o'clock at night, we landed ſafely in the harbour of Centuri. I learnt that Signor Giaccomini of this place, to whom I was recommended by Count Rivarola, was juſt dead. He had made a handſome fortune in the Eaſt Indies; and having had a remarkable warmth in the cauſe of liberty during his whole life, he ſhewed it in the ſtrongeſt manner in his laſt will. He bequeathed a conſiderable ſum of money, and ſome pieces of ordinance, to the nation. He alſo left it in charge to his heir, to live in Corſica, and be firm in the patriotick intereſt; and if ever the iſland ſhould again be reduced under the power of the Genoeſe, he ordered him to retire with all his effects to Leghorn. Upon theſe conditions only could his heir enjoy his eſtate.

I was directed to the houſe of Signor Giaccomini's couſin, Signor Antonio Antonetti at Morſiglia, about a mile up the country. The proſpect of the mountains covered with vines and olives, was extremely agreeable; and the odour of the myrtle and other aromatick ſhrubs and flowers that grew all around me, was very refreſhing. As

I walked along, I often saw Corsican peasants come suddenly out from the covert; and as they were all armed, I saw how the frightened imagination of the surgeon's mate had raised up so many assassins. Even the man who carried my baggage was armed, and had I been timorous might have alarmed me. But he and I were very good company to each other. As it grew dusky, I repeated to myself these lines from a fine passage in Ariosto.

> E pur per selve oscure e calli obliqui
> Insieme van senza, sospetto aversi.
> ARIOST. Canto I.
> Together through dark woods and winding ways
> They walk, nor on their hearts suspicion preys.

I delivered Signor Antonnetti the letter for his deceased cousin. He read it, and received me with unaffected cordiality, making an apology for my frugal entertainment, but assuring me of a hearty welcome. His true kindly hospitality was also shewn in taking care of my servant, an honest Swiss, who loved to eat and drink well.

I had formed a strange notion that I should see every thing in Corsica totally different from what I had seen in any other country. I was therefore much surprised to find Signor Antonetti's house quite an Italian one, with very good furniture, prints, and copies of some of the famous pictures. In particular, I was struck to find here a small copy from Raphael, of St. Michael and the Dragon. There was no necessity for its being well done. To see the thing at all was what surprised me.

Signor Antonetti gave me an excellent light repast, and a very good bed. He spoke with great strength of the patriotick cause, and with great veneration of the General. I was quite easy, and liked much the opening of my Corsican tour.

The next day, being Sunday, it rained very hard; and I must observe that the Corsicans with all their resolution, are afraid of bad weather, to a degree of effeminacy. I got indeed a drole but a just enough account of this, from one of them. 'Sir, said he, if you were as poor as a 'Corsican, and had but one coat, so as that after 'being wet, you could not put on dry cloaths, 'you would be afraid too.' Signor Antonetti would not allow me to set out while it rained, for, said he, 'Quando si trova fuori, patienza; 'ma di andare fuori è cattivo. If a man finds 'himself abroad, there is no help for it. But to 'go deliberately out, is too much.'

When the day grew a little better, I accompanied Signor Antonetti and his family, to hear mass in the parish church, a very pretty little building, about half a quarter of a mile off.

Signor Antonetti's parish priest was to preach to us, at which I was much pleased, being very curious to hear a Corsican sermon.

Our priest did very well. His text was in the Psalms. 'Descendunt ad infernum viven-
'tes.' They go down alive into the pit.'

After endeavouring to move our passions with a description of the horrours of hell, he told us 'Saint Catherine of Siena wished to be
'laid on the mouth of this dreadful pit, that
'she might stop it up, so as no more unhappy
'souls should fall into it. I confess, my bre-
'thren, I have not the zeal of holy Saint Ca-
'therine. But I do what I can; I warn you
'how to avoid it.' He then gave us some good practical advices and concluded.

The weather being now cleared up, I took leave of the worthy gentleman to whom I had been a guest. He gave me a letter to Signor Damiano Tomasi Padre del Commune at Pino, the next village. I got a man with an ass to carry my baggage. But such a road I never

S

saw. It was absolutely scrambling along the face of a rock overhanging the sea, upon a path sometimes not above a foot broad. I thought the ass rather retarded me; so I prevailed with the man, to take my portmanteau and other things on his back.

Had I formed my opinion of Corsica from what I saw this morning, I might have been in as bad humour with it, as Seneca was, whose reflections in prose are not inferiour to his epigrams. 'Quid tam nudum inveniri po-
'test, quid tam abruptum undique quam hoc
'saxum? quid ad copias respicienti jejunius?
'quid ad homines immansuetius? quid ad ip-
'sum loci situm horridius? Plures tamen hîc
'peregrini quam cives consistunt? usque eò ergo
'commutatio ipsa locorum gravis non est, ut
'hic quoque locus a patria quosdam abduxerit (*a*).
'What can be found so bare, what so rugged
'all around as this rock? what more barren
'of provisions? what more rude as to its in-
'habitants? what in the very situation of the
'place more horrible? what in climate more in-
'temperate? yet there are more foreigners than
'natives here. So far then is a change of place

(*a*) Seneca de Consolatione.

' from being disagreeable, that even this place
' hath brought some people away from their
' country.'

At Pino I was surprised to find myself met by some brisk young fellows drest like English sailors, and speaking English tolerably well. They had been often with cargoes of wine at Leghorn, where they had picked up what they knew of our language, and taken clothes in part of payment for some of their merchandise.

I was cordially entertained at Signor Tomasi's. Throughout all Corsica except in garrison towns, there is hardly an inn. I met with a single one, about eight miles from Corte. Before I was accustomed to the Corsican hospitality, I sometimes forgot myself, and imagining I was in a publick house, called for what I wanted, with the tone which one uses in calling to the waiters at a tavern. I did so at Pino, asking for a variety of things at once; when Signora Tomasi perceiving my mistake, looked in my face and smiled, saying with much calmness and good-nature, ' Una cosa dopo un altra,
' Signore. One thing after another, Sir.'

In writing this Journal, I shall not tire my readers, with relating the occurrences of each particular day. It will be much more agreeable to them, to have a free and continued account of what I saw or heard, most worthy of observation.

For some time, I had very curious travelling, mostly on foot, and attended by a couple of stout women, who carried my baggage upon their heads. Every time that I prepared to set out from a village, I could not help laughing, to see the good people eager to have my equipage in order, and roaring out, ' Le Donne, Le Donne. The Women, The Women.'

I had full leisure and the best opportunities to observe every thing, in my progress through the island. I was lodged sometimes in private houses, sometimes in convents, being always well recommended from place to place. The first convent in which I lay, was at Canari. It appeared a little odd at first. But I soon learnt to repair to my dormitory as naturally as if I had been a friar for seven years.

The convents were small decent buildings, suited to the sober ideas of their pious inhabi-

tants. The religious who devoutly endeavour to
' walk with GOD,' are often treated with raillery
by those whom pleasure or business prevents from
thinking of future and more exalted objects. A
little experience of the serenity and peace of mind
to be found in convents, would be of use to temper the fire of men of the world.

At Patrimonio I found the seat of a provincial magistracy. The chief judge was there, and
entertained me very well. Upon my arrival, the
captain of the guard came out, and demanded
who I was? I replied 'Inglese English.' He
looked at me seriously, and then said in a tone
between regret and upbraiding, 'Inglese, c'erano
' i nostri amici; ma non le sono più. The En
' glish. They were once our friends; but they
' are so no more.' I felt for my country, and was
abashed before this honest soldier.

At Oletta I visited Count Nicholas Rivarola,
brother to my friend at Leghorn. He received
me with great kindness, and did every thing in
his power to make me easy. I found here a
Corsican who thought better of the British, than
the captain of the guard at Patrimonio. He talked of our bombarding San Fiorenzo, in favour

of the patriots, and willingly gave me his horse for the afternoon, which he said he would not have done to a man of any other nation.

When I came to Morato, I had the pleasure of being made acquainted with Signor Barbaggi, who is married to the niece of Paoli. I found him to be a sensible intelligent well-bred man. The mint of Corsica was in his house. I got specimens of their different kinds of money in silver and copper, and was told that they hoped in a year or two, to strike some gold coins. Signor Barbaggi's house was repairing, so I was lodged in the convent. But in the morning returned to breakfast, and had chocolate; and at dinner we had no less than twelve well-drest dishes, served on Dresden china, with a desert, different sorts of wine and a liqueur, all the produce of Corsica. Signor Barbaggi was frequently repeating to me, that the Corsicans inhabited a rude uncultivated country, and that they lived like Spartans. I begged leave to ask him in what country he could shew me greater luxury than I had seen in his house; and I said I should certainly tell wherever I went, what tables the Corsicans kept, notwithstanding their pretensions to poverty and temperance. A good deal of pleasantry passed upon this. His lady was a genteel woman, and appeared to be agreeable, though very reserved.

From Morato to Corte, I travelled through a wild mountainous rocky country, diversified with some large valleys. I got little beasts for me and my servant, sometimes horses, but oftener mules or asses. We had no bridles, but cords fixed round their necks, with which we managed them as well as we could.

At Corte I waited upon the supreme council, to one of whom, Signor Boccociampe, I had a letter from Signor Barbaggi. I was very politely received, and was conducted to the Franciscan convent, where I got the apartment of Paoli, who was then some days journey beyond the mountains, holding a court of syndicato at a village called Sollacarò.

As the General resided for some time in this convent, the fathers made a better appearance than any I saw in the island. I was principally attended by the Priour, a resolute divine, who had formerly been in the army, and by Padre Giulio, a man of much address, who still favours me with his correspondence.

S 4

These fathers have a good vineyard and an excellent garden. They have between 30 and 40 bee-hives in long wooden cases or trunks of trees, with a covering of the bark of the cork tree. When they want honey, they burn a little juniper wood, the smoak of which makes the bees retire. They then take an iron instrument with a sharp-edged crook at one end of it, and bring out the greatest part of the honey-comb, leaving only a little for the bees, who work the case full again. By taking the honey in this way, they never kill a bee. They seemed much at their ease, living in peace and plenty. I often joked them with the text which is applied to their order, ' Nihil habentes et omnia possidentes. Having nothing, and yet possessing all things.'

I went to the choir with them. The service was conducted with propriety, and Padre Giulio played on the organ. On the great altar of their church is a tabernacle carved in wood by a Religious. It is a piece of exquisite workmanship. A Genoese gentleman offered to give them one in silver for it; but they would not make the exchange.

These fathers have no library worth mentithing; but their convent is large and well built. I looked about with great attention, to see if I could find any inscriptions; but the only one I found was upon a certain useful edifice.

> Sine necessitate huc non intrate,
> Quia necessaria sumus.

A studied, rhiming, Latin conceit marked upon such a place was truly ludicrous.

I chose to stop a while at Corte, to repose myself after my fatigues, and to see every thing about the capital of Corsica.

The morning after my arrival here, three French deserters desired to speak with me. The foolish fellows had taken it into their heads, that I was come to raise recruits for Scotland, and so they begged to have the honour of going along with me; I suppose with intention to have the honour of running off from me, as they had done from their own regiments.

I received many civilities at Corte from Signor Boccociampe, and from Signor Massesi the Great Chancellor, whose son Signor Luigi a young gentleman of much vivacity, and natural politeness, was so good as to attend me constantly as my conductour. I used to call him my governour.

I liked him much, for as he had never been out of the island, his ideas were entirely Corsican.

Such of the members of the supreme council as were in residence during my stay at Corte, I found to be solid and sagacious, men of penetration and ability, well calculated to assist the General in forming his political plans, and in turning to the best advantage, the violence and enterprise of the people.

The university was not then sitting, so I could only see the rooms, which were shewn me by the Abbé Valentini, procuratour of the university. The professours were all absent except one Capuchin father whom I visited at his convent. It is a tolerable building, with a pretty large collection of books. There is in the church here a tabernacle carved in wood, in the manner of that at the Franciscans, but much inferiour to it.

I went up to the castle of Corte. The commandant very civilly shewed me every part of it. As I wished to see all things in Corsica, I desired to see even the unhappy criminals. There were then three in the castle, a man for the murder of his wife, a married lady who had hired one of her servants to strangle a woman of whom she was jealous, and the servant who had actually perpetrated this barbarous action. They were brought out from their cells, that I might talk with them. The murderer of his wife had a stupid hardened appearance, and told me he did it at the instigation of the devil. The servant was a poor despicable wretch. He had at first accused his mistress, but was afterwards prevailed with to deny his accusation, upon which he was put to the torture, by having lighted matches held between his fingers. This made him return to what he had formerly said, so as to be a strong evidence against his mistress. His hands were so miserably scorched, that he was a piteous object. I asked him why he had committed such a crime, he said, ‘ Perche era senza spirito. Because I was without understanding.’ The lady seemed of a bold and resolute spirit. She spoke to me with great firmness, and denied her guilt, saying with a contemptuous smile, as she pointed to her servant, ‘ They can force that creature to say what they please.’

The hangman of Corsica was a great curiosity. Being held in the utmost detestation, he durst not live like another inhabitant of the island. He was obliged to take refuge in the caftle, and there he was kept in a little corner turret, where he had juft room for a miferable bed, and a little bit of fire to drefs fuch victuals for himfelf as were fufficient to keep him alive, for nobody would have any intercourfe with him, but all turned their backs upon him. I went up and looked at him. And a more dirty rueful fpectacle I never beheld. He feemed fenfible of his fituation, and held down his head like an abhorred outcaft.

It was a long time before they could get a hangman in Corfica, fo that the punifhment of the gallows was hardly known, all their criminals being fhot. At laft this creature whom I faw, who is a Sicilian, came with a meffage to Paoli. The General who has a wonderful talent for phyfiognomy, on feeing the man, faid immediately to fome of the people about him, ' Ecco il boia. Behold our hangman.' He gave orders to afk the man if he would accept of the office, and his anfwer was, ' My grandfather was a hangman, my father was a hangman. I have been a hangman myfelf, and am willing to continue fo.' He was therefore immediately put into office, and the ignominious death difpensed by his hands, had more effect than twenty executions by fire arms.

It is remarkable that no Corsican would upon any account consent to be hangman. Not the greatest criminals, who might have had their lives upon that condition. Even the wretch, who for a paultry hire, had strangled a woman, would rather submit to death, than do the same action, as the executioner of the law.

When I had seen every thing about Corte, I prepared for my journey over the mountains, that I might be with Paoli. The night before I set out, I recollected that I had forgotten to get a passport, which, in the present situation of Corsica, is still a necessary precaution. After supper therefore the Priour walked with me to Corte, to the house of the Great Chancellor, who ordered the passport to be made out immediately, and while his secretary was writing it, entertained me by reading to me some of the minutes of the general consulta. When the passport was finished, and ready to have the seal put to it, I was much pleased with a beautiful, simple incident. The Chancellor desired a little boy who was playing in the room by us, to run to his mother, and bring the great seal of the kingdom. I thought myself sitting in the house of a Cincinnatus.

Next morning I set out in very good order, having excellent mules, and active clever Corsican guides. The worthy fathers of the convent who treated me in the kindest manner while I was their guest, would also give me some provisions for my journey; so they put up a gourd of their best wine, and some delicious pomegranates. My Corsican guides appeared so hearty, that I often got down and walked along with them, doing just what I saw them do. When we grew hungry, we threw stones among the thick branches of the chestnut trees which overshadowed us, and in that manner we brought down a shower of chestnuts with which we filled our pockets, and went on eating them with great relish; and when this made us thirsty, we lay down by the side of the first brook, put our mouths to the stream, and drank sufficiently. It was just being for a little while, one of the ' prisca gens morta-' lium, the primitive race of men,' who ran about in the woods eating acorns and drinking water.

While I stopped to refresh my mules at a little village, the inhabitants came crouding about me as an ambassadour going to their General. When they were informed of my country, a strong black fellow among them said, 'Inglese! sono 'barbari; non credono in Dio grande. English! 'they are barbarians; they don't believe in the 'great God.' I told him, Excuse me Sir. We do believe in God, and in Jesus Christ too. 'Um, said he, e nel Papa? and in the Pope?' No. 'E perehe? And why?' This was a puzzling question in these circumstances; for there was a great audience to the controversy. I thought I would try a method of my own, and very gravely replied, 'Perche siamo troppo lontani. Because 'we are too far off.' A very new argument against the universal infallibility of the Pope. It took however; for my opponent mused a while, and then said, 'Troppo lontano! La Sicilia è tanto 'lontana che l'Inghilterra; e in Sicilia si credono nel 'Papa. Too far off! Why Sicily is as far off as En-'gland. Yet in Sicily they believe in the Pope. 'O, said I, noi siamo dieci volte più lontani che 'la Sicilia! We are ten times farther off than 'Sicily. Aha!' said he; and seemed quite satisfied.

In this manner I got off very well. I question much whether any of the learned reasonings of our protestant divines would have had so good an effect.

My journey over the mountains was very entertaining. I past some immense ridges and vast woods. I was in great health and spirits, and fully able to enter into the ideas of the brave rude men whom I found in all quarters.

At Bastelica where there is a stately spirited race of people, I had a large company to attend me in the convent. I liked to see their natural frankness and ease; for why should men be afraid of their own species? They just came in making an easy bow, placed themselves round the room where I was sitting, rested themselves on their muskets, and immediately entered into conversation with me. They talked very feelingly of the miseries that their country had endured, and complained that they were still but in a state of poverty. I happened at that time to have an unusual flow of spirits; and as one who finds himself amongst utter strangers in a distant country has no timidity, I harangued the men of Bastelica with great fluency. I expatiated on the bravery of the Corsicans, by which they had purchased liberty, the most valuable of all possessions, and rendered themselves glorious over all Europe. Their poverty, I told them, might be remedied by a proper cultivation of their island, and by engaging a little in commerce. But I bid them remember, that they were much happier in their present state than in a state of refinement and vice, and that therefore they should beware of luxury.

What I said had the good fortune to touch them, and several of them repeated the same sentiments much better than I could do. They all expressed their strong attachment to Paoli, and called out in one voice that they were all at his command. I could with pleasure, have passed a long time here.

At Ornano I saw the ruins of the seat where the great Sampiero had his residence. They were a droll enough society of monks in the convent at Ornano. When I told them that I was an Englishman, 'Aye, aye, said one of them, 'as was well observed by a reverend bishop, 'when talking of your pretended reformation, 'Angli olim angeli nunc diaboli. The English 'formerly angels now devils.' I looked upon this as an honest effusion of spiritual zeal. The Fathers took good care of me in temporals.

When I at last came within sight of Sollacarò, where Paoli was, I could not help being under considerable anxiety. My ideas of him had been greatly heightened by the conversations I had held with all sorts of people in the island, they having represented him to me as something above humanity. I had the strongest desire to see so exalted a character; but I feared that I should be unable to give a proper account why I had presumed to trouble him with a visit, and that I should sink to nothing before him. I almost wished yet to go back without seeing him. These workings of sensibility employed my mind till I rode through the village and came up to the house where he was lodged.

Leaving my servant with my guides, I past through the guards, and was met by some of the General's people, who conducted me into an antichamber, where were several gentlemen in waiting. Signor Boccociampe had notified my arrival; and I was shewn into Paoli's room. I found him alone, and was struck with his appearance. He is tall, strong, and well made; of a fair complexion, a sensible, free, and open countenance, and a manly, and noble carriage. He was then in his fortieth year. He was drest in green and gold. He used to wear the common Corsican habit, but on the arrival of the French he thought a little external elegance might be of use to make the government appear in a more respectable light.

He asked me what were my commands for him. I presented him a letter from Count Rivarola, and when he had read it, I shewed him my letter from Rousseau. He was polite, but very reserved. I had stood in the presence of many a prince, but I never had such a trial as in the presence of Paoli. I have already said, that he is a great physiognomist. In consequence of his being in continual danger from treachery and assassination, he has formed a habit of studiously observing every new face. For ten minutes we walked backwards and forwards through the room, hardly saying a word, while he looked at me, with a stedfast, keen and penetrating eye, as if he searched my very soul.

This interview was for a while very severe

upon me. I was much relieved when his reserve wore off, and he began to speak more. I then ventured to address him with this compliment to the Corsicans. 'Sir, I am upon my 'travels, and have lately visited Rome. I am 'come from seeing the ruins of one brave 'and free people: I now see the rise of ano-'ther.'

He received my compliment very graciously; but observed that the Corsicans had no chance of being like the Romans, a great conquering nation, who should extend its empire over half the globe. Their situation, and the modern political systems, rendered this impossible. But, said he, Corsica may be a very happy country.

He expressed a high admiration of M. Rousseau, whom Signor Buttafoco had invited to Corsica, to aid the nation in forming its laws. It seems M. de Voltaire had reported, in his rallying manner, that the invitation was merely a trick which he had put upon Rousseau. Paoli told me that when he understood this, he himself wrote to Rousseau, enforcing the invitation. Of this affair I shall give a full account in an after part of my Journal.

Some of the nobles who attended him, came into the room, and in a little we were told that dinner was served up. The General did me the honour to place me next him. He had a table of fifteen or sixteen covers, having always a good many of the principal men of the island with him. He had an Italian cook who had been long in France; but he chose to have a few plain substantial dishes, avoiding every kind of luxury, and drinking no foreign wine.

I felt myself under some constraint in such a circle of heroes. The General talked a great deal on history and on literature. I soon perceived that he was a fine classical scholar, that his mind was enriched with a variety of knowledge, and that his conversation at meals was instructive and entertaining. Before dinner he had spoken French. He now spoke Italian, in which he is very eloquent.

We retired to another room to drink coffee. My timidity wore off. I no longer anxiously thought of myself; my whole attention was employed in listening to the illustrious commander of a nation.

He recommended me to the care of the Abbé Rostini, who had lived many years in France. Signor Colonna, the lord of the manor here being from home, his house was assigned for me to live in. I was left by myself till near supper time, when I returned to the General, whose conversation improved upon me, as did the society of those about him, with whom I gradually formed an acquaintance.

Every day I felt myself happier. Particular marks of attention were shewn me as a subject of Great Britain, the report of which went over to Italy, and confirmed the conjectures that I was really an envoy. In the morning I had my chocolate served up upon a silver salver adorned with the arms of Corsica. I dined and supped constantly with the General. I was visited by all the nobility, and whenever I chose to make a little tour, I was attended by a party of guards. I begged of the General not to treat me with so much ceremony; but he insisted upon it.

One day when I rode out I was mounted on Paoli's own horse, with rich furniture of crimson velvet, with broad gold lace, and had my guards marching along with me. I allowed myself to indulge a momentary pride in this parade, as I was curious to experience what could really be the pleasure of state and distinction with which mankind are so strangely intoxicated.

When I returned to the continent after all this greatness, I used to joke with my acquaintance, and tell them that I could not bear to live with them, for they did not treat me with a proper respect.

My time passed here in the most agreeable manner. I enjoyed a sort of luxury of noble sentiment. Paoli became more affable with me. I made myself known to him. I forgot the great distance between us, and had every day some hours of private conversation with him.

From my first setting out on this tour, I wrote down every night what I had observed during the day, throwing together a great deal, that I might afterwards make a selection at leisure.

Of these particulars, the most valuable to my readers, as well as to myself, must surely be the memoirs and remarkable sayings of Paoli, which I am proud to record.

Talking of the Corsican war, ' Sir, said he, if the event prove happy, we shall be called great defenders of liberty. If the event shall prove unhappy, we shall be called unfortunate rebels.

The French objected to him that the Corsican nation had no regular troops. We would not have them, said Paoli. We should then have the bravery of this and the other regiment. At present every single man is as a regiment himself. Should the Corsicans be formed into regular troops, we should lose that personal bravery which has produced such actions among us, as in another country would have rendered famous even a Marischal.

I asked him how he could possibly have a soul so superiour to interest. 'It is not superiour, said he; my interest is to gain a name. I know well that he who does good to his country will gain that: and I expect it. Yet could I render this people happy, I would be content to be forgotten. I have an unspeakable pride, "Una superbia indicibile." The approbation of my own heart is enough.'

He said he would have great pleasure in seeing the world, and enjoying the society of the learned, and the accomplished in every country. I asked him how with these dispositions, he could bear to be confined to an island yet in a rude uncivilized state; and instead of participating Attick evenings, 'noctes coenaeque Deûm,' be in a continual course of care and of danger. He replied in one line of Virgil.

Vincet amor patriae laudumque immensa cupido.

This uttered with the fine open Italian pronunciation, and the graceful dignity of his manner, was very noble. I wished to have a statue of him taken at that moment.

I asked him if he understood English. He immediately began and spoke it, which he did tolerably well. When at Naples, he had known several Irish gentlemen who were officers in that service. Having a great facility in acquiring languages, he learnt English from them. But as he had been now ten years without ever speaking it, he spoke very slow. One could see that he was possessed of the words, but for want of what I may call mechanical practice, he had a difficulty in expressing himself.

I was diverted with his English library. It consisted of

Some broken volumes of the Spectatour and Tatler.

Pope's Essay on Man.

Gulliver's Travels.

A History of France, in old English.

And

Barclay's Apology for the Quakers.

I promised to send him some English books *.

He convinced me how well he understood our language; for I took the liberty to shew him a Memorial which I had drawn up on the advantages to Great Britain from an alliance with Corsica, and he translated this memorial into Italian with the greatest facility. He has since given me more proofs of his knowledge of our tongue by his answers to the letters which I have had the honour to write to him in English, and in particular by a very judicious and ingenious criticism on some of Swift's works.

He was well acquainted with the history of Britain. He had read many of the parliamentary debates, and had even seen a number of the North

* I have sent him the Works of Harrington, of Sidney, of Addison, of Trenchard, of Gordon, and of other writers in favour of liberty. I have also sent him some of our best books of morality and entertainment, in particular the Works of Mr. Samuel Johnson, with a compleat set of the Spectatour, Tatler and Guardian; and to the University of Corte, I have sent a few of the Greek and Roman Classicks, of the beautiful editions of the Messieurs Foulis at Glasgow.

Briton. He shewed a considerable knowledge of this country, and often introduced anecdotes and drew comparisons and allusions from Britain.

He said his great object was to form the Corsicans in such a manner that they might have a firm constitution, and might be able to subsist without him. Our state, said he, is young, and still requires the leading strings. I am desirous that the Corsicans should be taught to walk of themselves. Therefore when they come to me to ask whom they should chuse for their Padre del Commune, or other Magistrate, I tell them, You know better than I do, the able and honest men among your neighbours. Consider the consequence of your choice, not only to yourselves in particular, but to the island in general. In this manner I accustom them to feel their own importance as members of the state.

After representing the severe and melancholy state of oppression under which Corsica had so long groaned, he said, We are now to our country like the prophet Elishah stretched over the dead child of the Shunamite, eye to eye, nose to nose, mouth to mouth. It begins to recover warmth, and to revive. I hope it shall yet regain full health and vigour.

I said that things would make a rapid progress, and that we should soon see all the arts and sciences flourish in Corsica. Patience Sir, said he. If you saw a man who had fought a hard battle, who was much wounded, who was beaten to the ground, and who with difficulty could lift himself up, it would not be reasonable to ask him to get his hair well drest, and to put on embroidered clothes. Corsica has fought a hard battle, has been much wounded, has been beaten to the ground, and with difficulty can lift herself up. The arts and sciences are like dress and ornament. You cannot expect them from us for some time. But come back twenty or thirty years hence, and we'll shew you arts and sciences, and concerts and assemblies, and fine ladies, and we'll make you fall in love among us, Sir.

He smiled a good deal, when I told him that I was much surprised to find him so amiable, accomplished, and polite; for although I knew I was to see a great man, I expected to find a rude character, an Attila king of the Goths, or a Luitprand king of the Lombards.

I observed that although he had often a placid smile upon his countenance, he hardly ever laughed. Whether loud laughter in general society be a sign of weakness or rusticity, I cannot say; but I have remarked that real great men, and men of finished behaviour, seldom fall into it.

The variety, and I may say versatility, of the mind of this great man is amazing. One day when I came in to pay my respects to him before dinner, I found him in much agitation, with a circle of his nobles around him, and a Corsican standing before him like a criminal before his judge. Paoli immediately turned to me, 'I am glad you are come, Sir. You protestants talk much against our doctrine of transubstantiation. Behold here the miracle of transubstantiation, a Corsican transubstantiated into a Genoese. That unworthy man who now stands before me is a Corsican, who has been long a lieutenant under the Genoese, in Capo Corso. Andrew Doria and all their greatest heroes could not be more violent for the republick than he has been, and all against his country.' Then turning to the man, 'Sir, said he, Corsica makes it a rule to pardon the most unworthy of her children, when they surrender themselves, even when they are forced to do so, as is your case. You have now escaped. But take care. I shall have a ſtrict eye upon you; and if ever you make the leaſt attempt to return to your traiterous practices, you know I can be avenged of you.' He ſpoke this with the fierceneſs of a lion, and from the awful darkneſs of his brow, one could ſee that his thoughts of vengeance were terrible. Yet when it was over, he all at once reſumed his uſual appearance, called out ' andiamo, come along;' went to dinner, and was as chearful and gay as if nothing had happened.

His notions of morality are high and refined, ſuch as become the Father of a nation. Were he a libertine, his influence would ſoon vaniſh; for men will never truſt the important concerns of ſociety to one they know will do what is hurtful to ſociety for his own pleaſures. He told me that his father had brought him up with great ſtrictneſs, and that he had very ſeldom deviated from the paths of virtue. That this was not from a defect of feeling and paſſion, but that his mind being filled with important objects, his paſſions were employed in more noble purſuits than thoſe of licentious pleaſure. I ſaw from Paoli's example the great art of preſerving young men of ſpirit from the contagion of vice, in which there is often a species of sentiment, ingenuity and enterprise nearly allied to virtuous qualities.

Shew a young man that there is more real spirit in virtue than in vice, and you have a surer hold of him, during his years of impetuosity and passion, than by convincing his judgement of all the rectitude of ethicks.

One day at dinner, he gave us the principal arguments for the being and attributes of GOD. To hear these arguments repeated with graceful energy by the illustrious Paoli in the midst of his heroick nobles, was admirable. I never felt my mind more elevated.

I took occasion to mention the king of Prussia's infidel writings, and in particular his epistle to Marischal Keith. Paoli who often talks with admiration of the greatness of that monarch, instead of uttering any direct censure of what he saw to be wrong in so distinguished a hero, paused a little, and then said with a grave and most expressive look, 'C'est une belle consolation pour
' un vieux general mourant, " En peu de tems
" vous ne serez plus." It is fine consolation for
' an old general when dying, " In a little while
" you shall be no more."

He observed that the Epicurean philosophy had produced but one exalted character, whereas Stoicism had been the seminary of great men. What he now said put me in mind of these noble lines of Lucan.

> Hi mores, haec duri immota Catonis
> Secta fuit, servare modum finemque tenere,
> Naturamque sequi, patriaeque impendere vitam,
> Nec sibi sed toti genitum se credere mundo.
> LUCAN. Pharsal. lib. ii. l. 380.
>
> These were the stricter manners of the man,
> And this the stubborn course in which they ran;
> The golden mean unchanging to pursue,
> Constant to keep the purpos'd end in view;
> Religiously to follow nature's laws,
> And die with pleasure in his country's cause.
> To think he was not for himself design'd,
> But born to be of use to all mankind.
> ROWE.

When he was asked if he would quit the island of which he had undertaken the protection, supposing a foreign power should create him a Marischal, and make him governour of a province; he replied, 'I hope they will believe I am more honest, or more ambitious; for, said he, to accept of the highest offices under a foreign power would be to serve.'

To have been a colonel, a general or a marifchal, said he, 'would have been sufficient for my table, for my taste in dress, for the beauty whom my rank would have entitled me to attend. But it would not have been sufficient for this spirit, for this imagination.' Putting his hand upon his bosom.

He reasoned one day in the midst of his nobles whether the commander of a nation should be married or not. 'If he is married, said he, there is a risk that he may be distracted by private affairs, and swayed too much by a concern for his family. If he is unmarried, there is a risk that not having the tender attachments of a wife and children, he may sacrifice all to his own ambition.' When I said he ought to marry and have a son to succeed him, 'Sir, said he, what security can I have that my son will think and act as I do? What sort of a son had Cicero, and what had Marcus Aurelius?"

He said to me one day when we were alone, 'I never will marry. I have not the conjugal virtues. Nothing would tempt me to marry, but a woman who should bring me an immense dowry, with which I might assist my country.'

But he spoke much in praise of marriage, as

U

an inftitution which the experience of ages had found to be the beft calculated for the happinefs of individuals, and for the good of fociety. Had he been a private gentleman, he probably would have married, and I am fure would have made as good a hufband and father as he does a fupreme magiftrate and a general. But his arduous and critical fituation would not allow him to enjoy domeftick felicity. He is wedded to his country, and the Corficans are his children.

He often talked to me of marriage, told me licentious pleafures were delufive and tranfient, that I fhould never be truly happy till I was married, and that he hoped to have a letter from me foon after my return home, acquainting him that I had followed his advice, and was convinced from experience, that he was in the right. With fuch an engaging condefcenfion did this great man behave to me. If I could but paint his manner, all my readers would be charmed with him.

He has a mind fitted for philofophical fpeculations as well as for affairs of ftate. One evening at fupper, he entertained us for fome time with fome curious reveries and conjectures as to the nature of the intelligence of beafts, with regard to which, he observed human knowledge was as yet very imperfect. He in particular seemed fond of inquiring into the language of the brute creation. He observed that beasts fully communicate their ideas to each other, and that some of them, such as dogs, can form several articulate sounds. In different ages there have been people who pretended to understand the language of birds and beasts. Perhaps, said Paoli, in a thousand years we may know this as well as we know things which appeared much more difficult to be known. I have often since this conversation, indulged myself in such reveries. If it were not liable to ridicule, I would say that an acquaintance with the language of beasts would be a most agreeable acquisition to man, as it would enlarge the circle of his social intercourse.

On my return to Britain I was disappointed to find nothing upon this subject in Doctour Gregory's Comparative View of the State and Faculties of Man with those of the Animal World, which was then just published. My disappointment however was in a good measure made up by a picture of society, drawn by that ingenious and worthy authour, which may be well ap-

plied to the Corficans. 'There is a certain pe-
'riod in the progrefs of fociety in which man-
'kind appear to the greateft advantage. In
'this period, they have the bodily powers,
'and all the animal functions remaining in full
'vigour. They are bold, active, fteady, ardent
'in the love of liberty and their native coun-
'try. Their manners are fimple, their focial af-
'fections warm, and though they are greatly
'influenced by the ties of blood, yet they are
'generous and hofpitable to ftrangers. Religi-
'on is univerfally regarded among them, though
'difguifed by a variety of fuperftitions (a).

Paoli was very defirous that I fhould ftudy the character of the Corficans. Go among them, faid he, the more you talk with them, you will do me the greater pleafure. Forget the mean- nefs of their apparel. Hear their fentiments. You will find honour, and fenfe and abilities among thefe poor men.

His heart grew big when he fpoke of his countrymen. His own great qualities appeared to unufual advantage, while he defcribed the virtues of thofe for whofe happinefs his whole

(a) Preface to Comparative View, p. 8.

life was employed. If, said he, I should lead into the field an army of Corsicans against an army double their number, let me speak a few words to the Corsicans, to remind them of the honour of their country and of their brave forefathers, I do not say that they would conquer, but I am sure that not a man of them would give way. The Corsicans, said he, have a steady resolution that would amaze you. I wish you could see one of them die. It is a proverb among the Genoese, 'I Corsi meritano la furca e la sanno soffrire. The Corsicans deserve the gallows, and they fear not to meet it.' There is a real compliment to us in this saying.

He told me, that in Corsica, criminals are put to death, four and twenty hours after sentence is pronounced against them. This, said he, may not be over catholick, but it is humane.

He went on, and gave me several instances of the Corsican spirit.

A sergeant, said he, who fell in one of our desperate actions, when just a dying, wrote to me thus. 'I salute you. Take care of my aged father. In two hours I shall be with the rest who have bravely died for their country.'

A Corsican gentleman who had been taken prisoner by the Genoese, was thrown into a dark dungeon, where he was chained to the ground. While he was in this dismal situation, the Genoese sent a message to him, that if he would accept of a commission in their service, he might have it. 'No, said he. Were I
' to accept of your offer, it would be with a de-
' termined purpose to take the first opportuni-
' ty of returning to the service of my country.
' But I will not accept of it. For I would not
' have my countrymen even suspect that I could
' be one moment unfaithful.' And he remained in his dungeon. Paoli went on. 'I defy Rome, Sparta or Thebes to shew me thirty years of such patriotism as Corsica can boast. Though the affection between relations is exceedingly strong in the Corsicans, they will give up their nearest relations for the good of their country, and sacrifice such as have deserted to the Genoese.'

He gave me a noble instance of a Corsican's feeling and greatness of mind. 'A criminal, said he, was condemned to die. His nephew came to me with a lady of distinction, that she might

solicit his pardon. The nephew's anxiety made him think that the lady did not speak with sufficient force and earnestness. He therefore advanced, and addressed himself to me, 'Sir, is it proper for me to speak?' as if he felt that it was unlawful to make such an application. I bid him go on. 'Sir, said he, with the deepest
' concern, may I beg the life of my uncle? If
' it is granted, his relations will make a gift
' to the state of a thousand zechins. We will
' furnish fifty soldiers in pay during the siege
' of Furiani. We will agree that my uncle shall
' be banished, and will engage that he shall never
' return to the island.' I knew the nephew to be a man of worth, and I answered him. You are acquainted with the circumstances of this case. Such is my confidence in you, that if you will say that giving your uncle a pardon would be just, useful or honourable for Corsica, I promise you it shall be granted. He turned about, burst into tears, and left me, saying, ' Non vor-
' rei vendere l'onore della patria per mille ze-
' chini. I would not have the honour of our
' country sold for a thousand zechins. And his uncle suffered.'

Although the General was one of the constituent members of the court of syndicato, he seldom took his chair. He remained in his own apartment; and if any of those whose suits were determined by the syndicato were not pleased with the sentence, they had an audience of Paoli, who never failed to convince them that justice had been done them. This appeared to me a necessary indulgence in the infancy of government. The Corsicans having been so long in a state of anarchy, could not all at once submit their minds to the regular authority of justice. They would submit implicitly to Paoli, because they love and venerate him. But such a submission is in reality being governed by their passions. They submit to one for whom they have a personal regard. They cannot be said to be perfectly civilized till they submit to the determinations of their magistrates as officers of the state, entrusted with the administration of justice. By convincing them that the magistrates judge with abilities and uprightness, Paoli accustoms the Corsicans to have that salutary confidence in their rulers, which is necessary for securing respect and stability to the government.

After having said much in praise of the Corſicans, 'Come, ſaid he, you ſhall have a proof of what I tell you. There is a crowd in the next room, waiting for admittance to me. I will call in the firſt I ſee, and you ſhall hear him. He who chanced to preſent himſelf, was a venerable old man. The General ſhook him by the hand, and bid him good day, with an eaſy kindneſs that gave the aged peaſant full encouragement to talk to his Excellency with freedom. Paoli bid him not mind me, but ſay on. The old man then told him that there had been an unlucky tumult in the village where he lived, and that two of his ſons were killed. That looking upon this as a heavy misfortune, but without malice on the part of thoſe who deprived him of his ſons, he was willing to have allowed it to paſs without enquiry. But his wife anxious for revenge, had made an application to have them apprehended and puniſhed. That he gave his Excellency this trouble to intreat that the greateſt care might be taken, leſt in the heat of enmity among his neighbours, any body ſhould be puniſhed as guilty of the blood of his ſons, who was really innocent of it. There was ſomething ſo generous in this ſentiment, while at the ſame time the old man ſeemed full of grief for the loss of his children, that it touched my heart in the most sensible manner. Paoli looked at me with complacency and a kind of amiable triumph on the behaviour of the old man, who had a flow of words and a vivacity of gesture which fully justified what Petrus Cyrnaeus hath said of the Corsican eloquence; 'Diceres 'omnes esse bonos causidicos. You would say 'they are all good pleaders.'

I found Paoli had reason to wish that I should talk much with his countrymen, as it gave me a higher opinion both of him and of them. Thuanus has justly said, 'Sunt mobilia Corsorum in- 'genia. The dispositions of the Corsicans are 'changeable.' Yet after ten years, their attachment to Paoli is as strong as at the first. Nay, they have an enthusiastick admiration of him. 'Questo grand' uomo mandato per Dio a libe- 'rare la patria. This great man whom God 'hath sent to free our country,' was the manner in which they expressed themselves to me concerning him.

Those who attended on Paoli were all men of sense and abilities in their different departments. Some of them had been in foreign service. One of them, Signor Suzzoni, had been long in Germany. He spoke German to me, and recalled to my mind, the happy days which I have paſt among that plain, honeſt, brave people, who of all nations in the world, receive ſtrangers with the greateſt cordiality. Signor Gian Quilico Caſa Bianca, of the moſt ancient Corſican nobility, was much my friend. He inſtructed me fully with regard to the Corſican government. He had even the patience to ſit by me while I wrote down an account of it, which from converſations with Paoli, I afterwards enlarged and improved. I received many civilities from the Abbé Roſtini, a man of literature, and diſtinguiſhed no leſs for the excellency of his heart. His ſaying of Paoli deſerves to be remembered. ' Nous ne craignons pas que notre General nous ' trompe ni qu'il ſe laiſſe tromper. We are not a-' fraid that our General will deceive us, nor that ' he will let himſelf be deceived.'

I alſo received civilities from Father Guelfucci of the order of Servites, a man whoſe talents and virtues, united with a ſingular decency and ſweetneſs of manners, have raiſed him to the honourable ſtation of ſecretary to the General. Indeed all the gentlemen here behaved to me in the moſt obliging manner. We walked, rode, and went a-ſhooting together.

The peaſants and ſoldiers were all frank, open, lively and bold, with a certain roughneſs of manner which agrees well with their character, and is far from being diſpleaſing. The General gave me an admirable inſtance of their plain and natural, ſolid good ſenſe. A young French Marquis, very rich and very vain, came over to Corſica. He had a ſovereign contempt for the barbarous inhabitants, and ſtrutted about (andava a paſſo miſurato) with prodigious airs of conſequence. The Corſicans beheld him with a ſmile of ridicule, and ſaid, ' Let him alone, he is young.'

The Corſican peaſants and ſoldiers are very fond of baiting cattle with the large mountain dogs. This keeps up a ferocity among them which totally extinguiſhes fear. I have ſeen a Corſican in the very heat of a baiting, run in, drive off the dogs, ſeize the half-frantick animal by the horns, and lead it away. The common people did not ſeem much given to diverſions. I obſerved ſome of them in the great hall of the houſe of Colonna where I was lodged, amuſing themselves with playing at a sort of draughts in a very curious manner. They drew upon the floor with chalk, a sufficient number of squares, chalking one all over, and leaving one open, alternately; and instead of black men and white, they had bits of stone and bits of wood. It was an admirable burlesque on gaming.

The chief satisfaction of these islanders when not engaged in war or in hunting, seemed to be that of lying at their ease in the open air, recounting tales of the bravery of their countrymen, and singing songs in honour of the Corsicans, and against the Genoese. Even in the night they will continue this pastime in the open air, unless rain forces them to retire into their houses.

The ambasciadore Inglese, The English ambassadour, as the good peasants and soldiers used to call me, became a great favourite among them. I got a Corsican dress made, in which I walked about with an air of true satisfaction. The General did me the honour to present me with his own pistols, made in the island, all of Corsican wood and iron, and of excellent workmanship. I had every other accoutrement. I even got one of the shells which had often sounded the alarm to liberty. I preserve them all with great care.

The Corsican peasants and soldiers were quite free and easy with me. Numbers of them used to come and see me of a morning, and just go out and in as they pleased. I did every thing in my power to make them fond of the British, and bid them hope for an alliance with us. They asked me a thousand questions about my country, all which I chearfully answered as well as I could.

One day they would needs hear me play upon my German flute. To have told my honest natural visitants, Really gentlemen I play very ill, and put on such airs as we do in our genteel companies, would have been highly ridiculous. I therefore immediately complied with their request. I gave them one or two Italian airs, and then some of our beautiful old Scots tunes, Gilderoy, the Lass of Patie's Mill, Corn riggs are Bonny. The pathetick simplicity and pastoral gaiety of the Scots musick, will always please those who have the genuine feelings of nature. The Corsicans were charmed with the specimens I gave them, though I may now say that they were very indifferently performed.

My good friends insisted also to have an English song from me. I endeavoured to please them in this too, and was very lucky in that which occurred to me. I sung them 'Hearts of 'oak are our ships, Hearts of oak are our men.' I translated it into Italian for them, and never did I see men so delighted with a song as the Corsicans were with Hearts of oak. 'Cuore di quer-'co, cried they, bravo Inglese.' It was quite a joyous riot. I fancied myself to be a recruiting sea-officer. I fancied all my chorus of Corsicans aboard the British fleet.

Paoli talked very highly on preserving the independency of Corsica. ' We may, said he, have foreign powers for our friends; but they must be ' Amici fuori di casa. Friends at arm's length.' We may make an alliance, but we will not submit ourselves to the dominion of the greatest nation in Europe. This people who have done so much for liberty, would be hewn in pieces man by man, rather than allow Corsica to be sunk into the territories of another country. Some years ago, when a false rumour was spread that I had a design to yield up Corsica to the Emperour. A Corsican came to me, and addressed me in great

agitation. 'What! shall the blood of so many
'heroes, who have sacrificed their lives for the
'freedom of Corsica, serve only to tinge the
'purple of a foreign prince!'

I mentioned to him the scheme of an alliance between Great Britain and Corsica. Paoli with politeness and dignity waved the subject, by saying, The less assistance we have from allies, the greater our glory. He seemed hurt by our treatment of his country. He mentioned the severe proclamation at the last peace, in which the brave islanders were called the Rebels of Corsica. He said with a conscious pride and proper feeling, Rebels! I did not expect that from Great Britain.

He however shewed his great respect for the British nation, and I could see he wished much to be in friendship with us. When I asked him what I could possibly do in return for all his goodness to me. He replied, 'Solamente disingannate il suo corte. Only undeceive your court. Tell them what you have seen here. They will be curious to ask you. A man come from Corsica will be like a man come from the Antipodes.'

I expressed such hopes as a man of sensibility

would in my situation naturally form. He saw at least one Briton devoted to his cause. I threw out many flattering ideas of future political events, imaged the British and the Corsicans strictly united both in commerce and in war, and described the blunt kindness and admiration with which the hearty, generous common people of England would treat the brave Corsicans.

I insensibly got the better of his reserve upon this head. My flow of gay ideas relaxed his severity, and brightened up his humour. Do you remember, said he, the little people in Asia who were in danger of being oppressed by the great king of Assyria, till they addressed themselves to the Romans. And the Romans, with the noble spirit of a great and free nation, stood forth, and would not suffer the great king to destroy the little people, but made an alliance with them?

He made no observations upon this beautiful piece of history. It was easy to see his allusion to his own nation and ours.

When the General related this piece of history to me, I was negligent enough not to ask him what little people he meant. As the story made a strong impression upon me, upon my return to

Britain I searched a variety of books to try if I could find it, but in vain. I therefore took the liberty in one of my letters to Paoli, to beg he would let me know it. He told me the little people was the Jews, that the story was related by several ancient authours, but that I would find it told with most precision and energy in the eighth chapter of the first book of the Maccabees.

The first book of the Maccabees, though not received into the Protestant canon, is allowed by all the learned to be an authentick history. I have read Paoli's favourite story with much satisfaction, and, as in several circumstances, it very well applies to Great Britain and Corsica, is told with great eloquence, and furnishes a fine model for an alliance, I shall make no apology for transcribing the most interesting verses.

' Now Judas had heard of the fame of the
' Romans, that they were mighty and valiant men,
' and such as would lovingly accept all that join-
' ed themselves unto them, and make a league of
' amity with all that came unto them.

' And that they were men of great valour.
' It was told him also of their wars and noble
' acts which they had done amongst the Galati-

'ans, and how they had conquered them, and
'brought them under tribute.

'And what they had done in the country of
'Spain, for the winning of the mines of the silver
'and gold which are there,

'And that by their policy and patience they
'had conquered all the place, though it were ve-
'ry far from them.

'It was told him besides, how they destroy-
'ed and brought under their dominion, all o-
'ther kingdoms and isles that at any time re-
'sisted them.

'But with their friends, and such as relied
'upon them, they kept amity: and that they
'had conquered kingdoms both far and near,
'insomuch as all that heard of their name
'were afraid of them:

'Also, that whom they would help to a
'kingdom, those reign; and whom again they
'would, they displace: finally, that they were
'greatly exalted:

'Moreover, how they had made for them-
'selves a senate-house, wherein three hundred
'and twenty men sat in council dayly, consult-
'ing alway for the people, to the end that they
'might be well ordered.

'In confideration of thefe things Judas chofe Eupolemus the fon of John the fon of Accos, and Jafon the fon of Eleazar, and fent them to Rome, to make a league of amity and confederacy with them.

'And to intreat them that they would take the yoke from them, for they faw that the kingdom of the Grecians did opprefs Ifrael with fervitude.

'They went therefore to Rome, which was a very great journey, and came into the fenate, where they fpake, and faid,

'Judas Maccabeus, with his brethren, and the people of the Jews, have fent us unto you, to make a confederacy and peace with you, and that we might be regiftered your confederates and friends.

'So that matter pleafed the Romans well.

'And this is the copy of the epiftle which the fenate wrote back again, in tables of brafs, and fent to Jerufalem, that there they might have by them a memorial of peace and confederacy.

'Good fuccefs be to the Romans, and to the people of the Jews, by fea and by land for ever. The fword alfo, and enemy be far from them.'

'If there come first any war upon the Romans, or any of their confederates, throughout all their dominions,

'The people of the Jews shall help them, as the time shall be appointed, with all their heart.

'Neither shall they give any thing unto them that make war upon them, or aid them with victuals, weapons, money or ships, as it hath seemed good unto the Romans, but they shall keep their covenant, without taking any thing therefore.

'In the same manner also, if war come first upon the nation of the Jews, the Romans shall help them with all their heart, according as the time shall be appointed them.

'Neither shall victuals be given to them that take part against them, or weapons, or money, or ships, as it hath seemed good to the Romans; but they shall keep their covenants, and that without deceit.

'According to these articles did the Romans make a covenant with the people of the Jews.

'Howbeit, if hereafter the one party or the other, shall think meet to add or diminish any thing they may do it at their pleasures, and

' whatsoever they shall add or take away, shall
' be ratified.

' And, as touching the evils that Demetrius
' doth to the Jews, we have written unto him,
' saying, Wherefore hast thou made thy yoke
' heavy upon our friends and confederates, the
' Jews?

' If therefore they complain any more against
' thee, we will do them justice, and fight with
' thee by sea and by land.'

I will venture to ask whether the Romans appear, in any one instance of their history, more truly great than they do here.

Paoli said, ' If a man would preserve the generous glow of patriotism, he must not reason too much. Mareschal Saxe reasoned; and carried the arms of France into the heart of Germany, his own country. I act from sentiment, not from reasonings.'

' Virtuous sentiments and habits, said he, are beyond philosophical reasonings, which are not so strong, and are continually varying. If all the professours in Europe were formed into one society, it would no doubt be a society very respectable, and we should there be entertained with the best moral lessons. Yet I believe I should find more real virtue in a society of good peasants in some little village in the heart of your island. It might be said of these two societies, as was said of Demosthenes and Themistocles, 'Illius dicta, hujus facta magis valebant. The one was powerful in words, but the other in deeds.'

This kind of conversation led me to tell him how much I had suffered from anxious speculations. With a mind naturally inclined to melancholy, and a keen desire of inquiry, I had intensely applied myself to metaphysical researches, and reasoned beyond my depth, on such subjects as it is not given to man to know. I told him I had rendered my mind a camera obscura, that in the very heat of youth I felt the 'non est tanti,' the 'omnia vanitas' of one who has exhausted all the sweets of his being, and is weary with dull repetition. I told him that I had almost become for ever incapable of taking a part in active life.

'All this, said Paoli, is melancholy. I have also studied metaphysicks. I know the arguments for fate and free-will, for the materiality and immateriality of the soul, and even the subtile arguments for and against the existence of matter.

' Ma lasciamo queste dispute ai oziosi. But let us leave these disputes to the idle. Io tengo sempre fermo un gran pensiero. I hold always firm one great object. I never feel a moment of despondency.

The contemplation of such a character really existing, was of more service to me than all I had been able to draw from books, from conversation, or from the exertions of my own mind. I had often enough formed the idea of a man continually such, as I could conceive in my best moments. But this idea appeared like the ideas we are taught in the schools to form of things which may exist, but do not; of seas of milk, and ships of amber. But I saw my highest idea realised in Paoli. It was impossible for me, speculate as I pleased, to have a little opinion of human nature in him.

One morning I remember, I came in upon him without ceremony, while he was dressing. I was glad to have an opportunity of seeing him in those teasing moments, when according to the Duke de Rochefoucault, no man is a hero to his valet de chambre. The lively nobleman who has a malicious pleasure in endeavouring to divest human nature of its dignity, by exhibiting partial views, and exaggerating faults, would have owned that Paoli was every moment of his life a hero.

Paoli told me that from his earliest years, he had in view the important station which he now holds; so that his sentiments must ever have been great. I asked him how one of such elevated thoughts could submit with any degree of patience, to the unmeaning ceremonies and poor discourse of genteel society, which he certainly was obliged to do while an officer at Naples. 'O said he, I managed it very easily. Ero connosciuto per una testa singolare, I was known to be a singular man. I talked and joked, and was merry; but I never sat down to play; I went and came as I pleased. The mirth I like is what is easy and unaffected. Je ne puis sonffrir long temps les diseurs de bons mots. I cannot endure long the sayers of good things,'

How much superiour is this great man's idea of agreeable conversation to that of professed wits, who are continually straining for smart remarks, and lively repartees. They put themselves to much pain in order to please, and yet please less than if they would just appear as they naturally feel themselves. A company of professed wits has always appeared to me, like a company of artificers employed in some very nice and difficult work, which they are under a necessity of performing.

Though calm and fully master of himself, Paoli is animated with an extraordinary degree of vivacity. Except when indisposed or greatly fatigued, he never sits down but at meals. He is perpetually in motion, walking briskly backwards and forwards. Mr. Samuel Johnson, whose comprehensive and vigorous understanding, has by long observation, attained to a perfect knowledge of human nature, when treating of biography, has this reflection. ' There are many invisible cir-
' cumstances which, whether we read as enqui-
' ries after natural or moral knowledge; whether
' we intend to enlarge our science, or increase our
' virtue, are more important than publick occur-
' rences. Thus Sallust the great master of nature,
' has not forgotten in his account of Catiline, to
' remark, that " his walk was now quick, and a-
' gain slow," as an indication of a mind revolv-
' ing something with violent commotion (*a*).' E-

(*a*) Rambler. number 60.

ver mindful of the wisdom of the rambler, I have accustomed myself to mark the small peculiarities of character. Paoli's being perpetually in motion, nay his being so agitated that, as the same Sallust also says of Catiline, 'Neque vigiliis, 'neque quietibus sedari poterat. He could not be 'quieted either by watching or by repose,' are indications of his being as active and indefatigable as Catiline, but from a very different cause. The conspiratour from schemes of ruin and destruction to Rome; the patriot from schemes of liberty and felicity to Corsica.

Paoli told me that the vivacity of his mind was such, that he could not study above ten minutes at a time. 'Lá testa mi rompa. My head is like to break,' said he. I can never write my lively ideas with my own hand. In writing, they escape from my mind. I call the Abbé Guelfucci, Allons presto, pigliate li pensieri. Come quickly, take my thoughts; and he writes them.'

Paoli has a memory like that of Themistocles; for I was assured that he knows the names of almost all the people in the island, their characters, and their connections. His memory as a man of learning, is no less uncommon. He has the best part of the classicks by heart, and he has a happy talent in applying them with propriety, which is rarely to be found. This talent is not always to be reckoned pedantry. The instances in which Paoli is shewn to display it, are a proof to the contrary.

I have heard Paoli recount the revolutions of one of the ancient states, with an energy and a rapidity which shewed him to be master of the subject, to be perfectly acquainted with every spring and movement of the various events. I have heard him give what the French call 'Une catalogue raisonnée' of the most distinguished men in antiquity. His characters of them were concise, nervous and just. I regret that the fire with which he spoke upon such occasions, so dazzled me that I could not recollect his sayings so as to write them down when I retired from his presence.

He just lives in the times of antiquity. He said to me, "A young man who would form his mind to glory, must not read modern memoirs; mà Plutarcho, mà Tito Livio; but Plutarch and Titus Livius.'

I have seen him fall into a sort of reverie, and break out into sallies of the grandest and noblest enthusiasm. I recollect two instances of this. 'What a thought? that thousands owe their happiness to you!' And throwing himself into an attitude, as if he saw the lofty mountain of fame before him. 'THERE; is my object, (pointing to the summit) if I fall, I fall at least THERE (pointing a good way up) magnis tamen excidit ausis.'

I ventured to reason like a libertine, that I might be confirmed in virtuous principles by so illustrious a preceptour. I made light of moral feelings. I argued that conscience was vague and uncertain; that there was hardly any vice but what men might be found who have been guilty of it without remorse. 'But, said he, there is no man who has not a horrour at some vice. Different vices and different virtues have the strongest impression, on different men; Ma il virtù in astratto è il nutrimento dei nostri cuori. But virtue in the abstract, is the food of our hearts.'

Talking of Providence, he said to me with that earnestness with which a man speaks who is anxious to be believed. 'I tell you on the word of an honest man, it is impossible for me not to be persuaded that GOD interposes to give freedom to Corsica. A people oppressed like the Corsicans, are certainly worthy of divine assistance. When we were in the most desperate circumstances, I never lost courage, trusting as I did in Providence.' I ventured to object; But why has not Providence interposed sooner? He replied with a noble, serious and devout air, ' Because his ways are unsearchable. I adore him for what he hath done. I revere him in what he hath not done.'

I gave Paoli the character of my revered friend Mr. Samuel Johnson. I have often regretted that illustrious men such as humanity produces a few times in the revolution of many ages, should not see each other; and when such arise in the same age though at the distance of half the globe, I have been astonished how they could forbear to meet.

' As steel sharpneth steel, so doth a man the
' countenance of his friend,' says the wise monarch. What an idea may we not form of an interview between such a scholar and philosopher as Mr. Johnson, and such a legislatour and general as Paoli!

I repeated to Paoli several of Mr. Johnson's sayings, so remarkable for strong sense and original humour. I now recollect these two.

When I told Mr. Johnson that a certain authour affected in conversation to maintain, that there was no distinction between virtue and vice, he said, 'Why Sir, if the fellow does not think
'as he speaks, he is lying; and I see not what
'honour he can propose to himself from having
'the character of a lyar. But if he does really
'think that there is no distinction between virtue
'and vice, why Sir, when he leaves our houses
'let us count our spoons.'

Of modern infidels and innovatours, he said
'Sir, these are all vain men, and will gratify
'themselves at any expence. Truth will not af-
'ford sufficient food to their vanity; so they have
'betaken themselves to errour. Truth Sir, is
'a cow which will yield such people no more
'milk, and so they are gone to milk the bull.'

I felt an elation of mind to see Paoli delighted with the sayings of Mr. Johnson, and to hear him translate them with Italian energy to the Corsican heroes.

I repeated Mr. Johnson's sayings as nearly

as I could, in his own peculiar forcible language, for which, prejudiced or little criticks have taken upon them to find fault with him. He is above making any anſwer to them, but I have found a ſufficient anſwer in a general remark in one of his excellent papers. ' Difference of thoughts will produce difference of language. He that thinks with more extent than another, will want words of larger meaning.' (*a*)

'I hope to be pardoned for this digreſſion, wherein I pay a juſt tribute of veneration and gratitude to one from whoſe writings and converſation I have received inſtructions of which I experience the value in every ſcene of my life.

During Paoli's adminiſtration, there have been few laws made in Corſica. He mentioned one which he has found very efficacious in curbing that vindictive ſpirit of the Corſicans, of which I have ſaid a good deal in a former part of this work. There was among the Corſicans a moſt dreadful ſpecies of revenge, called ' Vendetta traſverſa, Collateral revenge,' which Petrus Cyrnaeus candidly acknowledges. It was

(*a*) Idler, number 70.

this. If a man had received an injury, and could not find a proper opportunity to be revenged on his enemy perfonally, he revenged himfelf on one of his enemy's relations. So barbarous a practice, was the fource of innumerable affaffinations. Paoli knowing that the point of honour was every thing to the Corficans, oppofed it to the progrefs of the blackeft of crimes, fortified by long habits. He made a law, by which it was provided, that this collateral revenge fhould not only be punifhed with death, as ordinary murther, but the memory of the offender fhould be difgraced for ever by a pillar of infamy. He alfo had it enacted that the fame ftatute fhould extend to the violatours of an oath of reconciliation, once made.

By thus combating a vice fo deftructive, he has, by a kind of fhock of oppofite paffions, reduced the fiery Corficans to a ftate of mildnefs, and he affured me that they were now all fully fenfible of the equity of that law.

While I was at Sollacarò, information was received, that the poor wretch who ftrangled the woman at the inftigation of his miftrefs, had confented to accept of his life, upon con-

Y

dition of becoming hangman. This made a great noise among the Corsicans, who were enraged at the creature, and said their nation was now disgraced. Paoli did not think so. He said to me 'I am glad of this. It will be of service. It will contribute to form us to a just subordination. We have as yet too great an equality among us. As we must have Corsican taylours and Corsican shoemakers, we must also have a Corsican hangman.'

I could not help being of a different opinion. The occupations of a taylour and a shoemaker though mean, are not odious. When I afterwards met M. Rousseau in England, and made him a report of my Corsican expedition, he agreed with me in thinking that it would be something noble for the brave islanders, to be able to say that there was not a Corsican but who would rather suffer death, than become a hangman; and he also agreed with me, that it might have a good effect to have always a Genoese for the hangman of Corsica.

I must however do the Genoese the justice to observe that Paoli told me, that even one of them had suffered death in Corsica, rather than consent to become hangman. When I, with a keeness natural enough in a Briton born with an abhorrence at tyranny, talked with violence against the Genoese, Paoli said with a moderation and candour which ought to do him honour even with the republick, 'It is true the Genoese are our enemies; but let us not forget, that they are the descendants of those worthies, who carried their arms beyond the Hellespont.

There is one circumstance in Paoli's character which I present to my readers with caution, knowing how much it may be ridiculed, in an age when mankind are so fond of incredulity, that they seem to pique themselves in contracting their circle of belief as much as possible. But I consider this infidel rage as but a temporary mode of the human understanding, and am well persuaded that e'er long we shall return to a more calm philosophy.

I own I cannot help thinking that though we may boast some improvements in science, and in short, superior degrees of knowledge in things where our faculties can fully reach, yet we should not assume to ourselves sounder judgements than those of our fathers; I will therefore venture to relate that Paoli has at times extraordinary impressions of distant and future events.

The way in which I difcovered it, was this. Being very defirous of ftudying fo exalted a character, I fo far prefumed upon his goodnefs to me, as to take the liberty of afking him a thoufand queftions with regard to the moft minute and private circumftances of his life. Having asked him one day when fome of his nobles were prefent, whether a mind fo active as his was employed even in fleep, and if he ufed to dream much. Signor Cafa Bianca faid with an air and tone which implied fomething of importance, 'Sì, fi fogna. Yes, he dreams.' And upon my asking him to explain his meaning, he told me that the General had often feen in his dreams, what afterwards came to pafs. Paoli confirmed this by feveral inftances. Said he, ' I can give you no clear explanation of it. I only tell you facts. Sometimes I have been miftaken, but in general, thefe vifions have proved true. I cannot fay what may be the agency of invifible fpirits. They certainly muft know more than we do; and there is nothing abfurd in fuppofing that GOD fhould permit them to communicate their knowledge to us.

He went into a moft curious and pleafing difquifition on a fubject, which the late ingenious Mr. Baxter has treated in a very philosophical manner, in his Inquiry into the Nature of the Human Soul; a book which may be read with as much delight, and surely with more advantage than the works of those who endeavour to destroy our belief. Belief is favourable to the human mind, were it for nothing else but to furnish it entertainment. An infidel I should think, must frequently suffer from ennui.

It was perhaps affectation in Socrates to say, that all he had learned to know was that he knew nothing. But surely it is a mark of wisdom, to be sensible of the limited extent of human knowledge, to examine with reverence the ways of GOD, nor presumptuously reject any opinion which has been held by the judicious and the learned, because it has been made a cloak for artifice, or had a variety of fictions raised upon it, by credulity.

Old Feltham says, ' Every dream is not to be
' counted of; nor yet are all to be cast away
' with contempt. I would neither be a stoick,
' superstitious in all; nor yet an Epicure, consi-
' derate of none (a).' And after observing how much the ancients attended to the interpretation of dreams, he adds, ' Were it not for the power

(a) Feltham's Resolves, Cent. I. Resol. 52.

'of the gospel, in crying down the vains* of men,
'it would appear a wonder how a science so
'pleasing to humanity, should fall so quite to
'ruin (*b*).'

The mysterious circumstance in Paoli's character which I have ventured to relate, is universally believed in Corsica. The inhabitants of that island like the Italians, express themselves much by signs. When I asked one of them, if there had been many instances of the General's foreseeing future events, he grasped a large bunch of his hair, and replied, 'Tante, Signore, So many Sir.'

It may be said that the General has industriously propagated this opinion, in order that he might have more authority in civilizing a rude and ferocious people, as Lycurgus pretended to have the sanction of the oracle at Delphos, as Numa gave it out that he had frequent interviews with the nymph Egeria, or as Marius persuaded the Romans, that he received divine communications from a hind. But I cannot allow myself to suppose that Paoli ever required the aid of pious frauds.

Paoli though never familiar, has the most per-

---

\* He means vanity.   (*b*) Feltham's Resolves, Cent. I, Resol. 52.

fect ease of behaviour. This is a mark of a real great character. The distance and reserve which some of our modern nobility affect is, because nobility is now little else than a name in comparison of what it was in ancient times. In ancient times, noblemen lived at their country seats, like princes, in hospitable grandeur. They were men of power, and every one of them could bring hundreds of followers into the field. They were then open and affable. Some of our modern nobility are so anxious to preserve an appearance of dignity which they are sensible cannot bear an examination, that they are afraid to let you come near them. Paoli is not so. Those about him come into his apartment at all hours, wake him, help him on with his clothes, are perfectly free from restraint; yet they know their distance, and awed by his real greatness, never lose their respect for him.

Though thus easy of access, particular care is taken against such attempts upon the life of the illustrious Chief, as he has good reason to apprehend from the Genoese, who have so often employed assassination merely in a political view, and who would gain so much by assassinating Paoli.

A certain number of soldiers are continually on guard upon him; and as still closer guards, he has some faithful Corsican dogs. Of these five or six sleep, some in his chamber, and some at the outside of the chamber-door. He treats them with great kindness, and they are strongly attached to him. They are extremely sagacious, and know all his friends and attendants. Were any person to approach the General during the darkness of the night, they would instantly tear him in pieces.

Having dogs for his attendants, is another circumstance about Paoli similar to the heroes of antiquity. Homer represents Telemachus so attended.

δύω κύνες ἀργοὶ ἕποντο.
HOMER Odyss. lib. ii. l. 11.
Two dogs a faithful guard attend behind.
POPE.

But the description given of the family of Patroclus applies better to Paoli.

Εννέα τῷ γε ἄνακτι τραπέζηες κύνες ἦσαν.
HOMER. Iliad lib. xxiii. l. 73.
nine large dogs domestick at his board.
POPE.

Mr. Pope in his notes on the second book of the Odyssey, is much pleased with dogs being in-

troduced, as it furnishes an agreeable instance of ancient simplicity. He observes that Virgil thought this circumstance worthy of his imitation, in describing old Evander. So we read of Syphax general of the Numidians, 'Syphax inter duos ca-
' nes stans, Scipionem appellavit*. Syphax stand-
' ing between two dogs called to Scipio.'

Talking of courage, he made a very just distinction between constitutional courage and courage from reflection. 'Sir Thomas More, said he, would not probably have mounted a breach so well as a sergeant who had never thought of death. But a sergeant would not on a scaffold, have shewn the calm resolution of Sir Thomas More.'

On this subject he told me a very remarkable anecdote, which happened during the last war in Italy. At the siege of Tortona, the commander of the army which lay before the town, ordered Carew an Irish officer in the service of Naples, to advance with a detachment to a particular post.

---

* I mention this on the authority of an excellent scholar, and one of our best writers, Mr. Joseph Warton in his notes on the Aeneid; for I have not been able to find the passage in Livy which he quotes.

Having given his orders, he whispered to Carew. 'Sir, I know you to be a gallant man. I have therefore put you upon this duty. I tell you in confidence, it is certain death for you all. I place you there to make the enemy spring a mine below you.' Carew made a bow to the general, and led on his men in silence to the dreadful post. He there stood with an undaunted countenance, and having called to one of the soldiers for a draught of wine, 'Here, said he, I drink to all those who bravely fall in battle.' Fortunately at that instant Tortona capitulated, and Carew escaped. But he had thus a full opportunity of displaying a rare instance of determined intrepidity. It is with pleasure that I record an anecdote so much to the honour of a gentleman of that nation, on which illiberal reflections are too often thrown, by those of whom it little deserves them. Whatever may be the rough jokes of wealthy insolence, or the envious sarcasms of needy jealousy, the Irish have ever been, and will continue to be, highly regarded upon the continent.

Paoli's personal authority among the Corsicans struck me much. I have seen a crowd of them with eagerness and impetuosity, endeavouring to approach him, as if they would have burst into his apartment by force. In vain did the guards attempt to restrain them; but when he called to them in a tone of firmness, 'Non c'è ora ricorso, No audience now,' they were hushed at once.

He one afternoon gave us an entertaining dissertation on the ancient art of war. He observed that the ancients allowed of little baggage, which they very properly called 'impedimenta;' whereas the moderns burthen themselves with it to such a degree, that 50,000 of our present soldiers are allowed as much baggage as was formerly thought sufficient for all the armies of the Roman empire. He said it was good for soldiers to be heavy armed, as it renders them proportionably robust; and he remarked that when the Romans lightened their arms, the troops became enfeebled. He made a very curious observation with regard to the towers full of armed men, which we are told were borne on the backs of their elephants. He said it must be a mistake; for if the towers were broad, there would not be room for them on the backs of elephants; for he and a friend who was an able calculatour, had measured a very large elephant at Naples, and made a computation of the space neceſſary to hold the number of men said to be contained in thoſe towers, and they found that the back of the broadeſt elephant would not be ſufficient, after making the fulleſt allowance for what might be hung by ballance on either ſide of the animal. If again the towers were high, they would fall; for he did not think it at all probable, that the Romans had the art of tying on ſuch monſtrous machines at a time when they had not learnt the uſe even of girths to their ſaddles. He ſaid he did not give too much credit to the figures on Trajans pillar, many of which were undoubtedly falſe. He ſaid it was his opinion, that thoſe towers were only drawn by the elephants; an opinion founded in probability, and free from the difficulties of that which has been commonly received.

Talking of various ſchemes of life, fit for a man of ſpirit and education; I mentioned to him that of being a foreign miniſter. He ſaid he thought it a very agreeable employment for a man of parts and addreſs, during ſome years of his life. 'In that situation said he, a man will insensibly attain to a greater knowledge of men and manners, and a more perfect acquaintance with the politicks of Europe. He will be promoted according to the returns which he makes to his court. They must be accurate, distinct, without fire or ornament. He may subjoin his own opinion, but he must do it with great modesty. The ministry at home are proud.'

He said the greatest happiness was not in glory, but in goodness; and that Penn in his American colony, where he had established a people in quiet and contentment, was happier than Alexander the Great after destroying multitudes at the conquest of Thebes. He observed that the history of Alexander is obscure and dubious; for his captains who divided his kingdom, were too busy to record his life and actions, and would at any rate wish to render him odious to posterity.

Never was I so thoroughly sensible of my own defects as while I was in Corsica. I felt how small were my abilities, and how little I knew. Ambitious to be the companion of Paoli, and to understand a country and a people which roused me so much, I wished to be a Sir James MacDonald\*.

The last day which I spent with Paoli, appeared of inestimable value. I thought him more than usually great and amiable, when I was upon the eve of parting from him. The night before my departure, a little incident happened which shewed him in a most agreeable light. When the servants were bringing in the desert after supper, one of them chanced to let fall a plate of walnuts. Instead of flying into a passion at what the man could not help, Paoli said with a smile, 'No matter;' and turning to me, 'It is a good sign for you, Sir, Tempus est spargere nuces, It is time to scatter walnuts. It is a matrimonial omen: You must go home to your own country, and marry some fine woman whom you really like. I shall rejoice to hear of it.

\* Sir James MacDonald baronet of the isle of Sky, who at the age of one and twenty, had the learning and abilities of a Professour and a statesman, with the accomplishments of a man of the world. Eton and Oxford will ever remember him as one of their greatest ornaments. He was well known to the most distinguished in Europe, but was carried off from all their expectations. He died at Frescati, near Rome, in 1765. Had he lived a little longer, I believe I should have prevailed with him to visit Corsica.

This was a pretty allusion to the Roman ceremony at weddings, of scattering walnuts. So Virgil's Damon says,

> Mopse novas incide faces: tibi ducitur uxor.
> Sparge marite nuces: tibi deserit Hesperus Oetam.
> VIRG. Eclog. viii. l. 30.
>
> Thy bride comes forth! begin the festal rites!
> The walnuts strew! prepare the nuptial lights!
> O envied husband, now thy bliss is nigh!
> Behold for thee bright Hesper mounts the sky!
> WARTON.

When I again asked Paoli if it was possible for me in any way to shew him my great respect and attachment, he replied, 'Ricordatevi che Io vi sia amico, e scrivetemi. Remember that I am your friend, and write to me.' I said I hoped that when he honoured me with a letter, he would write not only as a commander, but as a philosopher and a man of letters. He took me by the hand, and said, 'As a friend.' I dare not transcribe from my private notes the feelings which I had at this interview. I should perhaps appear too enthusiastick. I took leave of Paoli with reget and agitation, not without some hopes of seeing him again. From having known intimately so exalted a character, my sentiments of human nature were raifed, while, by a fort of contagion, I felt an honeſt ardour to diſtinguiſh myſelf, and be uſeful, as far as my ſituation and abilities would allow; and I was, for the reſt of my life, ſet free from a ſlaviſh timidity in the preſence of great men, for where ſhall I find a man greater than Paoli?

When I ſet out from Sollacarò, I felt myſelf a good deal indiſpoſed. The old houſe of Colonna, like the family of its maſter, was much decayed; ſo that both wind and rain found their way into my bed-chamber. From this I contracted a ſevere cold, which ended in a tertian ague. There was no help for it. I might well ſubmit to ſome inconveniences, where I had enjoyed ſo much happineſs.

I was accompanied a part of the road by a great ſwarthy prieſt, who had never been out of Corſica. He was a very Hercules for ſtrength and reſolution. He and two other Corſicans took a caſtle, garriſoned by no leſs than fifteen Genoeſe. Indeed the Corſicans have ſuch a contempt for their enemies, that I have heard them ſay, 'Baſterebbero le donne contra i Genoveſi, Our women would be enough againſt the Genoese.' This priest was a bluff, hearty, roaring fellow, troubled neither with knowledge nor care. He was ever and anon shewing me how stoutly his nag could caper. He always rode some paces before me, and sat in an attitude half turned round, with his hand clapped upon the crupper. Then he would burst out with comical songs about the devil and the Genoese, and I don't know what all. In short, notwithstanding my feverishness, he kept me laughing whether I would or no.

I was returning to Corte, but I varied my road a little from the way I had come, going more upon the low country, and nearer the western shore.

At Cauro I had a fine view of Ajaccio and its environs. My ague was sometime of forming, so I had frequent intervals of ease, which I employed in observing whatever occurred. I was lodged at Cauro in the house of Signor Peraldi of Ajaccio, who received me with great politeness. I found here another provincial magistracy. Before supper, Signor Peraldi and a young Abbé of Ajaccio entertained me with some airs on the violin. After they had shewn me their taste in fine improved musick, they gave me some original Corsican airs, and at my desire, they brought up four of the guards of the magistracy, and made them shew me a Corsican dance. It was truly savage. They thumped with their heels, sprung upon their toes, brandished their arms, wheeled and leaped with the most violent gesticulations. It gave me the idea of an admirable war dance.

During this journey I had very bad weather. I cannot forget the worthy rectour of Cuttoli, whose house afforded me a hospitable retreat, when wet to the skin, and quite overcome by the severity of the storm, which my sickness made me little able to resist. He was directly such a venerable hermit as we read of in the old romances. His figure and manner interested me at first sight. I found he was a man well respected in the island, and that the General did him the honour to correspond with him. He gave me a simple collation of eggs, chestnuts and wine, and was very liberal of his ham and other more substantial victuals to my servant. The honest Swifs was by this time very well pleased to have his face turned towards the continent. He was heartily tired of seeing foreign parts, and meeting with scanty meals and hard beds, in an island which he could not comprehend the pleasure of visiting. He said to me, 'Si J'etois encore une fois retourné à mon pais parmi ces montagnes de Suisse dont monsieur fait tant des plaisanteries, Je verrai qui m'engagera à les quitter. If I were once more at home in my own country, among those mountains of Switzerland, on which you have had so many jokes, I will see who shall prevail with me to quit them.'

The General out of his great politeness, would not allow me to travel without a couple of chosen guards to attend me in case of any accidents. I made them my companions, to relieve the tediousness of my journey. One of them called Ambrosio, was a strange iron-coloured fearless creature. He had been much in war; careless of wounds, he was cooly intent on destroying the enemy. He told me, as a good anecdote, that having been so lucky as to get a view of two Genoese exactly in a line, he took his aim, and shot them both through the head at once. He talked of this, just as one would talk of shooting a couple of crows. I was sure I needed be under no apprehension; but I don't know how, I desired Ambrosio to march before me that I might see him.

I was upon my guard how I treated him. But as sickness frets one's temper, I sometimes forgot myself, and called him 'bestia, blockhead;' and once when he was at a loss which way to go, at a wild woody part of the country, I fell into a passion, and called to him 'Mi maraviglio che un uomo si bravo può esser si stupido. I am amazed that so brave a man can be so stupid.' However by afterwards calling him friend, and speaking softly to him, I soon made him forget my ill humour, and we proceeded as before.

Paoli had also been so good as to make me a present of one of his dogs, a strong and fierce animal. But he was too old to take an attachment to me, and I lost him between Lyons and Paris. The General has promised me a young one, to be a guard at Auchinleck.

At Bogognano I came upon the same road I had formerly travelled from Corte, where I arrived safe after all my fatigues. My good fathers of the Franciscan convent, received me like an old acquaintance, and shewed a kind concern at my illness. I sent my respects to the Great Chancellor, who returned me a note, of which I insert a translation as a specimen of the hearty civility to be found among the highest in Corsica.

'Many congratulations to Mr. Boswell on his return from beyond the mountains, from his servant Massesi, who is at the same time very sorry for his indisposition, which he is persuaded has been occasioned by his severe journey. He however flatters himself, that when Mr. Boswell has reposed himself a little, he will recover his usual health. In the mean time he has taken the liberty to send him a couple of fowls, which he hopes, he will honour with his acceptance, as he will need some refreshment this evening. He wishes him a good night, as does his little servant Luiggi, who will attend him to-morrow, to discharge his duty.'

My ague distressed me so much, that I was confined to the convent for several days. I did not however weary. I was visited by the Great Chancellor, and several others of the civil magistrates, and by Padre Mariani rectour of the university, a man of learning and abilities, as a proof of which, he had been three years at Madrid in the character of secretary to the General of the Franciscans. I remember a very eloquent expression of his, on the state of his country. 'Corsica, said he, has for many years past, been bleeding at all her veins. They are now closed. But after being so severely exhausted, it will take some time before she can recover perfect strength.' I was also visited by Padre Leonardo, of whose animating discourse I have made mention in a former part of this book.

Indeed I should not have been at a loss though my very reverend fathers had been all my society. I was not in the least looked upon as a heretick. Difference of faith was forgotten in hospitality. I went about the convent as if I had been in my own house; and the fathers without any impropriety of mirth, were yet as chearful as I could desire.

I had two surgeons to attend me at Corte, a Corsican and a Piedmontese; and I got a little Jesuit's bark from the spiceria or apothecary's shop, of the Capuchin convent. I did not however expect to be effectually cured, till I should get to Bastia. I found it was perfectly safe for me to go thither. There was a kind of truce between the Corsicans and the French. Paoli had held two different amicable conferences with M. de Marboeuf their commander in chief, and was so well with him, that he gave me a letter of recommendation to him.

On one of the days that my ague disturbed me least, I walked from the convent to Corte, purposely to write a letter to Mr. Samuel Johnson. I told my revered friend, that from a kind of superstition agreeable in a certain degree to him, as well as to myself, I had during my travels, written to him from LOCA SOLENNIA, places in some measure sacred. That as I had written to him from the Tomb of Melancthon, sacred to learning and piety, I now wrote to him from the palace of Pascal Paoli, sacred to wisdom and liberty; knowing that however his political principles may have been represented, he had always a generous zeal for the common rights of humanity. I gave him a sketch of the great things I had seen in Corsica, and promised him a more ample relation.

Mr. Johnson was pleased with what I wrote here; for I received at Paris an answer from him which I keep as a valuable charter. 'When

' you return, you will return to an unaltered,
' and I hope, unalterable friend. All that you
' have to fear from me, is the vexation of difap-
' pointing me. No man loves to fruftrate expec-
' tations which have been formed in his favour,
' and the pleafure which I promife myfelf from
' your journals and remarks, is fo great, that per-
' haps no degree of attention or difcernment will
' be fufficient to afford it. Come home however
' and take your chance. I long to fee you, and
' to hear you; and hope that we fhall not be
' fo long feparated again. Come home, and
' expect fuch a welcome as is due to him whom
' a wife and noble curiofity has led where per-
' haps, no native of this country ever was before.'

I at length fet out for Baftia. I went the firft night to Roftino, hoping to have found there Signor Clemente de' Paoli. But unluckily he had gone upon a vifit to his daughter; fo that I had not an opportunity of feeing this extraordinary perfonage, of whom I have given fo full an account, for a great part of which I am indebted to Mr. Burnaby.

Next day I reached Vefcovato, where I was received by Signor Buttafoco, who proved fuperiour to the character I had conceived of him from the letter of M. Rousseau. I found in him the incorrupted virtues of the brave islander, with the improvements of the continent. I found him in short, to be a man of principle, abilities and knowledge; and at the same time a man of the world. He is now deservedly raised to the rank of colonel of the Royal Corsicans, in the service of France.

I past some days with Signor Buttafoco, from whose conversation I received so much pleasure, that I in a great measure forgot my ague.

As various discourses have been held in Europe, concerning an invitation given to M. Rousseau to come to Corsica; and as that affair was conducted by Signor Buttafoco, who shewed me the whole correspondence between him and M. Rousseau, I am enabled to give a distinct account of it.

M. Rousseau in his Political Treatise, entitled Du Contract Social, has the following observation. ' Il est encore en Europe un pays capable de législation; c'est l'isle de Corse. La valeur et la constance avec laquelle ce brave peuple a su recouvrer et défendre sa liberté mériteroit bien que quelque homme sage lui apprit à la conserver. J'ai quelque pressentiment qu'un jour cette petite isle etonnera l'Europe. (*a*) There is yet one country in Europe, capable of legislation; And that is the island of Corsica. The valour and the constancy with which that brave people hath recovered and defended its liberty, would well deserve that some wise man should teach them how to preserve it. I have some presentiment that one day that little island will astonish Europe.'

Signor Buttafoco, upon this, wrote to M. Rousseau, returning him thanks for the honour he had done to the Corsican nation, and strongly inviting him to come over, and be that wise man who should illuminate their minds.

I was allowed to take a copy of the wild philosopher's answer to this invitation; it is written with his usual eloquence.

' Il est superflu, Monsieur, de chercher à ex-
' citer mon zele pour l'entreprise que vous me pro-
' posez. Sa seule idée m'eleve l'ame et me trans-
' porte. Je croirois la reste de mes jours bien
' noblement, bien vertueusement et bien heureuse-

---

(*a*) Du Contract Social. liv. ii. chap. 10.

'ment employés. Je croirois meme avoir bien
' racheté l'inutilité des autres, si je pouvois rendre
' ce triste reste bon en quelque chose à vos braves
' compatriotes; si je pouvois concourir par quel-
' que conseil utile aux vûes de votre digne Chef
' et aux votres; de ce coté la donc soyez sur de
' moi. Ma vie et mon coeur sont à vous.'

' It is superfluous Sir, to endeavour to excite
' my zeal for the undertaking which you propose
' to me. The very idea of it elevates my soul and
' transports me. I should esteem the rest of my
' days very nobly, very virtuously, and very happi-
' ly employed. I should even think that I well re-
' deemed the inutility of many of my days that
' are past, if I could render these sad remains of
' any advantage to your brave countrymen. If by
' any useful advice, I could concur in the views of
' your worthy Chief, and in yours. So far then
' you may be sure of me. My life and my heart
' are devoted to you.'

Such were the first effusions of Rousseau. Yet before he concluded even this first letter, he made a great many complaints of his adversities and persecutions, and started a variety of difficulties as to the proposed enterprise.

The correspondence was kept up for some

time, but the enthusiasm of the paradoxical philosopher gradually subsiding, the scheme came to nothing.

As I have formerly observed, M. De Voltaire thought proper to exercise his pleasantry upon occasion of this proposal, in order to vex the grave Rousseau, whom he never could bear. I remember he used to talk of him with a satyrical smile, and call him, 'Ce Garçon, That Lad;' I find this among my notes of M. de Voltaire's conversations, when I was with him at his Chateau de Ferney, where he entertains with the elegance rather of a real prince than of a poetical one.

To have Voltaire's assertion contradicted by a letter under Paoli's own hand, was no doubt a sufficient satisfaction to Rousseau.

From the account which I have attempted to give of the present constitution of Corsica, and of its illustrious Legislatour and General, it may well be conceived that the scheme of bringing M. Rousseau into that island, was magnified to an extravagant degree by the reports of the continent. It was said, that Rousseau was to be made no less than a Solon by the Corsicans, who were implicitely to receive from him a code of laws.

This was by no means the scheme. Paoli was

too able a man to submit the legislation of his country to one who was an entire stranger to the people, the manners, and in short to every thing in the island. Nay I know well that Paoli pays more regard to what has been tried by the experience of ages, than to the most beautiful ideal systems. Besides, the Corsicans were not all at once to be moulded at will. They were to be gradually prepared, and by one law laying the foundation for another, a compleat fabrick of jurisprudence was to be formed.

Paoli's intention was to grant a generous asylum to Rousseau, to avail himself of the shining talents which appeared in his writings, by consulting with him, and catching the lights of his rich imagination, from many of which he might derive improvements to those plans which his own wisdom had laid down.

But what he had principally in view, was to employ the pen of Rousseau in recording the heroick actions of the brave islanders. It is to be regretted that this project did not take place. The father of the present colonel Buttafoco made large collections for many years back. These are carefully preserved, and when joined to those made by the Abbé Roftini, would furnifh ample materials for a Hiftory of Corfica. This, adorned with the genius of Rouffeau, would have been one of the nobleft monuments of modern times.

Signor Buttafoco accompanied me to Baftia. It was comfortable to enter a good warm town after my fatigues. We went to the houfe of Signor Morelli, a counfellor at law here, with whom we fupped. I was lodged for that night by a friend of Signor Buttafoco, in another part of the town.

Next morning I waited on M. de Marboeuf. Signor Buttafoco introduced me to him, and I prefented him the letter of recommendation from Paoli. He gave me a moft polite reception. The brilliancy of his levee pleafed me; it was a fcene fo different from thofe which I had been for fome time accuftomed to fee. It was like paffing at once from a rude and early age, to a polifhed modern age; from the mountains of Corfica, to the banks of the Seine.

My ague was now become fo violent, that it got the better of me altogether. I was obliged to ask the French general's permiffion to have a chair fet for me in the circle. When M. de

Marboeuf was informed of my being ill, he had the goodness to ask me to stay in his house till I should recover; 'I insist upon it, said he, I have a warm room for you. My servants will get you bouillons, and every thing proper for a sick man; and we have an excellent physician. I mention all these circumstances to shew the goodness of M. de Marboeuf, to whom I shall ever consider myself as under great obligations. His invitation was given in so kind and cordial a manner, that I willingly accepted of it.

I found M. de Marboeuf a worthy openhearted Frenchman. It is a common and a very just remark, that one of the most agreeable characters in the world is a Frenchman who has served long in the army, and has arrived at that age when the fire of youth is properly tempered. Such a character is gay without levity, and judicious without severity. Such a character was the Count de Marboeuf, of an ancient family in Britanny, where there is more plainness of character than among the other French. He had been Gentilhomme de la Chambre to the worthy King Stanislaus.

He took a charge of me as if he had been my near relation. He furnished me with books and every thing he could think of to amuse me. While the phyſician ordered me to be kept very quiet, M. de Marboeuf would allow nobody to go near me, but payed me a friendly viſit alone. As I grew better, he gradually encreaſed my ſociety, bringing with him more and more of his officers; ſo that I had at laſt the honour of very large companies in my apartment. The officers were polite agreeable men: ſome of them had been priſoners in England, during the laſt war. One of them was a Chevalier de St. Louis, of the name of Douglas, a deſcendant of the illuſtrious houſe of Douglas in Scotland, by a branch ſettled near to Lyons. This gentleman often came and ſat with me. The idea of our being in ſome ſort countrymen, was pleaſing to us both.

I found here an Engliſh woman of Penrith in Cumberland. When the Highlanders marched through that country in the year 1745, ſhe had married a ſoldier of the French picquets in the very midſt of all the confuſion and danger, and when ſhe could hardly underſtand one word he ſaid. Such freaks will love ſometimes take.

> Sic visum Veneri; cui placet impares
> Formas atque animos sub juga ahenea
>    Saevo mittere cum joco.
>
> HORAT. lib. I. Od. 33.
>
> So Venus wills, whose power controuls
> The fond affections of our souls;
> With sportive cruelty she binds
> Unequal forms, unequal minds.
>
> FRANCIS.

M. de la Chapelle was the physician who attended me. He had been several years physician to the army at Minorca, and had now the same office in Corsica. I called him the physician of the isles. He was indeed an excellent one. That gayeté de coeur which the French enjoy, runs through all their professions. I remember the phrase of an English common soldier who told me, ' that at the battle of Fontenoy, his captain received a shot in the breast, and fell, said the soldier, with his spontoon in his hand, as prettily killed as ever I see'd a gentleman.' The soldier's phrase might be used in talking of almost every thing which the French do. I may say I was prettily cured by M de la Chapelle.

But I think myself bound to relate a circumstance which shews him and his nation in the genteelest light. Though he attended me with the greatest assiduity, yet, when I was going away, he would not accept of a single Louis d'or. " No Sir, said he, I am nobly paid by my king. I am physician to his army here. If I can at the same time, be of service to the people of the country, or to any gentleman who may come among us, I am happy. But I must be excused from taking money. M. Brion the surgeon major behaved in the same manner.

As soon as I had gathered a little strength, I walked about as well as I could; and saw what was to be seen at Bastia. Signor Morelli was remarkably obliging. He made me presents of books and antiques, and of every other curiosity relating to Corsica. I never saw a more generous man. Signor Caraffa, a Corsican officer in the service of France, with the order of St. Louis, was also very obliging. Having made a longer stay in Corsica than I intended, my finances were exhausted, and he let me have as much money as I pleased. M. Barlé, secretary to M. de Marboeuf, was also very obliging. In short, I know not how to express my thankfulness to all the good people whom I saw at Bastia.

The French seemed to agree very well with

the Corsicans. Of old, those islanders were much indebted to the interposition of France, in their favour. But since the days of Sampiero, there have been many variances between them. A singular one happened in the reign of Lewis XIV. The Pope's Corsican guards in some fit of passion insulted the French ambassadour at Rome. The superb monarch resolved to revenge this outrage. But Pope Alexander VII. foreseeing the consequences, agreed to the conditions required by France; which were, that the Corsican guards should be obliged to depart the ecclesiastical state, that the nation should be declared incapable ever to serve the holy see, and, that opposite to their ancient guard-house, should be erected a pyramid inscribed with their disgrace (*a*).

Le Brun, whose royal genius could magnify and enrich every circumstance in honour of his sovereign, has given this story as a medaillon on one of the compartments of the great gallery at Versailles. France appears with a stately air, shewing to Rome the design of the pyramid; and Rome, though bearing a shield marked S. P. Q. R. receives the design with most submissive humility.

(*a*) Corps Diplomatique anno 1664.

I wish that France had never done the Corsicans greater harm than depriving them of the honour of being the pope's guards. Boisseux and Maillebois cannot easily be forgotten; nor can the brave islanders be blamed for complaining that a powerful nation should interpose to retard their obtaining entire possession of their country, and of undisturbed freedom.

M. de Marboeuf appeared to conduct himself with the greatest prudence and moderation. He told me that he wished to preserve peace in Corsica. He had entered into a convention with Paoli, mutually to give up such criminals as should fly into each others territories. Formerly not one criminal in a hundred was punished. There was no communication between the Corsicans and the Genoese; and if a criminal could but escape from the one jurisdiction to the other, he was safe. This was very easily done, so that crimes from impunity were very frequent. By this equitable convention, justice has been fully administered.

Perhaps indeed the residence of the French in Corsica, has, upon the whole, been an advantage to the patriots. There have been markets twice a week at the frontiers of each garrison-town, where the Corsican peasants have sold all sorts of provisions, and brought in a good many French crowns; which have been melted down into Corsican money. A cessation of arms for a few years has been a breathing time to the nation, to prepare itself for one great effort, which will probably end in a total expulsion of the Genoese. A little leisure has been given for attending to civil improvements, towards which the example of the French has in no small degree contributed. Many of the soldiers were excellent handi-craftsmen, and could instruct the natives in various arts.

M. de Marboeuf entertained himself by laying out several elegant pieces of pleasure ground; and such were the humane and amicable dispositions of this respectable officer, that he was at pains to observe what things were most wanted in Corsica, and then imported them from France, in order to shew an example to the inhabitants. He introduced in particular, the culture of potatoes, of which there were none in the island upon his arrival. This root will be of considerable service to the Corsicans, it will make a wholesome variety in their food; and as there will thereby, of confequence, be lefs home confumption of cheftnuts, they will be able to export a greater quantity of them.

M. de Marboeuf made merry upon the reports which had been circulated, that I was no lefs than a minifter from the Britifh court. The Avignon gazette brought us one day information, that the Englifh were going to eftablifh Un Bureau de Commerce in Corfica. 'O Sir, faid he, the fecret is out. I fee now the motive of your deftination to thefe parts. It is you who are to eftablifh this Bureau de Commerce.'

Idle as thefe rumours were, it is a fact that, when I was at Genoa, Signor Gherardi, one of their fecretaries of ftate, very ferioufly told me, 'Monfieur, vous m'avez fait trembler quoique je ne vous ai jamais vu. Sir, you have made me tremble although I never faw you before.' And when I fmiled and affured him that I was juft a fimple traveller, he fhook his head; but faid, he had very authentick information concerning me. He then told me with great gravity, 'That while I travelled in Corfica, I was dreft in fcarlet and gold; but when I payed my refpects to the Supreme Council at Corte, I appeared in a full fuit of black.' These important truths I fairly owned to him, and he seemed to exult over me.

I was more and more obliged to M. de Marboeuf. When I was allowed by my physician, to go to his Excellency's table, where we had always a large company, and every thing in great magnificence, he was so careful of me, that he would not suffer me to eat any thing, or taste a glass of wine, more than was prescribed for me. He used to say, 'I am here both physician and commander in chief; so you must submit.' He very politely prest me to make some stay with him, saying, 'We have taken care of you when sick, I think we have a claim to you for a while, when in health.' His kindness followed me after I left him. It procured me an agreeable reception from M. Michel, the French chargé d'affaires at Genoa; and was the occasion of my being honoured with great civilities at Paris, by M L'Abbé de Marboeuf conseiller d'etat, brother of the Count, and possessing similar virtues in private life.

I quitted Corsica with reluctance, when I thought of the illustrious Paoli. I wrote to him from Bastia, informing him of my illness, which I said, was owing to his having made me a man of so much consequence, that instead of putting me into a snug little room, he had lodged me in the magnificent old palace, where the wind and rain entered.

His answer to my first letter is written with so much spirit, that I begged his permission to publish it, which he granted in the genteelest manner, saying, 'I do not remember the contents 'of the letter; but I have such a confidence in 'Mr. Boswell, that I am sure, he would not pu- 'blish it, if there was any thing in it improper 'for publick view; so he has my permission.' I am thus enabled to present my readers with an original letter from Paoli.

## TO JAMES BOSWELL, Esq;

### OF AUCHINLECK, SCOTLAND.

STIMATISSIMO SIGNOR BOSWELL,

RICEVEI la lettera che mi favorì da Bastia, e mi consolo assai colla notizia di essersi rimessa in perfetta salute. Buon per lei che cadde in mano di un valente medico! Quando altra volta il disgusto de' paesi colti, od ameni lo prendesse, e lo portasse in questa infelice contrada, procurerò che sia alloggiata in camere più calde, e custodita di quelle della casa Colonna in Sollacarò; ma ella ancora dovrà contentarsi di non viaggiare quando la giornata, e la stagione vogliono che si resti in casa per attendere il tempo buono. Io resto ora impaziente per la lettera che ha promesso scrivermi da Genova, dove dubito assai che la delicatezza di quelle dame non le abbia fatto fare qualche giorno di quarantena, per ispurgarsi di ogni anche più leggiero influsso, che possa avere portato seco dell'aria di questo paese; e molto più, se le fosse venuto il capriccio di far vedere quell'abito di veluto Corso, e quel berrettone, di cui i Corsi vogliono l'origine dagli elmi antichi, ed i Genovesi lo dicono inventato da quelli, che, rubando alla strada, non vogliano essere conosciuti: come se in tempo del loro governo avessero mai avuta apprensione di castigo i ladri pubblici? Son sicuro però, che ella presso avrà il buon partito con quelle amabili, e delicate persone, insinuando alle medesime, che il cuore delle belle è fatto per la compassione, non per il disprezzo, e per la tirannia; e così sarà rientrato facilmente nella lor grazia. Io ritornato in Corte ebbi subito la notizia del secreto sbarco dell'Abbatucci nelle spiaggie di

Solenzara. Tutte le apparenze fanno credere che il medesimo sia venuto con disegni opposti alla pubblica quiete; pure si è costituito in castello, e protesta ravvedimento. Nel venire per Bocognano si seppe, che un capitano riformato Genovese cercava compagni per assassinarmi. Non potè rinvenirne e vedendosi scoperto si pose alla macchia, dove è stato ucciso dalle squadriglie che gli tenevano dietro i magistrati delle provincie oltramontane. Queste insidie non sembrano buoni preliminari del nostro accomodamento colla repubblica di Genova. Io sto passando il sindicato a questa provincia di Nebbio. Verso il 10. dell'entrante anderò per l'istesso oggetto in quella del Capocorso, ed il mese di Febrajo facilmente mi tratterrò in Balagna. Ritornerò poi in Corte alla primavera, per prepararmi all'apertura della consulta generale. In ogni luogo avrò presente la sua amicizia, e sarò desideroso de' continui suoi riscontri. Frattanto ella mi creda

Suo affettuosissimo amico

PATRIMONIO,
23 Decembre 1765.

PASQUALE DE' PAOLI

## MUCH ESTEEMED Mr. BOSWELL,

I RECEIVED the letter which you wrote to me from Baftia, and am much comforted by hearing that you are reftored to perfect health. It is lucky for you that you fell into the hands of an able phyfician. When you fhall again be feized with a difguft at improved and agreeable countries, and fhall return to this ill-fated land, I will take care to have you lodged in warmer and better finifhed apartments than thofe of the houfe of Colonna, at Sollacarò. But you again fhould be fatisfied not to travel when the weather and the feafon require one to keep within doors, and wait for a fair day. I expect with impatience the letter which you promifed to write to me from Genoa, where I much fufpect that the delicacy of the ladies will have obliged you to perform fome days of quarantine, for purifying you from every the leaft infection, which you may have carried with you from the air of this country: and ftill more fo, if you have taken the whim to fhew that fuit of Corfican velvet * and that bonnet of which the

---

* By Corfican velvet he means the coarfe ftuff made in the ifland, which is all that the Corficans have in ftead of the fine velvet of Genoa.

Corsicans will have the origin to be from the ancient helmets, whereas the Genoese say it was invented by those who rob on the high way, in order to disguise themselves; as if during the Genoese government, publick robbers needed to fear punishment. I am sure however, that you will have taken the proper method with these amiable and delicate persons, insinuating to them, that the hearts of beauties are formed for compassion, and not for disdain and tyranny: and so you will have been easily restored to their good graces. Immediately on my return to Corte, I received information of the secret landing of Abbatucci*, on the coast of Solenzara. All appearances make us believe, that he is come with designs contrary to the publick quiet. He has however surrendered himself a prisoner at the castle, and protests his repentance. As I passed by Bogognano, I learnt that a disbanded Genoese officer was seeking associates to assassinate me. He could not succeed, and finding that he was discovered, he betook himself to the woods; where he has been slain by the party detached by the magistrates of the the provinces on the other side of the mountains,

* Abbatucci, a Corsican of a very suspicious character.

in order to intercept him. These ambuscades do not seem to be good preliminaries towards our accommodation with the republick of Genoa. I am now holding the syndicato in this province of Nebbio. About the 10th of next month, I shall go, for the same object, into the province of Capo Corso, and during the month of February, I shall probably fix my residence in Balagna. I shall return to Corte in the spring, to prepare myself for the opening of the General Consulta. Wherever I am, your friendship will be present to my mind, and I shall be desirous to continue a correspondence with you. Meanwhile believe me to be

Your most affectionate friend

PATRIMONIO,}
28 December, 1765.}

PASCAL PAOLI.

Can any thing be more condescending, and at the same time shew more the firmness of an heroick mind, than this letter? With what a gallant pleasantry does the Corsican Chief talk of his enemies! One would think that the Queens of Genoa should become Rival Queens for Paoli. If they saw him, I am sure they would.

I take the liberty to repeat an observation made to me by that illustrious minister, whom Paoli calls the Pericles of Great Britain. ' It may be said of Paoli, as the Cardinal de Retz said of the great Montrose, " C'est un de ces hommes qu'on ne trouve plus que dans les Vies de Plutarque. He is one of those men who are no longer to be found but in the lives of Plutarch."

THE END.